Change for the Better

Self-Help Through Practical Psychotherapy

Second Edition

Elizabeth Wilde McCormick

CASSELL

For Tony and all the Cognitive Analytic Therapists

Cassell
Wellington House
125 Strand
London WC2R 0BB

370 Lexington Avenue
New York
NY 10017-6550

First edition published 1990
Second edition published 1996

Reprinted 1998, 1999

British Library Cataloguing-in-Publication Data
A catalogue record for this book is available from the British Library

ISBN 0–304–33530–4

Typeset by Action Typesetting Limited, Northgate Street, Gloucester
Printed and bound in Great Britain by Biddles Limited, Guildford
and King's Lynn

Contents

Contents

Acknowledgements

This book is based upon the work carried out by Dr Anthony Ryle at Guy's and St Thomas's Hospitals in the field of Cognitive Analytic Therapy, CAT for short. Since 1984 CAT and CAT therapists have grown in numbers, and this method of time-limited, focused therapy is now taught and used in different settings within the health service. I am grateful to Tony Ryle for encouraging me to write a self-help book based on his work, and for his help with the first draft, as well as his support for this second edition. He read all of the new material and contributed clarity and focus, especially in the new chapter for couples.

Annalee Curran and Shakir Ansari also read some of the early drafts for the first edition and made helpful additions. I am grateful for their continued support in my efforts at writing. My thanks to them and to my other CAT colleagues, particularly Norma Maple, Cherry Boa, Dilys Davies, Val Coumont, Deirdre Haslam, Angela Wilton, Mark Dunn, all of whom contributed ideas and cases for this book.

The other psychological influence shaping these pages comes from the Centre for Transpersonal Psychology. I am grateful to Barbara Somers and Ian Gordon Brown for their influence on my understanding of unconscious material, visualization, dreams and active imagination.

A special thank-you goes to all the patients who agreed to have their life stories, charts, letters and diagrams used for publication. All names and some details have been changed to protect their identities. Their examples show us how difficulties can be faced and how lives can be changed.

I am grateful to Professor J. P. Watson for agreeing to write the foreword and for his ongoing support and encouragement for CAT.

I would also like to thank Bee Willey for her imaginative illustrations.

Change for the Better has had a curious passage since its first publication by Unwin Hyman in 1990. It became an 'orphan book' when its publishers were taken over by HarperCollins two weeks after publication, and for the years following was not readily available in bookshops. Nevertheless it survived, largely thanks to the continued interest in CAT and the growth in training programmes for therapists at ACAT. *Change for the Better* has also found its way into different organizations keen to focus on change and self-help: universities, day centres, career counselling and GP practices. I am grateful for the interest in the book and to the number of readers who have written to me about how they have been able to make use of it. I am particularly grateful for the support of ACAT.

Lastly I would like to thank Cassell for commissioning this new edition and for their interest in achieving such a fine production with its new illustrations and revised content.

The author and publishers would like to acknowledge and thank the following for permission to quote lines from; *My Father's House* reproduced with permission of Virago Press, copyright Sylvia Fraser; *Understanding Women* (Penguin Books, 1985) copyright Louise Eichenbaum and Susie Orbach 1983; *Type A Behaviour and Your Heart* (Fawcett Crest) by Meyer Friedman and Ray Rosenman; *Woman, Her Changing Image* by Ann Shearer (Grapevine, an imprint of Thorsons Publishing Group, Wellingborough); the *Evening Standard* a report by Anne de Courcey; *You* magazine, interview by David Levin; 'The Dream' a poem by Felix Pollak from *Subject to Change* (Juniper Press, 1978).

Foreword to the first edition

Psychotherapy is a curious business and arouses strong feelings, for or against. 'Why does (s)he devote so much time to therapy, twice a week for five years, and still seem no better?' or, 'I couldn't have survived without therapy: after ten years I'm just beginning to find myself' or, 'I went to the psychiatrist and all I got was pills, not really *treatment*'. And so on.

For many, 'therapy' has to do with psychonanalysis or its derivatives, and the assumption that 'real' or 'ideal' treatment should involve prolonged exposure to a wise and highly trained exponent of the psychoanalytic art. This book is not about that type of therapy.

Change for the Better has emerged from a psychotherapeutic setting with three important features which give it structure. First, the therapeutic methods it presents have been developed and tested in the cauldron of the British National Health Service. Secondly, the methods have been assessed in a series of ongoing research studies. So we know some of the ways in which people may be helped by the treatment, and also that effective therapists may begin from many different professional backgrounds.

The third point concerns the nature of the therapeutic methods themselves. The treatment is time-limited and usually brief (these are not the same thing). It draws upon varied theoretical frameworks, including psychoanalytic notions, cognitive and social psychology and also behavioural therapy traditions. It has been evolved by Anthony Ryle at St Thomas's and Guy's Hospitals.

I have know Dr Ryle for many years, due to a shared interst in the Personal Construct Theory of George Kelly and the repertory grid methods of investigation to which it gave rise. It has been a great pleasure to be associated with him in the explorations which have made this book possible. The academic psychiatric department at Guy's/St Thomas's, which I chair, has always been keen to promote psychological treatments for patients attending NHS clinics in ordinary places, such as inner London, where our practice has been based. It seems to me of very great importance indeed that Dr Ryle's treatment has been shown to be applicable to many patients in the general run of NHS settings.

Equally important is the fact that the treatment is relatively economical of therapist time. Even so, the NHS in the Britain of the 1980s and 1990s finds extreme difficulty in understanding that such treatment should be funded. I hope that this book will significantly promote a climate of opinion that will encourage the allocation of resources to this activity.

Along with the route which has led to this book, a substantial number of psychotherapists with unorthodox backgrounds – that is, those without the prior experience of hospitals or psychiatry – have come to Guy's and St Thomas's to gain clinical experience and to learn Dr Ryle's treatment. Elizabeth McCormick was one such therapist who brought her own relevant, but not 'mental health professional', experience to the task. There is now no doubt that therapists can acquire the skills required to provide and then teach Cognitive Analytic Therapy through supervised experience such as Dr Ryle has developed. I hope this book will increase the health and social service authorities' awareness of the contribution which could be made by these talented and self-motivated people for whom, until recently, such authorities have usually found it impossible to provide paid full-time or sessional work.

J. P. Watson MD FRCP FRCPsych
London, 1990

Foreword to the second edition

New developments in psychotherapy, psychiatry or other helping professions are often brought about by rare people with special talents and the ability and energy to use them. The uncomfortable possibility always arises that the new development is *entirely* dependent on founder charisma. Hence the period after the departure of the founder is always a crucial time for a new organization. Can the new creation survive?

Since the first edition of this book, Dr Anthony Ryle has retired from the NHS. He continues, however, to write, teach and research; indeed, a striking feature of the therapy world is the number of therapists who go on improving, like good claret, with age, often until well after ordinary retirement might have been expected. The important thing is that Cognitive Analytic Therapy has survived its founder. An increasing number of people in an increasing number of places, are discovering that *there is definitely something important in it*. Not only that, but its time-limited and focused structure, as well as being good for therapy, seems likely to find an increasingly prominent place in public therapy provision, and to figure in purchasing plans.

Patients, clinicians, managers and purchasers will all benefit from this book, which continues to be an excellent introduction to this form of accessible and 'sensible' psychotherapy.

J. P. Watson MD FRCP FRCPsych
London, February 1995

About Cognitive Analytic Therapy

Cognitive Analytic Therapy is a time-limited, integrated psychotherapy pioneered by Dr Anthony Ryle at Guy's and St Thomas's Hospitals in London. It has been used with increasing demand in numerous different settings within the British health service since 1983, and brings together several different traditions.

The main theoretical sources of ideas and methods are as follows:

- From **Psychoanalysis**: concepts of conflict, defence, object relations and countertransference. The theory is restated in cognitive terms, and therapists' interventions are more active and various than in psychoanalytical therapies.
- From **Kelly's Personal Construct Theory** and work with **repertory grids**: a focus on how people make sense of their world (man/woman as scientist) and on common-sense cooperative work with patients.
- From **cognitive-behavioural approaches**: the step-by-step planning and measurement of change, teaching patients self-observation of moods, thoughts and symptoms.
- From **developmental** and **cognitive psychology** and **artificial intelligence**: an information-processing model of how experience and actions are organized.

Introduction

How many times in a day do we think about change? I wish. I wish I hadn't. I wish they didn't. I wish I could. How often when things go wrong do we wish it were different, that perhaps *we* were different? And how often do these wishes remain as remote dreams that can only come true with the help of a magic wand?

Perhaps we try hard at something. We strive hard to make it work, employing everything we know. We work at our jobs, at being nice to people, at making relationships, developing hobbies; we try something new. But still we feel inside that something is wrong; we feely unhappy, lost, hopeless, doomed. Things go wrong outside: we don't fit in, our jobs perish, partners leave, or we can't rid ourselves of habits or thoughts that make us feel bad. So we try to make changes – a new look, job, partner, house – and for a while we are glad, and things are different. But then the same bad old things start happening again and we feel worse – worse because our hope of change fades. We feel stuck or jinxed and anger and helplessness begin to well up. Perhaps we are beginning to believe we actually are that miserable, stuck person we see in the mirror every morning at whom we want to lash out.

This book is about change. It sets out methods of identifying just what we *can* change about ourselves and our behaviour and suggests ways to go about this:

- We *can* learn to become better observers about what happens to us.
- We *can* identify the patterns, based on our earlier need to survive, that dominate how we conduct ourselves.
- We *can* revise these old survival beliefs which we take for granted, but which become redundant when they get in our way.

- We *can* then allow space for our *real* selves to leap into life.
- We *can* help this real self by identifying and practising different ways of expressing ourselves.
- We *can* change, by recognizing the difference between the old survival self, dominated by faulty thinking, and the real self that needs time, understanding and nourishment.

When we change the old assumptions and attitudes based on our early need to survive, we change our lives.

We don't, however, change the fundamental core of our being, the individual seed of our real selves with which we were born, and I will explain that more fully in Chapter 1. But we can change the hold that survival-self thinking has on our life: the way it limits our choices and leads to things going wrong. We are usually unaware that such processes inform our everyday choices because we learned them very early on, and they are all we know. The wild deer in the forest who wounds her leg might lie low so as not to be seen and preyed upon. Alternatively, she may remain with the other deer, but limp behind at a distance; she may even find someone who will shelter her for life. People are no different in their survival responses. If we survive a harsh early life by developing a brittle coping self, we come through the hard times when otherwise we might have gone under. However, we emerge into adulthood with survival presumptions that make it hard to get close to others or to be touched by life's beauties. And the difference between the deer and a human being is that we are able to contemplate alternatives. And it is when life challenges us through our difficult feelings or habits, or when things have gone very wrong for us, that we confront aspects of ourselves we had previously taken for granted.

This book aims to help people who wish to do something active about their lives, who find themselves saying: 'Wait a minute, I don't want to settle for this kind of thing ...' or 'Does it have to be like this?' It will provide methods for individual self-examination, for checking out patterns, for self-monitoring, for making personal maps to illustrate the kind of thinking webs we weave that ensnare us. And it will offer ways for changing the patterns that are no longer working.

Here is an outline of the steps we shall follow:

1. We identify problems and the thinking and feelings that accompany them.

2. We begin to name the sequences or patterns of thinking that we take for granted, but which actually limit our choices.
3. We write our individual life story, how it has been for us since the beginning, and link what has happened to us with the traps, dilemmas and snags that have become our everyday reality.
4. We begin to notice the sequences when they occur in daily life, and write them down.
5. We make maps that show us the sequences to help us in our everyday life.
6. We make realistic goals for challenging and changing the sequences.
7. We begin to experience 'real' bits of ourselves, because for the first time, we have more space and energy in our lives.
8. We process and bear the shifts that come with change.
9. We find helpful ways to hold on to change.

The psychotherapeutic way of working outlined in this book is based upon the time-limited psychotherapy project developed by Dr Anthony Ryle and researched at Guy's and St Thomas's Hospitals in London. The section of the book entitled 'Naming the Problem', is an enlarged version of the psychotherapy file given to patients at their first session of a CAT brief therapy. Many other projects in this kind of therapy are currently working in a variety of different settings throughout Britain. Many of the examples, stories and experiences are related by people who have been working in this way with myself or my colleagues at Guy's and St Thomas's, and who have generously given their permission for their stories to be published. All names and personal details have been changed in order to protect their identities. Each story gives a living example of how people can work towards change, and change for the better.

The changes we may make from this book are achieved by using conscious will and effort to revise old patterns that are no longer working. Once we do our part, using strengths developed by actively thinking about how we operate, we often stimulate other changes which are less conscious in origin. For example, many people who actively engage in the process of helping themselves and looking within find they begin to dream and remember dreams. In addition, there is often a greater awareness of meaningful patterns in life generally, and of the numerous threads running through our individual lives which have a lot to tell us; we begin to feel that there is more in life than the tunnelled-vision way of keeping going that many of us are reduced to when things are not going well. We all carry a part of us which is wounded in some way. How we carry this wound makes the difference between a passive attitude of 'I am a depressive, no one can help me' and the active, 'There is a part of me which is depressed and I take care of it'. Once we engage with ourselves in this way we are much more open to enjoy and use our inner world of imagination, dream and insight, and to accept ourselves as valuable beings embarked on a journey in life which has the possibility of joy and of soul.

Each of us has the right to take up the challenge of looking at ourselves afresh: to see what things we can change and to accept those we cannot, and to know the difference. Setting aside time to ponder on what we can change, and actively working to achieve those changes, means that we are freeing ourselves from the presumed restrictions of the past, and that our changes are changes for the better.

Part 1
All About Change

Why change?

Everyone seeks change for different reasons – to feel less anxious, perhaps, to overcome debilitating problems like depression or phobia, to feel more in control of life, to stop making destructive relationships. Or perhaps we seek change because we feel sad or bad, unhappy or empty, but aren't quite sure why. We may not necessarily be aware that change is what we want until we begin to look more closely at ourselves and at the way we have become used to doing things. Just being prepared to look afresh at ourselves from a different perspective is already embracing change.

We come into life as a seed with an inherent pattern of growth already inside us which is a mixture of genetic patterning and something uniquely ours we call 'self'. This 'seed self' contains our potential – who we might become, what we might be like, the traits, talents, gifts, tendencies we might have. The 'seed self' is our real self. It is planted into the soil within the garden of the family. The growth of the seed is bound up with the nature and effort of the soil. We cannot isolate ourselves from our context within culture, language, family and history. Inevitably some seeds will be planted in an acid soil when their growth is more suited to alkaline. Others may be pruned too early as their shoots are only just beginning to grow, and some will be thrown onto stony ground. Some seeds, which are perhaps destined to become peaches or pears experience alienation when others expect oranges or apples to grow and their own pearness or peachness goes unrecognized. All of us must find ways of meeting these early experiences, sometimes returning via reflection or therapy to reconnect with the seed of the real self from which we may have been diverted.

Survival self and real self

Very few seeds are given the soil that is completely right for their natural growth. The robust healthy tree in Figure 1 is one model or idea of how the seed 'might' have grown in an 'ideal' world. But neither nature nor culture are 'ideal' in terms of an ultra-controlled environment. Each restricts and assaults the seed's growth. Nature is constantly forging change. It brings wind, rain, frost, snow, earthquake, disease and plague, and its laws decree devastation and death, as well as care and nurture. Just as nature constantly shows us its creative adaptations, so most 'human' seeds have to develop a 'survival self' in order to manage the conditions of their early life. Developing this survival self, together with a package of coping tactics for adapting to a difficult, hostile or just strange environment, is always necessary, and a mark of the human capacity for change. Human beings are extremely creative!

But the 'survival self' is not the sum total of who we really are. Understanding the difference between the survival self, with its adapted way of proceeding, and the real self, the self we came into life with, is the heart of the work of psychotherapy.

We begin by looking at how life has been for us so far, and how we've built the sense of ourselves out of what has happened to us. When we can look afresh at our survival self and the everyday details of how we think about ourselves and our choices, we are able to challenge those patterns that are no longer useful and which actually make things worse. In so doing, we give space and energy for the real self to come forward, and allow our creativity to connect with this real self.

No-go areas and adapted procedures

If we have had to bend a long way from our intended path of natural growth (see Figure 1) in order to manage our early life, there will be some 'no-go' areas inside us. They may be to do with painful life events such as bereavement or illness, or they may concern aspects of ourselves that were misunderstood, judged harshly, or even punished and banished. They remain 'no-go' areas full of difficult feelings, because any association with them tends to frighten us. And we've learned to cope by proceeding in an adapted way – for example, by avoidance or

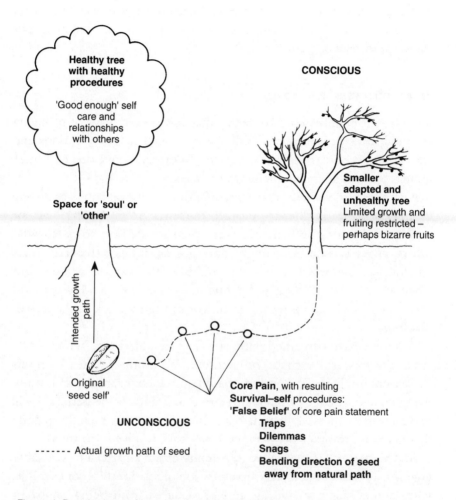

Figure 1 Development of 'seed' self and 'survival' self

self-negation, or by losing ourselves in activity. So we tend not to look too closely until life pushes us into them again. A broken relationship can often trigger earlier feelings of loss that had been left unresolved. And we often carry on judging or punishing ourselves in the way we've experienced earlier because this is what we know.

Until we can begin to describe them these 'no-go' areas remain as blocks to our natural growth and limit our range of choices of response. A clear description of how things have been, together with an understanding of the ways we've learned to cope, help to begin the process of change. Revising our old learned adapted ways of proceeding offers freedom from old patterns that hinder and limit us, so widening our choices and releasing energy.

Traps, dilemmas and snags

Survival-self patterns tend to decree that *only* certain ways of behaving are valid, thus presenting us with a very limited range of options and choices about how to express ourselves. In this book, we describe these limited options as traps, dilemmas or snags.

A **trap** occurs when we carry into adulthood survival habits that were developed in early life to protect ourselves from feeling bad or unwanted. Pleasing and smiling even when we are hurt so as to avoid others' anger or rejection, might have got us through the early years when it was important to be told 'you're such a *good* girl or boy'. But when we carry on pleasing and giving in to others, we tend to get used and abused, and end up feeling even worse, angrily stuck in the trap of placation.

When we have bargained with ourselves in a black and white way – either I'm this, or I'm that – or we think, 'If I do this ... then I am this ...', we end up living at one end of a **dilemma**. For example: 'If I'm not living on a knife edge of having to strive constantly to be perfect, I will make a terrible mess'. Dilemmas can also form an 'if ... then ...' quality: 'If I get close to other people *then* I will have to give in to them.'

And a **snag** occurs when we apparently create a pattern of self-sabotage. We are just about to take up a new job or relationship, for example, when something goes wrong and prevents us from being happy or successful.

The different forms that traps, dilemmas and snags can take in different lives are described and amplified throughout this book, together with suggestions and examples of ways to name and understand our own patterns, and to facilitate change.

Core pain

As you can see, skirting around no-go areas and living 'as if' we had only a range of limited options reduces our choice of how to be in the world, and tends to keep us linked to the past. While it is important to recognize and value the ways we learned to survive, we need to free ourselves from the rigid hold these old habits can have. Indeed, these old ways may be not only redundant but actually contribute to the things that keep going wrong.

The other reason for revising old adapted procedures is the extent to which the internal pain we carry will always cry out for healing. People often ask: 'But why do I *always* end up living with people who criticize me and make me feel bad?'; 'Why do bad things always happen just as I'm about to get going?'; 'Why do I never feel really happy or comfortable inside, despite what I've achieved?' These are cries of pain. And while the very fact of living means that some internal pain is inevitable, the way we carry a sense of woundedness and how we care for it can be destructively passive or usefully active.

It has always been noted by many psychologists, Jung in particular, that the human psyche dislikes lopsidedness. The 'seed self' inside will always seek to achieve a balance. If our life is 'on hold' in some way, externally because of disabling symptoms, but internally by unhealed core pain, life will lead us to this place until the pain is acknowledged consciously. And while the *fact* of distressing early beginnings – rejection, abandonment, abuse, cruelty, loss, pain and illness – cannot be removed, the wound that these events or attitudes inflicted can be accepted by us and carried consciously. And the procedures which we learned in order to cope with the pain inside, but which in adulthood limit our life, can be revised. This gives us an opportunity to change, by learning to have a wider range of options for how to express ourselves and our needs.

An undressed, abandoned wound may fester for years, or suppurate and burst. A treated wound, however, tends to feel very different once it has begun to receive the attention it needs. It is always moving to see just how far people can transform their lives.

Our internal core pain will be unique to us. It is based upon what, for us, was both the nature of, and our response to, the people, atmosphere and events of our early life. And it's important to stress, as we do throughout this book, that in searching the past to look at how we've constructed our internal maps, we are not allocating blame. It is not *just* what happens to us, but what we *make* of what happens to us, as well as what we bring into this life from our unique 'seed', that is important.

Different approaches to looking at the inner life of a human being offer varying ideas and theories about the nature of an individual's life patterns. Many people carry a strong sense of 'past', contained within the stories and myths of their families, tribes or cultures. This may affect their lives deeply, and may require acknowledgement rather than psychological analysis. The task of the focused psychotherapeutic approach outlined in this book is to offer the tools for revision, adjustment, healing or forgiveness only *where it is needed*.

The growing interest in the transpersonal psychologies and ancient religious systems, which incorporate the idea of soul and spirit into their maps of the human developmental journey, perhaps indicates a current thirst for a deeper meaning. Such systems certainly posit a deeper and wider view of the life journey (that we come from somewhere and go to somewhere), as well as offering an understanding of past life and collective unconscious influences, together with an awareness of how the many different energy levels – from the chakra, auric, karmic and ethereal systems – can influence us.

These different approaches may all prove helpful in our own search for an understanding and acceptance of the core pain and life patterns we carry. While the concept of the 'seed' in the individual comes from my work in transpersonal pyschology, and is one of the central themes in this book, I have chosen to concentrate on how to name and change the procedural patterns that obstruct us in this life. An exploration of the value of belief systems and the contribution of soul psychologies to change and healing are the main subjects of another book.

What is always important is our present-day act of *recognition*. Although the 'reality principle' ('Yes, my father's death was not communicated to me for over a year and I thought he'd left because I was bad'; or, 'Yes, I was beaten with a thin cane in the toolshed and no one ever believed me') is often vital in order to make sense of our difficulties, this book seeks to spotlight *how* we live with what we feel and *how* we have adjusted, and what changes, if any, are needed. I would also like to add that I have met many people who seem to carry an overwhelming sense of pain and suffering for reasons that are unclear. Not every-thing has a linear cause. We can only bear witness to the suffering we experience in ourselves or in others, and honour its reality as it lives within the individual, and not seek to concretize or rationalize its source.

Core pain and feelings and core pain statements

We can look at core pain in two ways: core pain feelings, and core pain statements – the 'as ifs' of our life. Here are some examples of core pain statements derived from core pain that lead to the patterns that are often hard to break:

1. *It is as if:* 'Only if I am allowed to have what I want on my own terms can I feel I exist.'

   The core pain feeling associated with this is terror of annihilation. As if our only hope for staying alive, or sane, is to make sure we have control over every interaction. As a consequence, people experience us as rigid and over-controlling, and if we do not have things on our own terms we experience depression and its associated sense of annihilation.

2. *It is as if:* 'No matter how hard I try to be perfect I can only ever be second best.'

   The core pain feeling here is one of rejection. We may devlop a determined perfectionism, striving always to come first, but we are snagged by this core feeling of limitation and judgement.
   We may end up exhausted and martyred, suffer burn-out, or even experience suicidal urges.

3. *It is as if:* 'When I have something nice it is bound to be taken away from me.'

   The core pain here is unbearable loss. We may have experienced the actual loss of someone or something precious early in life. Perhaps we carry an irrational guilt about something for which we were not responsible that makes us disallow or sabotage the good. We then build a sense of ourselves which involves vowing never to let anything become that important to us again. We might feel as if we are living 'on hold', lonely, unable to get close or choose joy, and our core pain may present itself as phobia, isolation or chronic anxiety.

You will see from these examples how important it is to get beneath the presenting symptoms or problems to the core of what limits or restricts us. The symptoms or problems that entrap us are the direct result of the patterns we've learned to cope with our core pain. Attending to the core pain beliefs and statements is the first step towards healing the pain.

Throughout the book we will see other examples of core pain and core pain statements. As you read, it will be helpful if you try to identify the traps, dilemmas and snags that operate in your own life, pondering on what your own core pain statement could be – the 'as if ...' It is often easier to realize this from looking at our life patterns, and then to acknowledge our core pain. In the Chapter 6 'Writing our Life Story' we will look at ways to get in touch with our own core statement.

The need to tell our own story

Stories have been an invaluable form of communication since time began. Long before psychology the storyteller was often experienced as the one who 'knew things'. He or she could be a wise person, mythmaker, keeper of secrets. The telling of fairy tales was an important form of entertainment in Europe until the turn of the last century, both for adults and children. The naming and telling of the 'story', however small, takes us into the world of 'once upon a time', 'how it all began', 'the dark and stormy night' and 'I remember when ...'. It moves us beyond our everyday lives and into the realm of imagination. Stories can be a way of dignifying and dramatizing the image of sufferer and suffering as hero and heroine, whose journey has a point or meaning. Stories honour experience, giving it shape as well as containment. And their sense of a continuum, of the spectre of past, present and future, widens the way we collect our ordinary life together. Stories, even about the most horrible and painful of situations, help to bring a dignity to our individual lives when it is *our* story: this is what happened to me; I felt this, I did this, I went there and it was as if ...

Everyone benefits from the opportunity to tell their story. In her book *Women Who Run With the Wolves,* Jungian analyst and storyteller Clarissa Pinkola Estés writes: 'Stories are medicine. They have such power. They do not require that we do, act, be anything, we need only listen.'

The stories we are sharing in this book are real-life individual stories: real-life dramas, with real-life players, scenery, atmosphere and plots. One thread will reveal the way of survival and the patterns this takes; the second will follow the 'seed' as it tries to live out the life its 'DNA' intended. The two strands weave together to give us the life story of that individual. All the stories are moving and graphically illustrate each person's struggle to live a life. And I thank again those people who have permitted their testimonies to be shared within these pages, and for allowing their themes to inspire us to look at our own lives afresh.

In Cognitive Analytic Therapy, the retelling of the life story, paying particular attention to the core pain, its statements and survival patterns, is called 'reformulation'. It is noteworthy that for many people who enter this form of therapy the storytelling is one of the most important ingredients. It marks the first step to being understood, and to understanding oneself; being in charge of one's patterns and one's life, and beginning the process of change.

What is it that changes?

One human life will encompass many phases and changes. Subtle shifts in our perceptions, feelings and our thinking go on all the time simply because of ordinary living, and we may change our style or belief because of outside influence. Indeed, today it is possible for people to have several kinds of work in one lifetime.

We have been looking at the idea that a human being has a 'seed self' and a 'survival self'. What does not change is the seed of ourselves with which we came into life. In fact, evidence seems to indicate that the pull of this seed gets stronger as we grow older. But perhaps this individual seed essence is most clearly apparent in the early months of life. Every baby is quite different and carries his or her own identity. And, depending on the nature of childhood, evidence of the individual's own nature tends to get woven into the family history and becomes the 'myth' of that person. The 'story' of what they are like, even if it is not entirely accurate, means that at least someone has noticed and acted as a sort of mirror. Because we are all so bound up with each other (we cannot even be a child without experiencing the mother's womb and being born), it is impossible to say that one thing stems from another. Our unique self has its own integrity at the same time as being implicated by and with other people and events.

What *can* change, however, is the nature of our survival self when this self has moved beyond its 'sell-by' date: when, like a snake's skin or chrysalis, it becomes redundant to the growing creature inside. The core pain statements fund a series of beliefs about ourselves that are very powerful but mistaken. As we will see, to proceed according to our mistaken beliefs prevents us from living fully, because we are trapped by living at one end of a dilemma, or snagged and unable to go forward.

Human beings are not fixed, although patterns of thinking can feel very rigid and dominating. We can challenge rigidities and free a space so that who we really are underneath can begin to breathe. But we cannot grow if we are living out of mistaken ideas. We cannot take in good things, however much they are offered, if inside we believe we are not entitled to receive them. We cannot relax or let go if we fear being persecuted or abused. And we cannot be assertive if we believe we will lose affection. So in order to change and grow we must challenge the presumptions that limit our freedom to be who we are.

Are there things better left unchanged?

There is an old superstition that it 'doesn't do to meddle with things you don't understand', and the myth of Pandora's box will be used to bear this out, as if all the things we've locked away will wreak havoc once exposed to the light of day. Then there are the old adages, 'Let sleeping dogs lie'; 'You've made your bed, you must lie on it'; 'Better the devil you know than the one you don't know'. These are powerful messages that would stop us seeking and searching and ultimately using our power of choice. On one level they encourage laziness and ensure that we are limited by fear. M. Scott Peck in his book *People of the Lie* goes further and names these attitudes as narrow-minded and evil, especially when they dominate other people's lives in relationships.

My feeling is that if you want to know your devils then make sure that you really do know them. If we fail to know them properly they have a habit of being projected onto other people, who then live them out for us, becoming the devils we fear; they pop up in relationships, in dreams, and they bind us into traps and dilemmas by remaining in the unconscious. In Jungian psychology what is called the Shadow contains all that we do not yet know, all that we fear and dislike in ourselves. Accepting that we have a Shadow, and that is is a valid part of being whole (there is no sun without shadow; no day without night), means that we know ourselves consciously. When things go wrong we are willing to look at the Shadow and see it for what it is, rather than projecting it out into the world and making other people or events carry it for us. Knowing and accepting it also means that is is less likely to attack and contain us unawares. We have it rather than it having us.

Looking at ourselves isn't easy or pain-free. But what we get out of it is an honest appraisal of ourselves and our choices, and a freedom from the burden of negative unconsciousness and traps.

Is there a burden in knowing ... and in knowing too much?

There are times when we are ready to know certain things about ourselves, and a time when we need to take action. The fact that you are reading this book might indicate that you have started a journey of self-exploration, and are already questioning things you've previously taken for granted. Because much of the meaningful work in psychotherapy is accomplished by the grace of insight, such insight will only come when we are ready for it. But we need to begin the process of self-questioning and exploration in order for insight to be forthcoming. Just knowing rationally is not enough; we need to open up our other senses – feeling, sensing, imagining. When we have opened up and are engaged in a process of unravelling and meaningful exploration we are freeing ourselves up to the possibility of developing our own powers of insight. From this point of view we cannot 'know' too much, the power itself will guide us to the right time to 'know'.

In her most moving book, *My Father's House*, Sylvia Fraser describes how for the first forty years of her life she split herself in two – the self that had a secret and the self that lived in the world. The secret self that had been split off leaked out via dreams, impulsive behaviour, irrational revulsions, in rages, incredible sadness and feelings of emptiness, until ultimately her marriage ended and she had a hysterectomy. She writes:

Though my restored memories came wrapped in terror, it is a child's terror that I realise I must feel in order to expel. Thus the adult me comforts the child, holds her hand, pities her suffering, forgives her for her complicity, assuages her guilt. She has carried the burden until I was prepared to remember our joint history without bitterness. I feel only relief, release, compassion, even elation. The mysteries of a lifetime, shadowy deeds dimly suspected, have been clarified.

Is there a right time to change?

Sometimes life gives us a jolt through a crisis that plunges us directly into new territory inside ourselves, and we are forced to change in order to get through. Sometimes problems become so serious that we have to seek professional help, and that in itself may be the beginning of change. One woman I knew flew back from an expensive holiday, for which she had spent years saving, a whole week early because she felt unwell and was convinced she had something seriously wrong with her. When it turned out only to be piles she realized the extent of her anxiety and took herself into therapy. She was then in her fifties. It was the appropriate time for her. At fifty-one Jane Fonda's husband left her. In an interview in *You* magazine she describes how she reacted:

We never know pleasure if we don't know pain. Life is difficult, period. If you don't realise that reality, you feel that life is supposed to be easy and that one day you will grow up and have all the answers. But that isn't the way life works. If you are lucky it is a continual process of struggle and hard work, growth, learning, setbacks and steps forward. The unfortunate ones are those who stop searching and give up; who don't stay open and are unwilling to grow. That is when the journey ends before it should. My journey is only beginning in fact.

Life has natural phases which involve great change. The greatest change we ever make is from girl to woman, boy to man; we change from little child to questing, questioning adolescent, struggling with emotions and changes in consciousness of all kinds. We change when we become parents, change jobs, move house, employ someone, own something precious, drive a car, fall in love. The new role, although only part of us and reflecting attitude rather than anything else, makes us look at our perspective. As we grow older we are forced to contemplate a different face and shape in the mirror and the fluctuations of our bodies. Mid-life, growing old, death – all these things involve us in change. So we are in fact changing all the time.

Developing an 'observer self'

We can consciously assist this process of change by looking inward and observing how we think and act. Thus we give ourselves a helping hand, preparing more solidly for what life may have to offer. Embracing the concept of change could be likened to a marathon runner preparing for the run of his life. He limbers up and stretches and does hours of warm-up exercises.

Psychotherapy can also be seen in this way: as preparation for changes which need to be made. Some of the changes brought about by psychotherapy are easy and natural, and are mainly concerned with shifts in thinking, perception and attitude. What is harder to change is the reflexive response to old messages. These old messages from the past may be known, even understood, and we may dilute their power considerably, but we have to actively learn not to act on them any more if they are no longer appropriate. This takes deliberate will and effort, and many different forms of exercises throughout this book will help with this process.

How to change

In order to change we have first of all to understand the nature of our survival self and our mistaken belief system. We must know something of how it might have developed and also a good deal about how mistaken thinking still operates within our life. Part 2 'Naming the Problem', will assist in this discovery process. Part 3, 'Gathering Information', is aimed at helping us to gather sketches about our early life: what happened and how our attitudes were shaped from our assimilation during this time. Much emphasis is laid upon self-reflection and self-analysis, with the assistance of detailed questionnaires and exercises. By writing down our life story, how things have been for us and how things have come to be as they are in our life, we also begin to look at what it is we need or wish to change. Part 4 'Making the Change', assists with this process and gives examples from other people who have made important changes for themselves in this way.

One does not have to be an engineer to drive a car and one certainly does not have to be a professional psychologist to live a life, but if things go wrong in either case it can be helpful to know something of how to go about tracing and remedying the trouble. The chapters are arranged in such a way that the simpler problems are described first; these earlier sections could be seen as a roadside manual, giving only partial explanations of the processes involved but aiming to provide enough to get the car back on the road. Later chapters give a fuller account of how we organize our lives and of the ways in which our sense of ourselves and of our relationships with others can be distorted. The basic assumption is that, in order to overcome our difficulties, we need to alter both how we see ourselves and our world and how we act.

The limits of self-help

It is important to say at this stage that not all difficulties and symptoms are the reflection of problems in living. Some are the effects of bodily processes and may need medical treatment. Many common symptoms, such as undue fatigue, headaches, indigestion or appetite changes, are most frequently the result of emotional stress, but can, in some instances, be caused by physical illness. If there is any doubt about the nature of such symptoms then medical advice should be sought. It is also the case that being badly depressed may cause, or may be caused by, physical changes in the nervous system which are best treated by drugs. Someone whose depression is severe, who suffers from marked physical or mental lethargy, or whose sleep is broken regularly in the small hours with gloomy wakefulness thereafter, should seek medical or psychiatric advice. More generally, if mental distress is severe or prolonged, with experiences of the mind not working normally, it would be appropriate and kind to the self to seek professional help.

Other problems are due to causes that are not primarily emotional, psychological or medical; they are social. The American writer Henry David Thoreau, in *Walden*, observed that 'the mass of men live lives of quiet desperation'. While much of this desperation may be rooted in the personal domain of marriage, family and career and might be eased by the methods discussed in this book, to be poor, unemployed, prematurely retired, discriminated against, badly housed, to have to work at intrinsically boring tasks under the arbitrary control of others are also potent causes of desperation. The impact of these factors is, of course, upon the feelings of individuals, but the appropriate action is political and beyond the scope of this book.

Preparation for reading this book

Having looked at some of the reasons we may wish to seek change, we now need to consider how we might engage in this process. This section suggests ways in which we might prepare for reading the self-help programme described in this book. Because you may be reading this book on your own, or sharing it with another person, some preparation is more pertinent than it might be if you were sharing the psychotherapy process with a therapist. No book can hope to take the place of a therapist, but there are one or two ways in which we can help ourselves assume the more contemplative approach to what we hope will be a journey of exploration and ultimately of change.

Co-counselling

You may like to share the process of reading this book with a friend. Each of you can help the other with the process of identifying attitudes, thinking and problem areas, and in answering the questionnaires. In co-counselling the aim is for the counsellor to be an objective observer and questioner to the counsellee, and for you each to take turns in this role. In Part 3 the questionnaires and the section called 'What Makes Us Tick?' are laid out in such a way that the counsellor may read out to the other and allow the counsellee time for reflection. Time for pondering is important, as is time usefully engaged in painting the images and impressions that are formed during the process of exploration. Help from another in writing the life story can also be important and can act as an encouragement and keep us at the task. If you decide upon co-counselling, set aside a certain time each week to meet in the privacy of one of your homes, and treat the time as you would a counselling session with a professional.

Going it alone

If you decide to read the book alone and to enter into the self-help programme, set aside some uninterrupted time to read the question-naires and to do the exercises. Part of the programme involves keeping notes, jotting down ideas and associations, keeping a journal of thoughts or ideas. For this you will perhaps need to allocate time for yourself in a way that you may not be used to. Marking out time in your diary can help, or setting aside particular days which you devote to self-reflection and keeping an eye on your aims for change. In each section there are instructions on how to proceed next, and examples from people who have already travelled along this path.

Notebook, pencil, colours and loose paper

Think of reading this book as going on a journey, and prepare yourself appropriately. A small notebook which will fit into your pocket is useful for jotting down thoughts and reactions as you go through each day. A larger notebook is helpful to keep a fuller journal if you so choose and is useful for writing down your dreams, ideas, fantasies, open letters to people who come up for you in the course of this programme, your life story, your target problems and aims, and any other pieces of writing – scribblings, drawings, cartoons, doodles – that intrigue you. Choose a notebook that you really like, that has a cover you enjoy, that you can claim as totally yours. Some people like to have loose-leaf files so that they can add more and more pages; others like hardbacked notebooks and journalists' pads. Richard Burton kept his life's diaries in lined Woolworth's notebooks, of which there were hundreds when he died. Keep your notes and thoughts as *you* would want to, not as others would, or for others.

The early five minutes

It is a very good idea when beginning a programme of self-examination to start each day with a few minutes' silence. If you only have five minutes when you are alone in the bathroom, then so be it; if you can get longer, excellent. For the first few weeks don't try and 'do' anything with this time, just quietly reflect upon yourself, how you feel, how your body feels, and gradually become aware of the first thoughts and stream-of-consciousness impressions you have about yourself. Jot down afterwards anything that strikes you as interesting and unusual, especially feelings. Most of us give very little time, if any, to pondering on how we feel emotionally or physically, and when we have problems we tend either to shut down and go on automatic, or feel flooded with uncontrollable feelings. This early five minutes will be a kind of anchor, a chance to be in silent communion with yourself at the very beginning of the day. And later on, when we've processed the difficulties into your story and your goals for change, you may like to use this time for contemplation of a more meditational kind.

Self-monitoring

In Part 4 'Making the Change', we look at ways in which we may help along the process of change. One of the most useful methods of keeping aware of what is happening inside ourselves is through self-monitoring, and details of how to accomplish this are described in this section. However, as you embark upon the reading of this book you might like to make a start by monitoring the number of times you think negatively about yourself, for example. Alternatively, monitor the times you have a bad headache or other physical symptoms. Monitoring when we feel depressed, by writing in a small pocket notebook the time of day, what is happening, what we are thinking about, can help us to see if there is any pattern to our mood swings, episodes of depression or angry outbursts. The same goes for any physical symptoms and panic or phobic attacks. As you read through the book you will see how monitoring the occasions when certain traps and dilemmas operate in your life can give you the insight and the clarity of control to get out of the trap or dilemma, and to choose to think and behave differently.

Choosing joy

We've said a lot so far about changing the negative patterns that have had a hold on our lives. Just as important is to value alongside this work the things we have done that we feel good about, the green shoots our seed has thrown up along the way. Sometimes just the fact of our survival is enough. To have survived a childhood of abuse and yet to be making our way in the world, working at what we can, trying again and again to make a relationship, is brave. Observe your own braveness, and wonder at this capacity you have for endurance!

Survival procedures and irrational guilt often prevent us from choosing joy or happiness. We think: 'I've got to get this done', or 'I can't be happy until ...', or 'If I allow myself to like this I will have to pay for it'. It's hard to have to live life in this way, as if we are waiting for permission to be happy. Several people I have met have said that they could envy a dying person, because they no longer had to struggle at life, they could just let go and be themselves. It is a sad thought that we have to wait to live until we are about to die. Sometimes just saying 'yes' to life and choosing a joyful attitude makes a difference. To walk in the street and see what is happening rather than what is not; to greet a person and recognize what is in their hearts rather than defending against what might hurt us. And the poets have been there before us. Their words can help:

> To see a World in a Grain of Sand
> And a Heaven in a Wild Flower,
> Hold Infinity in the palm of your hand
> And Eternity in an hour.
>
> 'Auguries of Innocence' by William Blake

Part 2
Naming the Problem

Chapter 1

Traps

Traps occur when the old belief system built by the survival self goes on informing the way we think and act long after it is appropriate. The way we learned to survive worked early on, but if it remains unrevised, what we think or do automatically as part of this survival tends to become a trap, and can actually make us feel worse.

In order to remove ourselves from a trap we need to revise what it is, in terms of our thinking, ideas or presumptions, that keeps us there.

The 'doing what others want' trap

When we fear being judged harshly, or feel uncertain of ourselves and our self-worth, we tend not to express ourselves freely but move towards the ideas, beliefs or desires of other people. We do as others dictate. We may please people, doing what they want, thinking their ideas, even feeling their feelings. (One woman said to me once, 'I felt I ought to cry because everyone else was so upset, but I didn't feel anything.') The idea behind our way of proceeding is, 'If I do what they want things are bound to be OK. They will like me, want me, want to be with me.' What tends to happen over a period of time is that our eagerness to please is taken advantage of. And we feel used and abused, angry, hurt and resentful that we should be treated in this way when we've tried so hard to receive someone's affection or attention. I often hear people saying, 'I gave him everything he wanted, never argued, never disagreed ... I even changed my hair colour/way of dressing to be as he wanted,' or, 'I stopped seeing the friends he didn't like,' or, 'I gave up my car/hobby for her, and then she went and left me for someone else who doesn't listen to a word she says.' When what one really wants

is affection, respect, care, love, it's bitterly disappointing to find it backfiring in this way.

What we need to challenge is the premise that we have to please others in order to be liked. Where has this idea come from? How often do we do it? Can we see after reading this that our learned way of coping with uncertainty about ourselves actually makes our situation worse? The more we are taken for granted and abused for our attempts to please, the more our uncertainty about ourselves is confirmed. As long as our energy is taken up with pleasing others, moving into their worlds to try to make our own safe, we are not developing our real inner selves as we might; we develop only a coping, or survival self.

When we feel let down or ignored because we are in the 'trying to please' trap our own actual needs *are* being ignored, which makes us feel resentful and needy. Sometimes these needs burst out in a childlike way when we don't want them to. We feel out of control, and because the pressure to please others, and our natural internal fury at this restriction, causes such tension, we may find that we put things off, actually let people down. Or we may hide away, increasing people's anger and displeasure with us, and thus compounding our uncertainty about ourselves. I knew a woman who was invited to a party she really wanted to go to on the same day that she had to attend her parents' golden wedding. She couldn't bear to upset either by saying no. As a result, she failed to reply to the party invitation, which made her appear rude and inconsiderate, and she arrived late for her parents' golden wedding because she was still trying to make a way clear to go to the other party.

Pat recognized herself as being caught in the 'doing what others want' trap, and she felt it applied to all her reactions. She could not bear to say 'no', or to feel she had let anyone down by being different in either opinion, view, dress, attitude, ideas or action. To her, failure to do what others wanted, pleasing them, meant dismissal and hostility, which she could not endure. In her self-monitoring of this trap she wrote:

'Bought a new dress. Didn't buy the one I wanted but the one the sales girl insisted looked the best. It was more expensive than I wanted and not the right colour, but somehow I couldn't refuse her, let her down, it seemed so important to her somehow that I bought this partic-ular dress. When I got home I just cried, I felt so upset and cross and so helpless. It wasn't what I wanted but I couldn't say "no".'

Pat also wrote about incidents with her children when she had given in to them over bedtimes. She had either felt bad about it and had shouted at them, or she had felt remorseful, given in to them, there'd been noisy, argumentative behaviour, and once again she'd lost her temper and felt aggrieved. 'I was giving them what they wanted and they threw it all back in my face.' She recalled similar incidents with her husband and friends, and one friend in particular to whom she had acted as 'agony aunt'. Pat had wanted to confide in her about her own problems, but the friend had cut her off sharply saying, 'I can't go into that now'. When Pat seemed tearful and hurt the friend suggested disgruntledly they meet in a café the following week. Pat duly turned up on time, but the friend arrived one hour later as Pat was boiling up inside with a rage she could not express and which only made her more fearful of losing her friend. She had convinced herself that it was her fault the friend was late, that she must have written down the wrong time, even though she knew this wasn't true. Pat couldn't speak because she was so upset, and the friend became cross and impatient. As a result of the encounter Pat felt guilty, alone and cross, but these feelings were hidden in her headache and sore feet.

When later we looked at the pattern of Pat's need to please and at what compelled her to keep doing this, she selected one of the images she'd written down during her monitoring and got into the feel of it. The trigger point for giving in to, and pleasing, others seemed to be linked to an expression in their eyes – a compelling and determined look. In staying with this image she was reminded of the look in a teacher's eye at her second school. This was her English teacher for whom she had written some good essays, and the teacher, who had been very nervous as it was her first job, looked to Pat when things got difficult in class. Pat became her anchor and help. Then Pat told me she'd realized that the look went further back, to her own mother, who had experienced similar feelings of insecurity, and had looked to Pat to help her and make life more comfortable. Pat's adaptation to having to do as others want began here. Her most basic fear was that if she did not respond to the eye call her mother would become cross, upset and withdrawn, and Pat's world would be in chaos. She dreaded her mother's cold silences, which made her feel isolated and abandoned, and which she interpreted as her own fault, as 'something wrong with her'. It was precisely to cope with such fear and pain that she developed the habit of pleasing. This mode had served her reasonably well during childhood and adolescence, because her mother responded and things were kept safe. But only on a superficial level, for underneath Pat wasn't developing her own voice or her own ways of being; she was bending and twisting to her mother's.

The habit of pleasing others went on into adult life and wasn't questioned until Pat came into therapy because of her depression. The depression was largely due to her living out of her survival self's need to please, at the huge expense of her real self. She felt guilty if she started work or had thoughts of her own. She married a man who greatly benefited from her pleasing skills and who was at first surprised and resentful when she would burst out angrily at the children, or when she did try and do work of her own that was different (she had recently given this up because she felt so guilty). Then everything was thrown into confusion by Pat's depression.

Looking at the placation trap, recognizing how much it controlled her everyday life, helped Pat to free herself from it. She chose to risk saying no, doing something different from others, to risk being disliked. She faced her worst fear. She saw that it was rooted in the world of her childhood and carried with it the force and pain of the child's fear. She recognized that if she wanted to grow and be free she had to take risks she couldn't have taken in childhood.

Although Pat's husband felt a little threatened at first by her change from placation to being more assertive, he came to recognize that his wife had many more 'real' qualities than he had seen before, that she did stop being depressed, and that it was a relief to have a positive response from her instead of feeling she was always so 'nice'. Pat had some surprises too: people she had previously feared would not like her actually took more notice, and the friend who had let her down said, 'I feel you're much more someone to be reckoned with rather than being taken for granted like a doormat.' In my experience people don't want doormats and placators, because in time they make them feel bad. To be 'too good' encourages others to behave badly – often in the hope of getting a real response. Also, if people are seen as 'too good', their underlying anger is more fearful because it is hidden.

Most of us want to please others, and it forms a useful and necessary skill in the making of relationships and in human interaction. But when it is all encompassing, when our entire life is lived through it, it becomes a damaging and self-negating trap, perpetuating our worst fears. On page 28 is a questionnaire for you to fill in about your own particular 'doing what others want' trap.

If you find that you have answered 'yes' to more than one question in each section then you are in the placation trap. Stay with what you have ticked and concentrate on the feelings you have identified. See if you can locate any images or memories that help you place these feelings. Make a note of them in your notebook and we will return to them more fully in Chapter 6, 'Writing Our Life Story'.

The 'depressed thinking' trap

We may have come to expect that we will do things badly or fail in some way because we feel we've done so in the past. One or two disappointments may well make us lose confidence, until we believe that we are in some way a failure. Thinking about oneself in a depressed way

---

Questionnaire: The 'doing what others want' trap

Do you act as if the following were true?

I fear not pleasing:
those close to me;
people I work for;
anyone and everyone/men/women/authority figures.

If I don't please them:
they won't like/love me;
I'll never get anywhere in life;
I'll be rejected/passed over/ignored/abandoned/criticized/hated/abused.

Pleasing people means:
doing what they want regardless of how I feel;
getting to know all about them and what makes them tick so I can feel confident of producing things they would like;
never getting cross or upsetting anyone, whatever they have done to me;
squashing what I *really* feel in case it slips out and I am rejected or criticized;
feeling dependent upon the goodwill of others to feel all right inside.

Sometimes this feeling I have to please can make me feel out of control, and my uncertainty about what to do to ensure the goodwill of others is increased. I then find myself:
putting things off because I'm unsure I've got it right and I can't bear to be wrong;
being unable to say 'no', and so ending up taking on too many tasks, agreeing to certain things that are inappropriate, and ultimately letting people down.

---

perpetuates the trap of feeling depressed. Although depression can be complex and have an actual physical basis which needs medication (see page 16) – and there are always deeper and more subtle reasons for feeling depressed, which I will look at more fully later – the depressed mood created by depressed thinking can be altered remarkably by following a few simple instructions.

Using self-monitoring, over the next week write down how many times you find yourself thinking, 'I'm not going to be able to do that.' 'I'm not going to get into this conversation because I don't know enough about it.' 'I look awful so I won't go out today.' 'I'm too tearful to do anything.' 'Last time I went near that place I couldn't bear it.' Any time, in fact, that you feel 'I'm bound to do this badly.'

Another form of self-monitoring is to make a chart like the one shown in Figure 2. Give yourself marks, from 1 to 10, for each hour of the day, to indicate the level of your depressed mood. A score of 1 would

	Mon	Tues	Wed	Thur	Fri	Sat	Sun
7 a.m.	10						
8 a.m.	10						
9 a.m.	9						
10 a.m.	9						
11 a.m.	9						
12 noon	7						
1 p.m.	7						
2 p.m.	6						
3 p.m.	7						
4 p.m.	5						
5 p.m.	7						
6 p.m.	4						
7 p.m.	4						
8 p.m.	3						
9 p.m.	5						
10 p.m.	5						

10 = very depressed, down, sad, not coping

7 = depressed but coping

5 = mildly depressed

3 = low, but able to take in other things and look around

1 = not depressed but enjoying the moment

Mark the chart for each hour for one week and see where your lowest and highest points come. You might like to use certain colours instead of numbers.

Figure 2 Chart for self-monitoring depressed mood

denote a lack of depression, whereas scoring 10 would signify a highly depressed state. This process asks us to be aware of our mood and what we are feeling; it also gives some loose structure to the shape of our day. So often when people feel depressed they choose to curl up in a ball and do nothing, presuming that whatever they do will not work. This simple exercise will help you in two ways. Firstly, it will let you see at what times you feel most depressed, and that you are probably not at number 10 all the time. If you find that you are, then perhaps some professional help should be sought, unless – and this requires honesty and self-observation – it may be that you are angry underneath your depression and don't want this to be relieved until you have been allowed to be angry. We will come back to this in Chapter 3. Secondly, by monitoring what it is you are thinking about at the times when you feel most low, you will get an indication of where your fears about yourself lie.

There are several ways in which this trap operates, and for everyone who recognizes it, it will have different origins. Malcolm, who had become very stuck in the 'depressed thinking' trap, felt he had got into an increasingly depressed way of looking at himself and life because of his disappointment with other people's failure to recognize the value of his work. On retirement he had hoped for greater acclaim and feared that he would be forgotten. Although on a deeper level his problems were largely to do with an early dilemma of 'having to be special or feeling empty and insignificant', which we will look at in Chapter 2, he was also caught in this particular trap. Every day he contributed to his depressed mood by thoughts such as, 'No one wants me any more.' 'There's no point writing to X because they probably won't reply.'

Malcolm began to see that he was approaching each day with the following attitude: 'I feel doomed before I start, so I jeopardize my own life by not valuing what I do, say or aim for.' One of the ways he got out of this trap was to start to value, and work at valuing, just what he had done and did do with his life. As an English teacher, he had many extremely grateful students and many fine examples of his work, but because a criterion for his acceptance and value was a fixed external idea of fame and public recognition, he could not see how much he was valued without realizing it for the many things he offered. Malcolm's depressed thinking about himself was accompanied by feelings of hope-lessness and pointlessness, and by thoughts of death, but fortunately he was angry enough about this feeling of 'stuckness' to use his anger to get out of it and to re-evaluate his approach.

We may also be trapped by our negative and depressed thinking in a passive way which makes us feel victimized. Clare felt very weak after a period in hospital for a knee operation. She had been feeling very depressed before this because she was unable to carry on with her work at home or at the consultant engineering company where she'd been a valued member of staff for five years. She was depressed when she was 'out of role', when the ordered world she knew was removed during her hospitalization, and afterwards when she felt she couldn't cope very well with everyday chores. She became more and more depressed, because she told herself, 'I'm useless.' 'I can't do anything.' 'No one will want to see me like this.' She feared that her husband would not understand her and that she would not be able to make him understand. Eventually, she got to the point where she was almost permanently in tears because of this trap.

She and her husband both attended a therapy session, where we drew up a self-monitoring chart to record her depressed mood (Figure 2). When she realized that she was not depressed all round the clock, but that there were some grey areas, she rallied enough to use the better hours to draw or paint what she was feeling and write down what she wanted to say. At first she dismissed all of what she wanted to say as, 'It's only silly, he'll never listen to this ...', but with the help of her husband she was able to make use of the less black periods and free herself from the more depressed times.

Questionnaire: The 'I'll only do things badly' trap

When you have monitored your own negative thoughts for a week (the 'I'll only do things badly' ideas), spend some time with your findings and try and see if you can identify where these thoughts and ideas stem from, and how much they are in fact self-perpetuating.

How much do you exaggerate your fear of doing things badly?

Use self-monitoring methods to get a really accurate picture together. Use the chart in Figure 2 or monitor the time and place when you expect a negative outcome to:
(a) a thought/idea;
(b) what you say;
(c) what you do;

If you feel you have done something badly, what were the ingredients of your involvement in that work? Were you:
doing something you liked?
doing something you wanted to do?
doing something new?
doing something you had admired others doing and presumed you would be unable to do yourself?

How much understanding did you have about what it entailed?

If you find that indeed your depression is made worse by constant depressed thinking that needs to be challenged and consciously adjusted, it will help to read on and perhaps find some clue to the source of your depressed feelings about yourself in further chapters.

The 'I'm better off on my own' trap

Sometimes we take the view that the trauma resulting from contact with other people just isn't worth it. We feel so anxious that people will find us boring and stupid and we get so hot and bothered when we have to talk to someone that we decide to avoid contact. It isn't that we'd rather be on our own; it's that we believe that because things don't go well for us socially we have no choice. When we are forced to make contact with others, and because of our internal beliefs about our abilities, we don't look at others properly, we find it difficult to know what to say and we appear actually unfriendly and standoffish. For these reasons people tend to leave us alone. This is the very opposite to what we really want, and, rather as with the pleasing trap, we are not developing the skills for meeting and talking to people that we need to gain confidence and break the negative cycle of the trap. The other aspect that tends to increase is the fantasy level of our ideas about our own incompetence. We can become phobic about it, building it up to dramatic proportions. Our sensitivity to other people's reactions to us can also be heightened, as we imagine rejections and criticisms in an exaggerated form. Jeff recalled his own experience of this: 'When I began to speak to a group of people at the party, I felt as if my whole being was lit up in stage lights and everyone was watching my performance.'

Paul decided very early on that being involved with people wasn't worth it. In his early life he had been in hospital for eighteen months. He had no conscious memory of that time, but it is not hard to imagine the powerful effect such a long separation would have on a small infant, and the way in which he might well have had to cut off and defend himself in order to cope with his feelings of loss inside. Then when he was six his mother became ill and died the following year. The rest of his childhood was particularly isolated: his father worked very hard and was absent for much of the time, leaving Paul with a grandmother whom he did not like. Paul withdrew into the world of study and encyclopaedias.

When we met, Paul had a successful career as a scientist, but tended to be very split inside himself. He felt he was either the powerful scientist at his word processor or the very lonely boy. One way in which he

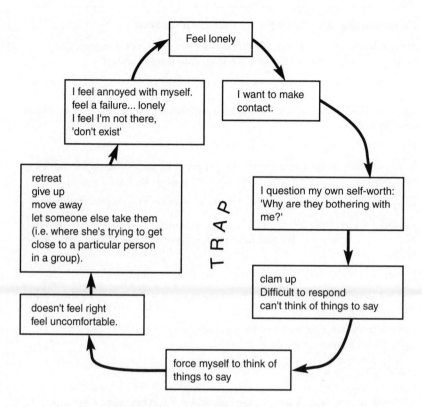

Feel lonely

I feel annoyed with myself.
feel a failure... lonely
I feel I'm not there,
'don't exist'

I want to make
contact.

retreat
give up
move away
let someone else take them
(i.e. where she's trying to get
close to a particular person
in a group).

T R A P

I question my own self-worth:
'Why are they bothering with
me?'

clam up
Difficult to respond
can't think of things to say

doesn't feel right
feel uncomfortable.

force myself to think of
things to say

Figure 3 Mary saw her problem in this way. The chart helped her to see how she was trapped into being 'better off on her own' as a way of coping

had ensured that this split would perpetuate itself was by falling into the 'I'm better off on my own' trap. Then he fell deeply in love and all his deeper feelings of longing, excitement, fusion, togetherness, needfulness and lovingness came to the surface. At first things were wonderful but when the initial wonder and magic was at all threatened he once again became the six-year-old boy who feared abandonment by the woman he loved (originally his mother). We will return to Paul's story in Chapter 2, but having identified the way in which he kept his split going by his isolation he was prepared to look more at his internal world, instead of the external, carefully controlled world of the scientist. He took risks in order deliberately not to isolate himself in situations at home, by going with the pain of his feelings and trying to find ways of expressing them.

Questionnaire: The 'I'm better off on my own' trap

Make a list of all the things you do on your own. Include activities like making breakfast, going to work, walking, shopping, holidays.

What is the nature of your work – in a busy office or factory, shop or organization, or freelance, a gardener or self-employed? How many people do you see every day? Make a chart showing the number of hours you are alone each day, for a week.

How much of your day do you spend alone?

If you do work within an organization where there might be opportunities to talk to others and form friendships, how often do you avoid contact?

Do you join clubs or associations, go to eat with others, stay on after work?

How do you tend to spend your time at weekends? Do you feel 'people have got to come to me' or, 'It's not worth making an effort as others never appreciate it'?

Do any of the following feelings about isolating yourself ring true?

I'm not used to being with people and don't know what to say to them when they start talking to me.

I'm not used to being with people because:
I don't have enough practice.
I don't meet people.
I don't join in at work.
I don't join outings.
I don't make sure that I set up meetings where I can practise being with people.

I expect people to talk to me because:
I don't feel I'm an outgoing person. (Where does this come from? Who said this? Is it really true? Check it out by asking someone.)
If people don't come to me then it's not worth it.
I don't feel I should have to make an effort. Nice things should just happen.

I lack confidence with others. I presume I will be:
rejected, that people won't like me;
criticized because I am not like others;
ignored – people will find me boring and stupid because I believe I'm not clever/attractive/rich/don't speak with the right accent.

When I do meet people I can't look at them, my hands sweat and I can't get my breath. I feel as if my whole body is lit up and that everyone is looking at me waiting for me to make a mistake.

I fear if I open my mouth I will:
say the wrong thing, and people will laugh at me;
get in a muddle, panic, perhaps become cross or start swearing, that I will say something awful.

Would you like to change the assumption that 'I'm better off on my own' and find ways to get out of this trap? If so, what is your image of how you would like to be with others? Describe the qualities you would like to have. Imagine yourself in this way.

Mark down in your notebook which of the above statements apply to you. Again, we are gathering important information, which we will use when we reconstruct our life story and make our plan for change.

The 'avoidance' trap

If we avoid things we find difficult, we will discover in the long run that our avoidance only increases our difficulties and our sense of ineffectiveness and lack of control in life. Perhaps the most powerful example of this is people who suffer from agoraphobia.

Every agoraphobic will have experienced something frightening outside, or when they were waiting in a bus queue or a shop, or just walking along a street. Sometimes it can happen in a cinema or other public place. Knees turn to jelly, pulse increases and it feels as if the heart might jump right out of the body; breathing becomes difficult, you feel faint or sick, buildings and surrounding vistas may become distorted and the overwhelming terror can be momentarily incapacitating. People have said, 'I really thought I was going to die.'

The physical manifestations of anxiety have always startled people with their depth and insistency, and can often easily be confused with real organic illness. The symptoms are identical, but the cause is different. What tends to happen in these instances is that the person becomes frightened to go out again in case the same thing happens. The feelings are *so* fearful that we become involved in the fear of the fear itself and stay indoors, thus avoiding the situation of the fear. This may give temporary relief, although many sufferers from agoraphobia also feel very anxious about being alone inside a house and project their anxiety onto families or friends, so that they only feel safe when everyone is home safely tucked up in bed. Avoidance of anything fearful may relieve us from the anxiety, but it is at considerable cost to our freedom and may restrict our life severely. Many agoraphobic sufferers do not go out of their houses for years.

We may not feel that we go to the extreme lengths experienced in agoraphobia, but may relate to all the feelings outlined in the next questionnaire in other situations in our lives. Some people avoid contact with others for fear of being rejected; others avoid making decisions in case they're the wrong ones; many people avoid telephoning in case they get a difficult response; others avoid their everyday tasks, leaving them for others to do or until they are forced to do them. All of which result in frustration and feeling bad – which can be worse than the fear the person is trying to avoid.

Most people get into the avoidance trap because they do not believe that they can cope with unforeseen or imagined circumstances. The sense of 'what if ...', followed by the dramatic scenario of rejection, anger, ridicule, or worse, can make us feel incapacitated, and so we avoid the situation.

Terry lost both his parents before he was three and was brought up by his grandmother. She felt very protective towards him, and he was never encouraged to go out and experience the world for himself. During his early school life he was often absent due to long periods of hospitalization to rectify a birth defect, and he missed out on a lot of schooling. When he was asked to give answers in class and found he couldn't reply, he felt embarrassed and 'stupid'. Later, when he wanted to ask a question about something he didn't understand, he avoided it lest he be called 'stupid' again.

Unused to having to deal with confrontation and nastiness, and with no preparation for an outside world that was so very different from life with his grandmother, Terry developed avoidance tactics to cope with potential stress, mistakenly believing that he couldn't handle whatever might be asked of him. The 'avoidance' trap meant that he didn't stay in any one job for long in case he was asked to take on more advanced things that he believed he wouldn't be able to handle. He had avoided making any commitment in terms of his work or future, and was plagued with the idea that he shouldn't have to ask but should just know. When he was able to face his imagined fears he took the risk of not avoiding things, and experienced all the physical symptoms described previously in relation to agoraphobia. But he did overcome his fears and entered into a training programme for a proper professional career.

Questionnaire: The 'avoidance' trap

I avoid things because of false beliefs: 'I'm no good at that so I won't try'.
Examine why you may have written something off. When did this attitude start? How far back does it go?
Who told you you were no good?
Have you been discouraged by not coming up to certain standards? Were they your own standards or those of others? (Important early figures: for example, father, mother, teacher.)
Has there been a period in your life when you felt left behind, when you didn't understand something and were unable to ask or get someone to go over it with you?

'Fear of failure means that I don't want to start anything.'
Have you put off starting a course, applying for jobs, making contact with people you know can help you?
What does failure mean to you?
When did you first come across it?
What are the examples of failure from your own life, or the lives of your family and friends?
If you feel you've failed to live up to your or others' expectations, do you feel it is what you attempted that hasn't worked out, or do you see it as a reflection of your lack of ability?
Have you identified your whole self with this, when it is only one aspect of what you do? For example, I may 'fail' to have my books accepted by a publisher, but 'I' am not a failure. I may 'fail' to look as smart as my mother only because I don't have the flair or figure for smart clothes. I may 'fail' my exams or my driving test, but I am not a failure. What I try for is not what I am.

Make a list of all the things you cope with by avoidance:
writing to friends;
inviting someone round;
applying for promotion;
starting a new course;
getting angry with someone;
reading something different because we envy others' knowledge about it;
trying something new;
sorting out sex problems;
confronting my partner;
being angry with someone who has hurt me;
mending something that's broken;
tidying up;
planning things to do with my toddler/children.

What are your fantasies about what will happen if you don't avoid things?
become ill;
rejection;
confrontation with things I don't like about myself;

> fear of getting it wrong, not knowing what to say, how to assert myself;
> get angry;
> make a mess;
> being judged.
>
> What is the personal price you are paying by your avoidance?

You will perhaps have recognized some of your deeply felt fears from this questionnaire. Give yourself time to allow an acceptance of these fears, because we do not go to the trouble of adopting avoidance behaviour unless our fears are profound. Write about it in your notebook. Knowing and naming what you fear is the first step to overcoming it. Working with your fear will be central to the development of your target problems and aims in Chapter 7.

The low self-esteem trap

Many people suffer from low self-esteem. This means they place little value on themselves or their contribution to life. And in feeling such worthlessness, they become self-effacing, automatically presuming they have nothing to offer. This might manifest itself in an obvious form, such as speaking negatively about themselves, putting themselves down or leaving themselves till last. Or it may take a more subtle form and remain hidden under a brittle, successful exterior or beneath the mask of a 'salt of the earth' coper who always manages. This subtle sense of uselessness may be so well hidden that friends and neighbours are shocked when the person they saw as marvellous and competent takes an overdose, revealing perhaps for the first time just how bad and worthless they feel.

People with low self-esteem find it hard to ask for anything for themselves, because they have very little sense of 'self' and therefore do not know what they might ask for, or they fear that in asking they will be blamed or punished. Feeling worthless tends to derive from having been criticized or judged as bad or wanting at some point in our development. We are left feeling that what we express, indeed often who we actually are and what we want, is in some way wrong or not up to scratch. How often have you heard someone say, 'I feel wrong' or, 'I feel bad'? And this can be said even by people who have accomplished much, or who are actually well loved. It's as if the self they wake up with in the mornings feels that it has no right to any self-expression or desire, or sometimes even to existence.

What is frequently most difficult about feeling worthless is that the standards we assume we 'should' be achieving are unclear; we are just sure that whatever we do it will never be good enough. Such a negative sense of self-worth means that we feel we cannot get what we want (a) because we don't know what we want and we feel weak and feeble, (b) because we fear being punished for even mentioning it, and (c) as if anything good we do receive is bound to be taken back or turn sour because, actually, we don't deserve it anyway.

This becomes a trap when we feel so hopeless about everything that we give up trying to express ourselves, at the same time as punishing ourselves for being weak. Such a circular movement in our thinking merely serves to confirm our sense of worthlessness.

Susan came into therapy because she felt unable to make any decisions in her life. As she described it: 'I don't know who to please for the best'. When, after the birth of her second child, a doctor told her that she was suffering from postnatal depression, she thought to herself, 'What does he mean, this is just how I always feel'. She identified feeling worthless, and had often been depressed, sometimes suicidal, claiming the only thing that had stopped her walking out in front of a car was her guilt about how the driver would feel.

She had very few early memories but many images of suffering, and some of these came forward more poignantly after her own children were born. She described her mother as 'hard-faced' and had experienced her as critical, demanding and conditional. Her mother boasted that she had 'never had a dirty nappy' from Susan, but that right from infancy she had been in the habit of 'holding her over a newspaper'. Later on Susan was left out in her pram in all weathers, even snow. Susan learned to survive this early start by expecting nothing from anyone and by fitting in with what other people wanted. She was terrified of feeling cold or hungry, and always wore too much clothing and carried food in her bag.

After the birth of her younger sister, the family's 'golden girl', she became 'mother's little helper' and rather than going to college left school early to help contribute to the family.

Despite these beginnings Susan had somehow held on to a belief that her life must have meaning. Towards this end she had joined several philosophical, political and religious societies, but still the feelings of worthlessness did not fade, as the groups could provide only outer rather than inner guides.

She expressed her understanding of her particular traps and dilemmas in the following way:

Feeling unsure of my worth and afraid of rejection, I try to please others by doing what they want. This results either in my being taken for granted and abused, when I feel angry, guilty and start to avoid people, which leads to isolation and confirms my low self-esteem. Or in my feeling confused about whom to please, leading to being frozen in indecision which makes me feel stupid and worthless.

Susan's dreams variously depicted her as a prisoner in a cage, a dead person underground who hears a voice bidding her to come out, and finally as someone who falls out of a tree but manages to somersault and land on her feet. As she worked with the dream themes and with the diagram of her trap (see Figure 4) she began to find a way out. She got in touch with her 'seed', her authentic rather than survival self, and began to let this self inform her of its value. This became a part of her which had its own sense of worth, meaning and direction, which was not dependent on the approval of others and which was able to make choices. She wrote:

I realize now that 'yes' to everything is wrong and 'no' to everything is wrong, and leads to a difficult existence. What I must brave is the disapproval of some people. It's hard, but no harder than the life I lead now.

Susan eventually decided to go to college to study for her O and A levels. About two years after her therapy she wrote the following:

I am going to do things on my own. Not carry food in my bag and eat it on the bus. I'll wait and buy something in a café. I'll sit at a table on my own and not feel I'm doing something wrong because there isn't anyone with me. When I was young I had an imaginary friend who travelled on buses with me and slept with me at night, who went everywhere I went. Here I felt on my own and obvious, so I'll bring that back to myself. I'll feel I've got myself with me and rely on that, not on what someone on the outside has to say.

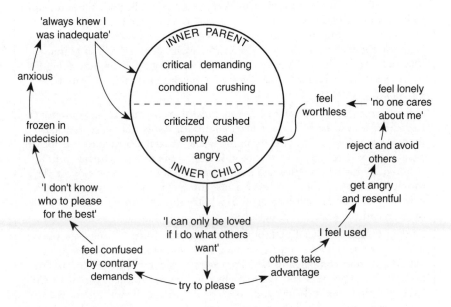

Figure 4 Susan's trap diagram

Exercise

Monitor for one week the occasions when you think in a 'I'm worthless' way, and make a note of them in your diary. Try and isolate a tone of voice, attitude or look that accompanies you at these times. See if you can give a shape or image to this internal judge. Does it remind you of anything from an earlier time in your life? If your internal judge is a parent, teacher, priest, nun, sibling, friend, write down all the things that person has said to you, and all the messages you have received. Read it out loud. Then ask yourself: 'Is this really true? Do I have to go on living my life according to this judgement, as if there were no court of appeal?'

Spend some time discussing these things with a friend you trust, and begin to value yourself in a new way, concentrating on what you find you *do* do and feel, rather than on what you do not. Everyone of us is worth something. We each deserve the chance to find something of our own truth, and it is this search which can help to both create and maintain our feelings of goodwill towards ourselves.

Questionnaire: The 'low self-esteem' trap

How do you rate your own value? What words do you use to describe yourself? If you are struggling in the worthless trap you probably have little sense of yourself at all and are afraid of thinking about yourself. Sometimes it helps to give yourself permission to take time, and as an experiment to just look at your face in the mirror. Notice what happens when you read this idea. Notice how you think about it. Do you think, 'I'm awful', 'I'm ugly', 'I'm nothing', 'I'm bad', 'I'm useless', 'I'll never amount to anything'? Or, 'I'm not going to do any of this, it's useless'? Just notice how much this thinking affects your mood and your sense of yourself.

If you notice that you think in this way, what part of yourself are you referring to? Is it your body, mind, feelings, spirit, or some other part? Or does the voice which says 'I'm bad' mean the whole of you? Go back to the mirror again, and be an observer to that face. If it were the face of a friend, you would probably be objective and find something positive to say about it. Try this approach now, still as an experiment. You might come up with nice eyes, hair or smile (try smiling into the mirror). Try this exercise each day for a few minutes and see what comes out of it.

Do you compare yourself with others? If so, which others? Think how you judge yourself. Is it by comparison with those you presume are superior or better? Are your comparisons fair? For example, Sibyl was always comparing herself with someone heroic she thought might represent the boy that would have made her parents happy and saved their marriage. It was a point she could never win, and her efforts merely reinforced the feelings she had about her own worthlessness. The question we must ask is how helpful is it to compare ourselves with what we were never intended to be? However you judge yourself, do you always find yourself wanting?

Do you presume that you and what you want are always 'wrong'? If so, try to isolate what this part of you *wants* to do or say, and let it have an airing. Then be your own judge as to whether it is 'wrong'.

Can you get help to express the bad feelings you have inside, and recognize where and when they originated? Can you see how much guilt you have assumed for not being what you thought others wanted, or guilt for some failure for which you could not possibly be responsible? Read Chapter 4, 'Snags and Self-sabotage', and see if this might throw any light on your experience of the worthless trap.

Have you got so used to feeling worthless that it has become a habit? Sometimes people are afraid to get out of the worthless trap because they feel that more will be demanded of them if they try. I've heard people say, 'If I did it well, people would expect it all the time. This way at least I can just be unhappy.'

Are you in touch with what you do well? It might be something straightforward like using your voice, keeping a nice home, being kind to others, writing letters. Make a list of what you feel you do well. If this feels too difficult, ask someone to help you with the list. When you have done something well, how did you respond to this inside yourself?

The 'fear of hurting others' trap

In this trap we believe that if we say what we think or feel, or just express ourselves to others, we will hurt them in some way. So we either avoid self-expression altogether, allowing others to ignore or abuse us, or we find our real feelings bursting out in a display of childish anger that surprises, even alarms, others, thus confirming our original feeling that what we think or express is harmful. And because we believe we will be hurtful, we avoid standing up for ourselves in case we are seen as aggressive.

So where does this idea that we might hurt others come from? Sometimes our early feedback emphasized that 'children should be seen and not heard'. Sometimes we have the impression that the way we express ourselves is just too demanding, and we get judged harshly, as if there were some better way to be. Anger is often a problematic emotion in families. It can be forbidden or punished, or evoke even more furious responses. We learn that to be angry is bad and dangerous, so we bottle it up fearing the 'devil' inside. Sometimes people have felt so oppressed in their early life, either by strict parenting or schooling, that they find it impossible to trust what they feel or need. It's as if their way of being has never been respected.

Sometimes we are frightened by the kind of thoughts and feelings we have inside. We fear that if we let these feelings out they will hurt others as we have been hurt. It's as if we have no way of judging the nature of our responses that we've bottled up. This sometimes applies to people who have been abused, either physically or sexually, early in life. They come to mistrust their own instincts and impulses, believing wrongly that it was something in them that made the bad things happen and that they, and what they feel inside, are not to be trusted.

The consequence of being bound in the 'fear of hurting others' trap is that we fail to assert ourselves with others or to stand up for our rights. We carry around a poor sense of what is reasonable, and are so afraid of expressing what we think that we do not develop our own ideas. Sometimes we feel stuck in a kind of childish sulk, weighed down by the unfairness of it all. We cope with this in a number of ways. We may turn what we believe our hurtful ways upon ourselves, inflicting harm by cutting or bruising, drinking or drug-taking. In so doing, we avoid contact or blot out the reality of what we feel, making ourselves so isolated that we become depressed and despairing.

Exercise: The 'fear of hurting others' trap

Monitor for one week the number of times you are aware that you fear hurting others when you are with them. Notice the way in which you think about yourself, or anticipate hurting others, and the words or images you use.

When you find yourself alone in a sulk or feeling badly because this fear you have has forced you to withdraw, notice the feelings you have and their nature. Keep a diary of them.

How angry do you feel? What are your ways of coping with anger or expressing it? Have you buried old anger?

How long have you felt like this? Was there a time when you felt that you *had* hurt someone? Who was this person? What did you either do or say that you feel was harmful to them? How old were you then? What were you feeling at this time? See if you can put words to the feeling. Did you feel angry, shamed, upset, abandoned? What has happened to those feelings now?

Ponder on how you carry your own hurt. What is its nature? How do you express it?

Take a piece of paper and crayons or paints, and draw or paint what you fear coming out of you. Don't censor it as you do with people. Just let the images form. Share them with someone you trust if you can, and see what they might be telling you about the fear involved in hurt.

Aggression and assertion

Many of us are helped out of the 'fear of hurting others' trap by a reappraisal of aggression and assertion. We may have been taught that to speak our own mind or stand up for ourselves is aggressive, and are put down for appearing this way. But aggression is part of our survival and we need to acknowledge its force and power. We can then claim our right to a relationship with it, as well as the right to choose how to express it. Mindless aggression leads to violence and the loss of power that often triggers it. Natural aggression becomes *assertion* when we use it to name or speak out about something important to us, and to stand up for our rights. It becomes our way of 'singing on the boundary' as the birds do in claiming their territory.

Chapter 2

Dilemmas

When we've not been free to be our real 'seed' selves, how we are inside becomes confused with role-playing, false identities and struggles of persona. When we are not free to 'be', we feel we have to 'do', and our choices about how to 'be' become polarized. Our ways of being and thinking are reduced to 'either/or' or 'if ... then', limiting us to perhaps only one choice of how to be. We restrict ourselves, because we believe the opposite is much worse. Many of us are aware of feeling stuck and limited in our choices of how to be and behave, but until we examine them we are not aware of the exact nature of our dilemmas.

When we become lopsided and live at one end of the pole of the dilemma, it is usually because what we see as the alternative is much worse. If we have recognized ourselves as being in the 'doing as others want' trap, it might be because inside we believe that if we fail to please or appear nice and good, we will be seen as unpleasant and bad, and that there is no middle way of proceeding. We choose that particular pole of the dilemma which has been more comfortable for our 'survival' self. If approval was gained by pleasing those whose approval we needed to feel loved and accepted, then pleasing will become our dominant mode of operating, even if it often expresses itself through not doing things or putting things off, which on the surface could be seen as non-pleasing.

The following are widely held dilemmas in being. Read through and see if any of these apply to you.

The 'perfect or guilty' dilemma

This dilemma is dominated by the need for perfection. In striving to be perfect we are trying to live up to an image of what we feel is expected of us. Being perfect might mean getting everything right all the time according to the accepted standard in our family. Every one of us will have a different model of what is 'perfect' for us. This dilemma tends to thrive in a fairly restricted family environment, where there were few choices of how to be. Trying to be perfect might encompass standards of excellence in work, behaviour, morals, lifestyle, accomplishments. Perfection for some might mean striving to meet ever higher standards or climbing one mountain after another; it can mean trying never to have a cross thought about anyone.

In this dilemma if we are not striving to follow the learned pattern of perfection we feel guilty, and the gap left by not striving makes us angry and dissatisfied. Because the dilemma is based on a false choice about how to be, it carries with it the weight of feeling we have to be a slave to a system that is not fully our own, and we become angry at the imposed restriction. Even the external 'success' that our perfect standards bring about does not relieve us.

Many people live with this dilemma for years, striving for the perfectionist standards they picked up from their early environment, but always aware of a nagging sense of meaninglessness and an irritability. There seems to be something missing. Even considerable achievements bring neither joy nor satisfaction. When you are caught up in this dilemma you have to go right on trying to be perfect, regardless of any success, until the dilemma is revised.

Perfectionists caught up in this dilemma tend to live on their nerves. If they try to be perfect they feel depressed and angry; if they don't try to be perfect they feel guilty, depressed and angry. Sometimes it is an admired and strict authoritarian role model in early life that stimulates the creation of this dilemma. 'If a job's worth doing, it's worth doing properly' might be a useful motto to follow if you need to be thorough and get things done correctly. But if it is adhered to too rigidly, with the unconscious message, 'You're nothing if you're not trying to be perfect', then psychological lopsidedness will be likely to ensue. (See Part 4, 'Making the Change'.)

Another way in which this dilemma can develop is in an environment where the person only feels safe if self-enforced models of perfection are brought about. Mary was the youngest daughter of a factory worker.

She was beaten and abused by her brother (eight years older) and teased at school for being clever and different. There were no books in her house, but she craved the life she escaped to in the safety of their pages. So she allowed her brother, who found ways to get books, to barter with her for them. She survived this deprived background by holding her feelings inside and never showing them or asking for anything, and by learning to despise the environment which we came to call 'in the grime'. Her way out of the grime was to work obsessively hard in order to get above those who persecuted her. Her coping mechanism worked

---

Questionnaire: The 'perfect or guilty' dilemma

I try to be perfect in the following way:
The way I am in my home. I have to be always cleaning and decorating, everything has to be in its place.

The way I am with other people. I have to be:
kind;
polite;
interesting;
helpful;
clever;
unselfish.

The way I dress. I have to be:
colour coordinated;
very neat;
fashionable;
young-looking;
smart.

I must get everything right by:
knowing what to do in all situations;
aiming for the best;
striving for the highest goal possible;
being always in control.

If I don't try to be perfect I feel:
depressed and empty;
in terror of being criticized;
vulnerable to being called names like 'lazy', 'sloppy', 'has been', 'no good';
envious of others who I perceive as getting it right;
frightened of being left behind;
angry that I should be caught up in this need: who's it for anyway?
lonely and lost without a goal;
frightened of chaos;
dissatisfied with myself, with life.

---

and she is now a successful doctor, but for years she has had to struggle with the depression caused by this dilemma. Her fear was that if she did not try to be perfect she would slide back into the grime, and she had been unable to develop a place that did not involve this slavery to perfection. Slowly she is separating herself from the rigidity of this dilemma – which also cuts her off from other people – and is starting to express not only what she really feels but also how to be content with 'good enough'. She has surprised herself with how philosophical she can be.

List in your notebook the number of times you recognize this dilemma. Record your frustration, depression, anger, petulance, or other difficult and unwanted feelings which may result from you or others failing to meet 'perfect' standards. Note any anxiety, guilt, fear or sadness which may be connected to your feeling prevented from reaching the state of perfection you seek. The search itself can become like a drug-induced 'fix', which, when withheld, causes withdrawal symptoms.

Experiment with allowing yourself to be in a less than perfect place from time to time. Allow the anxious or guilty feelings. Begin to accept and care for them. In Part 3, 'Gathering Information' you will be able to look at the source of this dilemma for you, and what fears or judgements you have learned to internalize which keep this dilemma going.

The 'perfect control or perfect mess' dilemma

This dilemma is dominated by the need for control. This may be to do with the way we express ourselves at work, at home, or in our dress. It may extend to our speech and thoughts and may be severe enough to involve all kinds of rituals of checking, touching, repetition of words or thoughts, or placing things and ourselves in certain positions at particular times. The need for perfection is linked to our need for control of, and freedom from, feeling guilty or messy. We may not be specifically aware of our fear of mess and its consequences, only dominated by the need to control it in particular ways. We may need to exert this control outside ourselves or inside. This may involve organizing things in such a way as to make sure we keep something safe and in order.

What may have begun as a ritual of protection in early years grows into something more rigid and seemingly detached from what it was originally meant to protect. We know from the work of Dr Donald Winnicott that children grow attached to objects early on – teddy bears, blankets, thumbs, fluff, cotton – and that these objects represent the safety of Mum, or whoever is the main carer, when that person isn't there. These objects help keep a child's inner world (which is the main world he or she understands) safe, so she can go about her daily tasks and be 'in the world' of outerness.

When the child is confronted by feelings for which she or he has no language, the child will project them onto the chosen object or fantasy: teddy is poorly today; the witch in the story is very, very wicked; the dragon in the dream breathes fire and crossness.

Sometimes our basic instincts get caught up in this use of objects or things outside for help. Overzealous wiping and changing of children who wet their pants may lead to the association that natural excretory functions are disgusting or very bad. In order to keep these difficult feelings at bay (whose expressions lead to our rejection), we may involve ourselves in various cleaning rituals which carry on into later life. It then becomes the floor, surfaces or door handles which carry our dirt and have to be repetitively cleaned. What we are struggling with inside is that primitive layer of feeling that we are trying to control. We might develop a similar view of sexual appetites and desires, which may also have been associated with disgust, filth and badness. When these mixtures of associations and feelings cannot be contained or held they tend to be projected onto things that feel a lot safer, and then we can actively engage in doing something about them, however tiring – wiping and cleaning, for example, or checking and counting.

We may experience our need for control in different ways, by limiting ourselves only to certain experiences. One of the most obvious ways of controlling our outer ways is by insisting on organization and order. We may seek to control our anxiety by limiting our lives only to areas we feel we can control and influence. Thus, we might respond to our anxiety about being attacked or invaded by arming ourselves with weapons, self-defence tactics, locks and alarms. Today this has become an appropriate response to urban and rural violence, but its outward expression may also tell us something about the nature of our struggle with internal invasions of feared violence upon our very person. Any early influence which restricted our natural growth, which was against us rather than for us, will be internalized and as such will carry on restricting us from inside in later life. We will continue to believe there is something frightening that must be controlled at all costs. We may have experienced these restrictions as frightening episodes of anger or temper, as an overemphatic concentration upon morals, or in the dogmatic insistence on 'right' and 'wrong' behaviour that is character-istic of religious fervour. We may also experience it via the obsessional or repetitive behaviour of those around us.

Susan was adopted by a couple who had already adopted a boy two years older. She spent her first few months with her biological mother, then time with her adoptive parents, and then her first Christmas with her biological mother. She was officially adopted when she was nearly two. Her family emphasized being in control, especially of anger and 'tantrums'. When she was three she remembers her grandmother saying, 'Put your anger in the wardrobe'. Her life was very contained, both by her tight family unit and by a strict school where little self-expression was encouraged and any kind of risk-taking severely restricted. At sixteen, on moving to a different school, Susan discovered an aspect of the world that felt 'wicked, naughty, dirty, sexy and very out of control' and which she was ill-equipped to handle.

Since this time, when she broke down under the strain, she has been bravely learning to cope with this different and difficult aspect of outside life triggering inside feelings, which threatens her safety. One of the ways she copes with strong feelings, especially negative feelings, and with her fear of sex and physical closeness, is to make sure that every-thing in her house is kept very clean. She may go over her doorknobs three or four times when she comes in from work, even though she knows that no one has been there during her absence. She explains:

If everything is in its place and tidy then I feel I can let myself off the hook and relinquish my obligations. I get cross if people mess up my order. If my bag isn't tidy and I haven't tidied up before I leave the house, then I'm all at sea and things will go wrong.

Susan sees her 'perfect control or perfect mess' dilemma as rooted in her early life's anxieties about being sent away or orphaned if she were not very good, which meant in her family being neat and controlled, especially with her feelings. This also kept her in a dependent position:

'If people feel I need them they'll stay around more than if they had a free choice.' She feels that if she gave up being dependent people might make decisions over which she would have no control.

Susan is an attractive, very intelligent woman who has done a great deal to separate herself from the early survival modes that helped her get through very difficult beginnings then, but which can sometimes get in the way of her current relationships now. She bravely monitors how she feels when the need to clean is at its most pressing, and these occasions are usually connected with a time of transition or change which threatens her security. She has recently taken the huge step of committing herself to a relationship where her fear of closeness, of sex and being out of control of what she most needs are challenged, and she is managing well. She has been able to express many of her hidden feelings about being adopted, and her sense that 'anyone could have picked me up', and the helplessness this puts her in touch with. She is working towards the possibility of freeing herself from the tyranny of 'perfect control' in the future by feeling more loved and 'allowed' as a person.

Questionnaire: The 'perfect control' or 'perfect mess' dilemma

If you recognize yourself in this dilemma, make a list of all the ways in which you need to keep in 'perfect control'. You may not be aware of some of the ways immediately, but let your awareness of this problem stay with you and inform you as you go about your everyday activities. Two of the most frequent ways of keeping in perfect control involve continuous cleaning and checking external situations. A young man came to see me because he had to get up three or four times in the night in order to re-clean his bathroom. When I asked him to describe exactly how he did the cleaning, he began to recite his ritual in great detail. Suddenly, as he was describing how he pulled on 'his pink rubber gloves', he exclaimed, 'I know ... it's all the dirt inside myself I want to clean out isn't it?' This sudden piece of insight allowed him to work back to the core issue of what he considered the 'dirt inside himself' to be. In unravelling how this idea had originated, he was able to release himself from the powerful internal terror of dirt which was manifest by his external, ritualistic cleanings, and which was threatening his everyday life and work. Glance through the following and see if any of the issues apply to you in any way. Write them down in your notebook.

Cleaning obsessively (more than is appropriate):
Going over the same area more than twice after it is already clean.
Cleaning something before you sit down, eat, go to bed or relax in any way.
Cleaning at inappropriate times.
Checking obsessively (more than is appropriate):
gas;

---

taps;
electricity;
windows;
valuables (jewellery, money, books, etc.);
things needed for work outside the home or journeys;
children;
telephone.

List how many times you have to check your 'perfect control' rituals. Count them. Write them down. The next time you feel compelled to move into a 'perfect control' mode, spend a few moments allowing your feelings to surface. Do not wory how vague they may seem to be. Do this on as many occasions as you can. When you have a sense of the feelings underneath the 'perfect control' mode, feel into what it is you are trying to achieve through the method of control. Are you:
keeping things (later on ask yourself, what things or feelings) safe;
keeping something out;
saving something;
blessing;
other?

What do you most fear will happen if you do not check, clean or control in any other way?
flooding;
invasion;
dirt;
contamination;
ruin;
disaster;
chaos;
annihilation;
death;
unbearable stress.

If any of the above did happen, what is it in you that tells you whether you would or wouldn't be able to cope or eventually ask for help in some way?

Then try to imagine how you would cope. What would you do? What could you do? Have you got an image of how others cope with such situations? If you have difficulty in imagining any coping strategies, it may be that it is difficult for you to imagine anything other than the 'distaste' itself. Is there a voice in you which tells you that you would be unable to cope? Or a voice which informs you that you would be helpless or unable to enlist help? One of the most useful positive thoughts to develop is the idea that, whatever happens, you will either find a way of coping, or you will ask for help. This is *all* you can expect to ask of yourself.

The 'greedy or self-punishing' dilemma

This dilemma is related to our basic needs and desires, which have, in some way, been thwarted from an early age. Left with a sense that we are not fully entitled to anything freely for ourselves, when we approach something we need or desire we inevitably feel as if we are being greedy. To cope with this we deny our needs because the pressure of the guilt about feeling greedy is unbearable, and we end up being miserable and punishing ourselves. This dilemma is very painful, and at its core lies our struggle to cope with early deprivation. Whichever end of the dilemma we inhabit, the experience is equally painful, and so often ritualistic toings and froings from one end to the other seem a way to cope.

One of the most symbolic ways in which this dilemma finds expression is in people who have problems with eating, sex, gambling, spending money, or any other ritual attached to something important which symbolizes having our needs met. The person suffering from bulimia, for example, will allow themselves a certain amount of food. If he or she goes beyond this limit, the solution is to vomit up the residue or take laxatives. Sometimes the self-imposed limit is very small, and the sufferer will feel in danger of becoming fat and being seen as out of control and greedy. Such is the terror that she or he enacts the self-punishing end of the dilemma by getting rid of the food. Equally, someone with a gambling compulsion will be able to have money for only a short time before he or she risks losing it. Some people will allow themselves to spend money on buying things, feel immediately greedy and have to store them away, never to be worn or used. Others may have decided that their needs are simply never going to be met, so they will deny all need or desire or pleasure and 'give themselves away' to anyone, being sexually profligate or exchanging body and sex for money and power.

Sometimes we may feel that the sense of deprivation inside is becoming unbearable and we desperately have to grab what we can in an attempt to fill the place that feels so empty and hurt. We may go on a binge of some sort – for example, eating or spending – or we may assume a compulsive pattern, grabbing at something or someone who we hope will fill the emptiness. We may get into debt, try to resist paying for things. (When you feel deprived inside it's hard to give out without resenting it somewhere in your being. This frequently expresses itself unconsciously, perhaps as hoarding, appearing 'mean', or by attaching an exaggerated anticipation on what other people may or may not give, which always disappoints.) But being torn in this way makes us feel miserable, and the misery may be turned against oneself. When someone in the grip of anorexia nervosa feels longing and hunger of an emotional as well as a physical kind, they are so terrified that punishment through strenuous exercise, or starving for days, soon follows. Other people are compelled to harm themselves by cutting, stabbing or damaging their bodies in some way.

This dilemma carries with it both a social stigma and a religious one, and thus the internal dilemma becomes more absolute as it is judged harshly by the moral tone of society or the Church. Greed is seen as a sin which deserves punishment. Perfectionism and high achievement are admired and encouraged. It may be that the truer source of greed comes, in fact, from the compulsive perfectionist's desire for bigger and better without reflection on need or appropriateness, rather than from the obviously equally compulsive strivings of someone labelled greedy by the exposure of their needs inside. Once basic needs are met – by each of us recognizing them for what they are, by having another recognize and name them, by a relationship with another, or by putting energy into something where our needs are satisfied and we are nourished – then the heat is taken out. Greed becomes recognized as need.

Rose started to look at her life closely when she realized that her spending of money had got out of hand. She would see something very beautiful, usually an antique, and couldn't resist buying it. She was very afraid of her husband's anger when he found out, because he said things she didn't want to hear: about her being out of control, greedy, irresponsible, wanting things 'above her stature and income'. She knew there was some truth in all of this, but she so desperately felt 'carried away by my tastes'.

Rose had been sexually abused first by her father between the ages of ten and fifteen and then by her uncle from fifteen to eighteen, when she managed to get right away to university. She came to see that, largely because of her secret and forbidden relationship with her father (which her mother refused to believe, and indeed made Rose feel dirty and guilty for revealing), she had linked all of her self-expression, her appetites and her desires and excitement, with guilt, shame and a sense that they were forbidden. She had married a man who helped her 'control' her appetites because he was 'strong, determined, disciplined' and very good at controlling money, which was his specialist field.

For a while she felt safe, that her appetites and tastes were under lock and key. But because she needed her instinctual nature and her appetites to allow her to express herself fully, they had to emerge somehow. (True seeds want to grow.) They tended to emerge guiltily, as in some of her compulsive eating bouts, and in her need to keep lovely 'delicacies' waiting in the fridge. And they started emerging through her compulsion to spend money on lovely things. The way in which her feelings and instincts surfaced frightened her, and at first served to refuel her old learned and mistaken belief that her appetites and tastes were dangerous and out of control and would lead to disaster.

Rose was a very wise professional woman who soon talked things over with her husband, got her own separate bank account, and began working on how her life had been controlled by the 'greedy or self-punishing' dilemma. One of her problems listed on the chart we made was: 'Pleasure, excitement, appetite, forbidden'. The aim was 'To free myself from the effect of past abuses and their grip. To allow a fuller range of feeling.' In the letter she wrote at the end of her therapy she says: 'The short therapy has been a wonderful vehicle for my release, and it showed me some of the ways I can manage the chaos that results from that release.' In allowing herself to get in touch with her instinctual nature she was able to revalue her creative 'seed' self, which had originally expressed itself through music until it had been put away, like all other instincts, when she became the scientific professional. She was also able to claim a much fuller relationship with her husband, no longer assigning him the 'controller' role, and has recently experienced the 'healing' joy of a second child.

Concentrate on the next questionnaire (p. 56) as you go through the rest of the book, and as you become more aware of your needs during your daily experience. As we build a picture of what you would most like to change we will also be building a picture of what you most need and desire in your life – something you may not have thought about. As well as actively changing old attitudes that are now redundant, we are also rebuilding a decent sense of who we are and the ingredients of what our 'seed' self most needs for its growth and development.

> **Questionnaire: The 'greedy or self-punishing' dilemma**
>
> In what ways do I experience myself as greedy?
> With food?
> With money?
> With possessions?
> With wanting more contact with others?
> With sex?
> Do I take on more than I need or can finish?
> Do I 'hoover up' experiences, books, others, time, events?
>
> What kinds of feelings are behind your experience of greediness?
> hunger;
> exasperation;
> need;
> desperation;
> hope;
> hate;
> love;
> longing;
> waiting;
> anticipation;
> fretfulness;
> shame;
> anxiety;
> emptiness.
>
> How do I cope with my experience of greed?
> Swinging from one end of the dilemma to the other.
> Living permanently at one end?
>
> Have I ever talked about it to anyone?
>
> What do I most hope will be resolved by this dilemma?
>
> How much is my body involved in this dilemma?
> What is my image of my body? Draw, look in the mirror, show a friend.
> Get in touch with the body which contains these feelings, carrying them out for me in a literal way. (See Chapter 9, 'Techniques for working through the process of change'.)
> Draw a picture of the hunger. What is it like, what does it need?
> What do you consider are the basic needs of a human body?
> Make a list of *your* basic needs as they come along. Include warmth, care, holding, rest, sleep, safety.

The 'busy carer or empty loner' dilemma

Most of us are familiar with the person who faithfully and selflessly devotes all of his or her life to others, either to a parent or family, or in serving a household or company way beyond the accepted call of duty. They end up, either in retirement or after the death of the parent or relative they've devoted their lives to, feeling lonely, anxious, unsure what to do with the rest of their lives and fearful of feeling out of control. Many people do serve others and find deep fulfilment without being caught in this dilemma, but here we are looking at those who, unless they are involved in looking after others and keeping up with their expected role of carer and server, suffer anxiety. It seems as if our whole identity is built upon the premise that we are lost without our job of serving the expectations of others.

This dilemma often originates from an early environment where we are encouraged to look after others, be involved in decisions of the adult world, and receive a lot of self-worth and praise for doing so. Many people are relieved to find they fit in, and can play a role that is useful. And if there is uncertainty about going out into the world alone, making a career or leaving a comfortable job to do something more risky or courageous, they will be glad to settle for a role where they become indispensable and their worth is reflected in everyday terms.

Out of this comes the need to be needed, a powerful exchange involving many of us. It is gratifying to be needed, especially if the need is something we can supply. In being needed we often don't have to attend to our own needs, which may feel terrifying. We may assume a 'holier than thou' pose, adopting a self-righteous and superior demeanour to save our inferior sense of self. If we are doing something worthwhile and selfless, many ways of life encourage this 'service not self' attitude. In communities where this is practised by everyone and there is more of a chance of everyone getting some of their needs met, this may work. But it is when our identities are caught up in believing we are nothing if not in the service of others that his dilemma becomes a tyranny.

When we are engaged in looking after another and their needs, and have devoted much of our energy to this (the person may not be ill or needy) we feel OK, and the reason for the dilemma is borne out. It is only when something happens (we are bereaved or told we are not needed any more), that we come face to face with our fears of coping with our *own* lives, and in particular with our own emotional and inner lives.

Sally was the sort of person who could be guaranteed to look after everyone and their problems. A jolly, large, cheerful person, nothing was ever too much trouble. She had four children, an unemployed husband, and worked as a nurse. In addition, she ran the Girl Guides and Sunday school, and took in animals and babies when people went away. She filled every moment of her life with other people's needs.

During her forties Sally began to get irritated with people, to snap at them and then feel remorseful and guilty. She began to get depressed, and put everything down to the 'change', until one Saturday when all her children were away and her husband absent, she wandered around the shopping centre wondering what to do with herself:

I sat down on one of the benches and looked at all the people milling around me. They all seemed to have somewhere to go, be doing something important. I saw my life as being one mad rush to get things done, and what for? I felt suddenly very frightened, horribly lonely, and I just started to cry, I couldn't stop.

This crisis brought Sally into counselling, where she needed to address her dilemma, be able to express some of her needs and understand that her irritation and bursts of anger towards others was not a 'madness' but the result of denying her own individual life and reality for so long.

Many people live with this dilemma in their relationships. Many women, particularly, have learned to be the carer, the one who thinks all around another, anticipates, who knows what the other – husband, partner, family, group – needs and wants, and who knows how to provide it. Many such women receive an early training from their mothers in the role of serving and giving, and in how to respond to another's needs without ever thinking of their own. From this way of being we absorb a lot of good feeling and security, and find a useful place in the community. But if our responding to another's needs is not based on a solid sense of ourselves – who we are, what our needs are – our own desires will surface in some uncontrollable way, making us feel guilty and angry. In *Understanding Women,* Louise Eichenbaum and Susie Orbach write:

A woman must learn to anticipate others' needs. Part of her social role as caregiver and nurturer of others involves putting her own needs second. Yet her needs do not remain merely secondary but often become hidden ... for if she herself does not have an emotional caregiver to turn to there is an imbalance in the giving. A woman then carries deep feelings of neediness.

Several men I have met over the years became carers in a different way from their women counterparts. The men expressed their caring through being good providers and by making sure their partners never needed for anything materially. They tended to choose partners who they secretly viewed as 'weak' and in need of looking after. Although this initially had the benefit of caring for the man's lonely 'inner female' self through its projection onto the partner, ultimately these relationships would become very stuck. The female partner would become infantalized into being the weak needy one who couldn't grow; the men remained in their loneliness, no nearer to claiming their neglected, lonely female selves or child selves.

Many people who have been busy carers for a long time have admitted that secretly they hoped that if they gave out enough to others, those others would turn round and recognize their own needs and desires and return in full the affection, attention and caring they had received. Alas, would it were so! If giving out is based on a denial of need and the underlying message is 'I don't need anything', 'I don't matter', 'I'm all sorted out, thank you', and if people who do try and give to busy carers are met with a rebuff because the carers cannot bear to think of themselves as having needs, it puts people off. Many busy carers are well defended. It's hard to reach them, because they feel invaded and vulnerable if their own needs are discussed. Perhaps the ultimate fear is that if carers really showed how they feel inside the outpouring would be unstoppable because the depth of feeling and need is so great.

If you have answered negatively to more than five of the items in the next questionnaire (p. 60) the chances are that you are caught in this dilemma and fear feeling out of control if your life and identity are not shaped by caring for others. Spend some time thinking about this dilemma, how it came about in your life, what really is at stake now in terms of claiming the right to your own life. You still have gifts for caring and giving. These will not go away. If you can develop a firmer sense of yourself, so that you can use your free time creatively, your skills at caring will be all the more nourished. You will be freer to give, and your giving will be enriched. You will not feel so out of control, but will have a greater sense of appropriate boundaries. Others will respect you more and demand less, because you are in firmer control of who you are and just how much you have to give out.

Many people realize that although they have given out all their lives

---

Questionnaire: The 'busy carer or empty loner' dilemma

How much of my daily energy is tied up with caring for others?
100%, 75%, 50%, 25%, 10%?

How much of my caring for others is caught up in the 'having to please' trap?

When people question my role as someone who cares and gives out to others all the time, what is my answer?
'I've no choice.'
'No one else would do it.'
'I can't let anyone down.'
'People need me. I can't help that.'
'I like to feel I'm doing something useful.'

What are my fantasies and dreams about the kind of lifestyle I would like to have?

How many things do I put off by saying, 'I'll do this when ...'? How much of my living is postposed until tomorrow?

How many things are there that I really want to do but daren't while I am in the role of main carer? Name them.

How often do I feel I can call upon the help of others to share my burdens, or do I feel I have to do it all myself all of the time?

When I do have time off or an afternoon by myself, how do I spend it? Buying or preparing for others, helping others, or doing something I really like?

How much can I recognize feeling anxious and lonely if people aren't expecting me to do things?

Perhaps I label my wanting to do things for myself as selfish. Do I want to be a selfless person?

Do I feel guilty when I think about not being a busy carer?

Feel into your loneliness or emptiness the next time you are about to fill it by caring for others. How does it feel? Can you paint or draw what you feel? Does it remind you of anything? How might you develop this image?

---

they have actually received very little thanks or regard for it. This makes us bitter and angry. Depression and a sense that it really wasn't worth it soon follow. Some people actually feel their lives have been wasted when they look back on years that have flown by in the service of others and at the expense of their own development.

I am not encouraging individual development at all costs, but I am discouraging lopsidedness. People who are centred, comfortable with themselves, who know how to say 'no' without the accompanying guilt, and have a quiet sense of themselves, are free to give with a joy that is beyond price. If we have tied ourselves to the dilemma that if we are not expected to do things for others then we become lonely, guilty and out of control, we are tying ourselves to a life of slavery. Although the caring role may have given us self-esteem and regard when we were small, to carry on inappropriately means building up underlying anger and resentment at the frittering away of our own precious life. Many murders are committed by wonderful carers who have suffered and been abused by their tyrannical charges, until one time they get pushed too far and boil over.

If you are reading this and getting in touch with your own anger, use it. Don't be afraid of it or consider it bad. Write down all the angry things you can think of; hit something (not someone), throw sticks, logs or cushions, go into a tunnel and scream. Get it out. Find out what your anger is like before it turns in on you and swamps you with depression and self-destruction. (See Chapter 9, 'Techniques for Working Through the Process of Change'.)

The 'bottled-up or burst-open' dilemma

This dilemma is related to how we cope with our feelings and emotions. Either we keep our feelings bottled up inside, or if we express what we feel we fear hurting others and being rejected ourselves. For us the world of feelings is dangerous and unknown, full of frightening unstable volcanoes about to erupt. For many people feelings carry a quality which they do not understand. Unlike the cool, clear rational world of thinking and reasoning, the world of feelings can resemble a raging fire, a stormy sea, a sweltering underground pool, a heavy earthen cave, damp and dark. It's a landscape many of us have difficulty painting. We often don't like what we feel inside and we don't like ourselves because we feel that way. We get used to bottling up feelings, because we don't know what else to do with them. It may be that feelings were not welcome currency early on in our lives and we were told to 'pull ourselves together' when we expressed something emotionally. We may have witnessed occasions where feelings got out of hand and the extremes of feeling were expressed, making us decide secretly never to get that way ourselves.

If we've known the extremes of the emotional and rational in our early lives we may feel we have to make a choice between them, and many of us choose the rational way because it feels safer, calmer and logical. Being a word-orientated society, many of us believe that clear words always prevail over the less decipherable world of feelings, which often come without words – in tears, anger, smouldering fury – or in hate, envy and fear which can be seen by body expression and are sometimes acted out, but which have to be interpreted via words before they can be understood. People are sometimes humiliated for expressing their feelings; they may be laughed at, or made to feel they are weak, at the mercy of anyone with a command of words.

As I have pointed out, we usually bottle up our feelings because we don't know what to do with them, and because we've learned and still presume that if they are let out they will be the cause of misery, mess, hurt and rejection. Most of us are unaware that we do this because, if it is still an unrevised dilemma, it remains the way things actually are for us. Sometimes we presume we don't actually have feelings, that we are 'not that type', but may yet find ourselves weeping at something apparently insignificant on the news or in a film, or find ourselves depressed and lonely for no 'good' reason. We may be aware of odd things happening in our bodies: feelings of apprehension or tension, constant stiff necks, backache, migraine headaches, skin trouble, pain in the chest, difficulty breathing. Although all these symptoms may well have other causes – and if there is a physical problem then this must be attended to – many people who bottle up their feelings do store them in their bodies. Bodies, exasperated at having to carry something that doesn't belong to them, will throw up symptoms. This may be the only clue we have to the fact that we bottle up feelings.

Paul, who was referred to in the 'I'm better off on my own' trap, (p. 32), would be overwhelmed by a surge of tears and sadness whenever he felt that someone was excluding him. He had a lump in his throat and wanted to cry. His frustration came out in anger against others for excluding him, which he was unable to express except by withdrawing into aloneness, and which others saw as a sulk. He experienced himself in a place where no one could reach him and all he had for comfort were the logic and facts of his encyclopaedias. He had learned no way to express his emotions, for in his early life there was no one to pick up the signals of what he was feeling or to interpret them. Thus, he had kept most of his feelings bottled up reasonably successfully for many years, through one marriage and its subsequent ending, and through the birth of his only child. It was only when he really fell in love for the first time at forty, that his feeling side welled up and yearned for expression, which he found extremely painful and difficult. He feared making a 'mess' and being unable to control this series of new (in his conscious life) expressions of feeling with which he was unfamiliar.

So most of us bottle up feelings, because to express them is worse, and feelings become our 'no-go area', the area we are least familiar with and fear most. If you feel you recognize yourself in this dilemma, spend some time pondering over the questionnaire on page 64.

Feelings that get bottled up tend to be behind most of the problems in life, as are the feelings that are displaced onto other people or things. Understanding the world of feelings plays a very important part in our growth process. Beginning to unravel the different feelings that affect you at different times and finding ways of using your feeling life creatively will be tremendously helpful. As you read on you will see how others have made this journey, and in Chapter 9 there are ideas to help

Questionnaire: The 'bottled-up or burst-open' dilemma

In what ways am I aware that I bottle up my feelings?

I keep everything inside me, no one ever sees what I truly feel.

When something emotional is going on I feel:

tense;	lost;
upset;	unsure
afraid;	eager to leave;
apprehensive;	hopeless.

Most of the time I am unaware of what I feel.

I presume I don't feel anything.

I experience physical symptoms:

stomach cramps;	wobbly legs;
tightness in the chest;	racing heart;
difficulty with breathing;	thumping heartbeats;
'lump in the throat';	dizziness;
difficulty swallowing;	pins and needles in hands and feet;
neck aches and headaches;	problems with eating, digestion, stomach.
clenched jaw;	
grinding teeth;	
back pain;	

I feel I do express some feelings but not others. I find the following feelings very difficult (you may only be aware of these in others, but they may well also apply to yourself):

anger;	happiness;
frustration;	success;
disappointment;	winning;
sadness;	envy;
when hurt by others;	jealousy;
praise;	mistrust;
shown affection;	hate;
love;	loathing;
admiration;	disapproval;
joy;	embarrassment.

I feel that if I don't bottle up feelings the following will happen:

I will get hurt by others who will take advantage of my weakness.

It will come out all wrong and I'll be embarrassed and want to disappear into a hole.

I will be rejected. No one really wants to know what I feel.

Everyone will see what a mess I am inside.

My whole world will be totally out of control. I will plunge into an abyss where the geography is unknown.

Feelings are messy and you should never wash your dirty linen in public.

If I really let out what I feel someone would get hurt. What I feel inside is violent, furious, out of control, intense, huge. The rage would be unstoppable, the tears would never stop, I would be:
(a) like a little baby almost choking myself on my screams, screaming into a void.
(b) swamped.
(c) drowned.

People would laugh at me and try to pull me down. They would call me names: cissy, mother's boy, wet, wimp, softie, cry-baby.

Whatever I feel it always comes out as tears, and I can't stand it.

Whatever I feel it always comes out as anger, and people don't understand.

On what sort of occasions am I aware of my feelings most strongly?

When alone.

When with others.

When with older people or those in authority.

After a row.

When watching a film or reading a book or news item.

Days after something important has happened.

When others are expressing strong feelings.

How were feelings handled in your family early on? Go to Part 3 ('Gathering Information') and consider the different kinds of feelings. Ponder on how they were or weren't expressed in your early life, and with whom each feeling was associated. How were feelings discussed, and if not experienced within the family, how were feelings discussed in association with others outside? What kind of family sayings or myths did you grow up with?

you to anchor what you are feeling and learn how to cope with the feelings of others.

The 'if I must ... then I won't' dilemma

Initially, this dilemma might appear quite difficult to understand, but just take a moment to examine the number of times in your life when you have felt totally overcome by instructions or orders or 'having to'. They may come from inside you or from other people. Sometimes we feel so restricted by these requests and demands that the only freedom is not to do them at all. The pattern would be, 'I've got to do this, I've got to do that, it's terribly important' – 'I've got no option.' The feeling is one of tremendous restrictiveness, a narrowing which sometimes can be claustrophobic, and the reaction is then not to do it. This is the only freedom you've got against this. This can operate in quite subtle ways: we may receive a letter from somebody which we feel we ought to answer but don't, perhaps there is a telephone call we need to make and we keep putting it off. A more extreme and damaging example might be that we fail to turn up for a job interview.

The seeds of this dilemma go back to very restrictive former years, where one felt bound by rules, regulations and obligations, sometimes in one's early family and sometimes in one's schooling, where the school is very strict (such as boarding school where the restrictions go on after study hours and into the weekend). We can feel so bound up within the rules and regulations that we have no self-expression whatsoever, and then our only self-expression is to say 'no'. The most graphic description of this particular kind of dilemma comes from the story of Oblomov, who lay in bed all the time because he couldn't bear any kind of obligations to get up and get dressed or go out. His dilemma consolidated itself to the point where he slowly dwindled away and died. That's this dilemma in its most extreme form.

I think it's true to say that this dilemma operates in most people's lives in some form. Most of us have experienced restrictions of one kind or another during our early life. But when the dilemma is severe it affects everything we do, and we are keeping up our sense of control in life mainly by default. It's not what we do but what we don't do that gives us a sense of control or power. But in time this backfires, as our inability to get anything done, because we feel impelled to move on as soon as restrictions from others appear to come along, means that we are never able to develop a decent sense of self-worth.

In the 'avoidance trap' we looked at Terry's story (p. 36), and how the restrictions placed upon him in early life led him to duck out of challenges to do with work. On a deeper level he experienced his early restrictions as coming from the demand of others that he be both grateful for being cared for by people who were not his parents, and for his (later) inheritance. Because he felt he owed it to his grandmother, and the family who later on adopted him, to 'be good' and do well, and because an over-protective environment meant that he hadn't developed the skills to deal with the challenges of outside life, he believed that the only way for him to cope was to not do anything at all. This was not a conscious decision, but an unconscious drive based upon the mistaken belief that his only option was to say 'no' to a demanding environment.

When Terry came into money at twenty-one, for which he was also unprepared, he took flight into heroin addiction. He could not cope with the demands the money made upon him, and he could not ask for

---

Questionnaire: The 'if I must ... then I won't' dilemma

How much does the dilemma 'if I must ... then I won't' operate in your life:
every day;
every week;
at work;
with friends;
with family;
in relationships with men/women?

If I feel obliged I feel:
restricted;
caged;
controlled by others.

This then makes me feel:
furious;
frightened;
belittled;
threatened;
defiant.

When I feel this way I want to:
hit out;
run away;
curl up;
want the world to make me disappear.

I see saying 'I will' as conforming to others' ways and ideas:
all of the time;
most of the time;
in certain situations (name them).

Saying 'I won't' gives me freedom from restrictions imposed by others. I have put this to use by:
creating my own life;
using my defiance to start something new.

Or I feel frustrated because I find I can only say 'no' or 'I won't'. I can only act 'against' and I have been unable to start anything of my own. The restrictions I feared from others have now turned against myself.

---

help from those whom he presumed he had to please and be grateful to. He did not believe he was entitled to his powerful and mixed feelings of grief over losing both of his parents, and he felt disloyal for talking about them.

Since this time, several years ago, he has been courageous and brave enough to get himself off heroin and to look at his life more fully. He has begun the painful process of grieving and mourning for his lost parents for the first time, and is releasing himself from his restrictions in thinking about his life and what he was entitled to. As he began to have more choices about how to respond, and as he allowed himself more freedom to take up choices about what to do, he has been able to release energy to put into tasks and training, has become professionally qualified and married. The energy that was tied up in the silent protest of 'if I must ... then I won't' has been well used.

If this dilemma is severely restricting your energy and your life, look carefully at where it originated and what your fears are about embracing something instigated by other people. If this dilemma is allowed to dominate it can take over and immobilize us to the point illustrated by Terry's heroin addiction. Feel into what your own inner restrictions are if you find yourself saying 'I won't' when you feel obliged by someone or something. See how many ways you can find to respond to the perceived restrictions, other than saying 'no' or 'I won't'. You may find you need to be angry, to hit out, to be sad and grieve, to find a way of thinking about things that stimulates you and which you allow. You will need to go through the 'pain barrier' felt by restriction and to find yourself on the other side – your own freedom.

The 'If I must not ... then I will' dilemma

Take a moment to explore this, even if you don't relate to it immediately. Again, as in the 'if I must ... then I won't' dilemma, this dilemma is concerned with our response to pressures, whether they come from inside ourselves or are imposed by others, especially those in some form of authority. In this case, it's as if the only proof of our existence is our resistance. In our fight against, in our protest, we are struggling to be *seen* for our real selves. But all too often this dilemma results in harm to ourselves, and in punishment rather than acceptance. We begin to break rules – even our own rules begin to feel too restricting – and so our frustration and fury with life escalate. Sometimes our attitude becomes so entrenched that we feel we will lose face even more if we give in or change our pattern, so we carry on piling up negative responses to command, thus tempting fate.

Many of us will perhaps relate to this dilemma during adolescence, when we need to lock horns or try out our strength against those in authority. The 'cult' of protest is active, and usually appropriate, during this growing time. And many of us forge our sense of ourselves against such testing of authority, especially parents or leaders, for our views on religion, politics, social welfare, dress and addictive substances! We emerge stronger and wiser and go on to occupy those positions of authority we once had to kick against, developing rules or structures we once found so frustrating.

But this dilemma can become a way of life, piling up our anger and resentment without a space to breathe or take stock. If it becomes entrenched, it may move us into circles of friends whose lives, behaviour and choices are all limited by this dilemma, creating a much greater force of 'must not'. Then the life itself can become like a brick wall which feels impossible to break down. Until properly revised and refreshingly challenged, this dilemma only serves to block our path and prevent us from having a life.

Sometimes we learn to resist as our *only* way of survival in a restricting environment, where our resistance ensures our actual body and soul survival. Like the mujaheddin in Afghanistan, who must fight for their very country and freedom, as well as for their families and villages, we learn to become guerrillas in our own families or environment, living on our nerves, hiding, being always on the attack against the enemy. And while all communities need this fighting *for* aspect, to challenge authority when it becomes limiting and oppressive, when we fight *against* simply because it has become a habit we court destruction rather than creation.

Many people do experience their lives as being oppressive in this way, as if they were the hunted minority. But if we persist with this behaviour after the war is over, we are not claiming our true freedom. The skills and determination we have learned during our resistance are actually needed much more for the creation of our own rules and standards, where we are forging a life for ourselves rather than having to defend against an imposed position.

Questionnaire: The 'If I must not ... then I will' dilemma

If you can see this dilemma operating in your life now, ask yourself:

In what areas of my life am I fighting the rule 'I must not ...'?
at home;
at school, work, college;
in religious belief;
in my social life and sexual or moral conduct;
over money?

Spend time examining exactly which rule you experience as 'I must not'.
Write it down. Try different responses to it in your imagination.

Monitor the number of times in a week you say 'I will' in response to
another's 'You will not'. Note the time, place, feeling, people or aspects
involved. See how these tie in with the first question.

How much of your life is taken up living in a 'must not' cult (friends, interests
etc.)? Does this serve your needs now?

Ask yourself what would happen if I examined my resistance more thoroughly? What are its qualities. On page 125 we look at 'subpersonalities',
aspects inside us that we can identify in a graphic form. Try and communicate
with your resistance now, and find out more about it.

The 'satisfied, selfish and guilty or unsatisfied, angry and depressed' dilemma

This dilemma is to do with getting what we want. If we get what we want and therefore attain some measure of satisfaction, we find that it is inevitably accompanied by feelings of selfishness and guilt. We feel like a spoiled child. At the other extreme, if we don't get what we want, we feel angry and depressed. This dilemma is related to our ability to receive something and possess it freely. At some point in our lives we've decided unconsciously that we're not allowed to have what we want. We may even have been told, 'Don't think you can get what you want' or, 'You can't always have your own way'. These kinds of statements, which are common currency during childhood and at school, can be inter-preted internally as 'if we get what we want it's actually at some cost'. So, like a spoiled child we feel rather guilty, because we're not really enti-tled to it.

At the opposite end of the pole, if we don't get what we want we feel very angry and depressed and obviously very deprived. This can lead to a kind of spoiling mechanism. Because we feel so guilty and childish when we get what we want, we actually don't allow ourselves anything – we don't even allow ourselves to receive things from other people. But at the same time, we feel permanently angry and depressed precisely *because* we're refusing to receive anything, either from ourselves or from others. We walk around like a martyr feeling absolutely dreadful.

We may find that our lives display a pattern of quite chronic illness – for example, migraine, stomach upset, back pain, colds and flu. It may be that, unconsciously, we have linked into this pattern of illness as the only way that we can actually freely receive something without feeling childish and guilty. This isn't to say that we make a conscious decision to become ill, but unconsciously this quite painful dilemma might allow the body to collude with the idea that we're not allowed anything unless we have some sort of permission – the permission of illness, the permission of imprisonment, or the permission of high achievement. But even then the dilemma still operates, because as long as it manifests itself in some powerful form, we're not really allowing ourselves to receive anything, and so once more we are plagued with guilt and feelings of childishness and anger.

> **Questionnaire: The 'satisfied, selfish and guilty or unsatisfied, angry and depressed' dilemma**
>
> Do I feel that I get what I want?
> at home;   with children;
> at work;   in sports;
> in relationships;   sexually.
>
> If you feel you've never addressed this issue, you might like to take a few minutes to consider what you want in your life. Write it down, and then ponder on which areas in your life are satisfactory and which are not.
>
> How do I know when I do get what I want? I feel:
> bad afterwards;   secretive;
> selfish;   joyous;
> guilty;   triumphant;
> greedy;   satisfied and happy.
> too big;
>
> If I get what I want, do I feel I will have to pay something back or that life or someone will get even with me sooner or later?
>
> What myths, sayings or 'old wives' tales' about being satisfied and getting what you want come from your early life? Where do they come from, whose voice do you hear when you remember them?
>
> If I don't get what I want, perhaps because of any of the above injunctions against it, I feel:
> angry;   spiteful;
> sad;   envious of others who seem to get what
> depressed;   they want;
> punished;   childish and want to cry;
> despised;   murderous;
> vindicated (i.e. 'They' –   ill.
> the voices in my head, the old
> messages, that say 'you can't'
> – are right);
>
> If you recognize a pattern of illness after disappointment, look to see if any of the above feelings could be hidden within the illness.
>
> Identify as clearly as you can the areas in which you believe you should deny yourself satisfaction. Notice the feelings you experience when you go along with something that you actually don't want, but have not yet developed a way of saying 'no' to. Note in your diary or notebook the times when this occurs and the feelings involved. Experiment with asking exactly for what you want in a direct, clear way and see what happens. When you have isolated the mistaken belief behind this dilemma, challenge it as best you can in your everyday approach to life.

Chapter 3

Problems and dilemmas within relationships

Relationships challenge all the ways in which we feel about and experience ourselves, and often bring forth new thoughts and feelings we didn't know we had before. It is through relationships with others that we experience fully the different aspects of the self and we learn much more about who we really are. This mirroring process can take many different forms and can involve many different journeys and paths. On one level relationships may appear superficial – we act out a role as teacher, friend, companion, instructor, game-player, tennis-player, bridge-player, bingo partner – but just below the surface is a deeper level where we have to confront the more powerful emotional feelings. It is on this interactional level, which brings up the more fragile and less known aspects of ourselves, that many of the difficulties within relationships arise.

Perhaps because relationships can so easily press on our core pain, some of us try and avoid involvement with other people by keeping our relationships as superficial as possible, only seeing friends at work, only talking on the telephone, only going out once a month and never getting involved on an interpersonal level. Whereas this may work to cope with what is feared in the entanglement of emotions, one nevertheless pays the price with superficiality, loneliness and isolation.

All relationships, when they get below the level of superficiality, and whether they are with the same or opposite sex, mean that we must face our vulnerability, our smallness, our need for closeness and intimacy, our internal and dependency fears, and that we face many ideas of roles and stereotypes. Relationships return us to the world of childhood, where things feel fair or unfair, we are in control or out of control, powerful or powerless, fearfully dependent or fiercely independent. Our very earliest relationships – with mother or father, aunt, uncle, brother, grandmother, sister, teacher, nurse, nanny – are repeated in our own relationships in an unconscious way, as if we were somehow being pushed back into the world of childhood in order to work something out, perhaps for the better.

Often it isn't until we have been in a relationship for some time, or have perhaps had a series of similar relationships, that we realize there are meaningful patterns at work. We are naturally drawn towards people who resemble in some way those figures who were significant in our early life and who have influenced us. As long as this is balanced by other mutual sharings and aspects this is no problem; but when we unconsciously seek out people who perhaps carry the more negative aspects of early powerful figures, we find ourselves caught up in potentially destructive patterns where we again become the child who felt humiliated or rejected, hurt or abandoned, lost, furious, uncared-for and needy.

In this section we look at the more complicated difficulties which arise from our relationships with other people, which press our core wound and inevitably push us back onto the relationship with the self. In order to understand this we need to look a little bit at the kind of patterns that emerge out of childhood, and the way that each of us develops in childhood.

Growth and development of the seed in the garden of the family

In Part 1 we looked at the way we come into life as a seed which contains all the essence of our being – who we are to become, all our potential – and at how this seed is planted into the garden of our early family. The growth of the seed is determined by the mixture and meeting of the seed with the qualities of the environment: for example, how the environment receives the little shoots of the seed as they start to emerge. In the beginning, as with seeds, our basic needs are for warmth, light, appropriate containment, holding, care and nourishment. If the seed's roots are not suitably cared for in the earth, the plant the seed is to become has no decent foundation in which to get started.

If the soil around the shoots is too loose the shoots will feel lost and rootless. The infant who started life in too loose a soil will tend to grow up into adulthood feeling somewhat 'dropped' and rejected and their antennae will be out ready to receive rejection and hurt. They will display a tendency not to express needs or ask for anything. As adults they may choose to lean on strong others, rather as a straggling plant always needs to be supported by a stake. Or they may become fiercely independent, acknowledging no needs: 'I can look after myself'. It may be very hard to get hold of a sense of self. The self may be hidden under a persona expressing a strong sense of unworthiness: 'I've no right to be here'. Sometimes people talk about having an emptiness inside.

Conversely a seed that is packed in too tightly soon becomes pot-bound, its growth restricted and hardened to take the shape of the pot. An infant who is held too tightly can be over-protected, over-controlled or overfed, becoming sluggish in its own growth, over-dependent upon others to give shape and meaning. As a result, when pot-bound children grow up into adulthood they carry a message which tells them that they either have to conform in order to cope with the outside world according to what's been learned early on, or they will have to rebel fiercely from any influence that is seen as over-containing, controlling and overbearing.

Parent and child reciprocal roles

The analogy of the soil and the seed provides an image for the effect that our early life has on us. When we grow up into adulthood all of us carry inside ourselves patterns of relating to others that we have learned. One pattern is connected to the way I feel towards others and my reaction to them, and the other pattern anticipates the way that I have learned that the other person is going to react towards me. So, for example, if my early experience has been with a mother who was perhaps absent for a lot of the time – either because of illness or depression or because of having to go to work, or simply because I didn't feel close to her – one of the images that I will carry inside is the image of myself as the abandoned or rejected child. I will also carry the image of the abandoning or rejecting other. Relationships in later life may well reflect those very early self-images and reciprocal images. Until revised, these two-way images form roles which we carry inside us and which act upon us. Sometimes our early reaction to quite small problems with parents, or small instances of absence or neglect, can be quite extreme, and until those reactions are modified and looked at afresh they do live on to inform the way we relate to others in quite a profound way.

We were also looking earlier at the fact that it isn't just the environment that affects what happens to us. We must also consider our own particular pattern or myth that we've come into life with, and to question what we are being asked to live out in terms of the kind of parenting or environment we have to deal with. It isn't just what happens to us, it's what we make of what happens to us. We are not looking at blame or something which is fixed and irredeemable in terms of our pattern of early life, but we're looking at that rich mixture of what happened, how we actually met this experience, and at what needs to be changed.

We're going to look next at some of the two-way roles that we get involved in early on in life: the one that is triggered off by the 'parental' role and the one that we carry inside us that is the 'child' (see Figure 5). Later on, in adulthood, we will carry both these roles inside us, and they will tend to be re-enacted, to a lesser or greater extent, depending upon the number of 'redeeming' factors that have accompanied our journey through childhood. The redeeming factors may include kindnesses from others, positive examples of care, however small, or the stimulation or our imaginative life which helps to support us by fantasy and dream which are meaningfully different from the environment we are being asked to endure. There are some people who survive the most neglectful and abusive of backgrounds. It may be that their seed self has contained the means by which to transcend what happens, or that this aspect of the individual is triggered by one good experience of a loving attitude.

Re-enactment of early life parent/child roles

What we learn from early experiences becomes a sort of hidden 'rule book' laying down patterns of relating. We can play *either* role, inviting others to play the reciprocal role. It is important to grasp that we learn *both* roles (the judged and the judging role, for example). As well as the 'coping child' role, we learn to force others to play the reciprocal role as well as treating ourselves in the same terms. Thus our *core wound* contains both the damaged and the damaging aspects we learned early on. One aspect contains the created core pain and the other acts as the core maintaining pain.

THE WAY WE EXPERIENCED EARLY CARE	WHAT WE ARE LEFT FEELING INSIDE (CORE WOUND)	WAYS WE COPE (SURVIVAL)
ABSENT rejecting abandoning	rejected abandoned	placating parental child (look after others)
CONDITIONAL judging belittling demanding	judged humiliated crushed	striving hypervigilant admired-or-rubbished split
TOO TIGHT overcontrolling fused dependency	restricted fearful	avoiding or rebelling flight into fantasy/ wrapped in bliss
TOO LOOSE anxious depressed abandoning	fearful fragile left 'nowhere world'	avoiding placating depression 'false self'
ENVIOUS	fearful hated	'magical guilt' self-sabotage
NEGLECTING physical emotional mental	neglected hurt angry fragmented	can't take care mood swings feel in bits self-neglect
ABUSIVE VIOLENT	abused hurt rage unexpressed	victim/bully swings hit out to self or others fantasy of 'perfect care'
GOOD ENOUGH not 'too good' not too bad loving caring	lovable reponsive secure cared for	good enough sense of self trusting loving healthy

Figure 5 Patterns of care that can dominate our relationships until we revise them

Figure 5 shows examples of the kinds of patterns we may carry from early life which affect both our relationship with others and with ourselves. There may be many variations in the actual words used to describe these experiences, and it is important for each of us to find our own. What we need to understand is that for each of these experiences of early care there are three variations of re-enactment in later life:

The internalized 'child' self
The internalized 'adult' self
The invited 'other'

For example, childhood experiences of punishment, either in an atmosphere of criticism and demand or acted out literally in beatings or abuse, may lead to someone carrying inside them both the child who felt punished and the adult 'other' who inflicted the punishment. The *internalized punished child self* expects others to behave in a punishing way towards them, possibly choosing others who display these characteristics, thus maintaining the core pain and coping devices such as over-striving or pleasing. Alternatively, the *internalized punishing adult self* may continue to behave in a punishing way towards themselves, creating demanding timetables or being overcritical about themselves, beating up on the internalized child self and maintaining a feeling of punishment. Or, they may behave in a punishing way towards others, particularly those who appear 'punishable', and press the core wound in situations where the choice is to either hit out or be hit oneself.

As another example, we could take the childhood experience of abandonment. This would involve the *internalized abandoned child*, whose experience was either of actual abandonment or of a parent or care-giver who felt remote, depressed or preoccupied. And then there would be the *internalized abandoning adult*, who continually abandons their 'child self' by not attending to needs, or who chooses an *abandoning 'other'* in relationships, which keeps the core wound in search of healing.

Given these patterns, we may expect all three 'roles' to be enacted at different times, or within the same relationship. It is when we begin to identify these patterns that we are able to see more clearly the nature of our core pain. In Chapter 1 we were looking at how the work of psychotherapy is to name the core pain which maintains the core pain statements and restricts our choices of how to be. In these internalized child and adult patterns it is both reciprocal role procedures that need our attention. It is important to recognize how each one maintains our earlier experience of pain. The child self who experiences core pain still feels helplessly bound up with it as if it were fresh, but it is maintained by the adult self who continues to inflict the similar kind of limiting patterns upon relationships, both internal and external. It is only when we recognize our core pain and the way it is maintained in these procedures that we begin to have a choice in how we can look after ourselves in more helpful ways.

Each situation which arises out of the patterns we may have been looking at in this section brings us to the point of crisis. We may say, 'What am I doing?' or, 'Help! I can't stand behaving like this'. We may suffer from several broken or destructive relationships, including the ones at work or with acquaintances, before we start looking at the patterns in which we are caught up internally. Once we start looking, however, our journey toward change has begun. Once we understand what it is that directs us to behave in such ways we are on our way to the practice of recognition, saying 'no' to old ways, and choosing new ones. We do not have to go on unconsciously repeating old patterns. Once old ways are recognized and refused, and core pain is allowed to be released, new ways of proceeding may be born. It then becomes possible to develop within ourselves the 'good enough' mother and father we never had.

Spend time writing in your journal some of your thoughts and images about the above. See if there are times from the past that you can remember feeling these fears, how you coped with them, what you did, what others' response was to you at that time. How much do any of these fears dominate your attitude to relationships? Consider your last relationship, or a current one in which you are having difficulties. (If you feel you do not have any relationship at present, even acquaintances at work, neighbours or family members, consider if any of the above apply to you and influence your aloneness.) How much of the above could be influencing what happens? What, if any, role do you feel you were unconsciously inviting the other person to take? What role, if any, were you caught up in yourself?

Exercise: Seed and survival

Stop for a moment now and consider where you feel you are in this section. Look at the flavour of your relationships with others so far and see if you can detect any pattern. This may be a painful exercise, and need considerably more of your time and understanding than the previous section. Take your time. The following short exercise may help to identify some of the qualities or fears that come up for you with others. You may not have realized how you feel in actual words, you may not have formed any descriptive language to frame what you feel.

If I get close to someone, I fear:
Ridicule: 'I'll be laughed at for what I feel.'
Humiliation: 'They will look down on me.'
Dependency: 'I don't want to have to need anyone.'
Being taken advantage of.
Being made to feel small and helpless.
Contempt: 'I will get spat upon.'
Being teased and taunted: 'They will get just within my reach and disappear with a laugh and a joke.'
Invasion: 'They'll get right inside me.'
Cruelty: 'I'll be beaten or shouted at.'
Lack of privacy: 'They are watching me all the time.'
It will never be enough to fill my longing.
I'll have to be on my 'best' behaviour all the time.
I'll be left just when I've let go.
I'll be abandoned in the end, no one will stay with me.
Having to be so tense and vigilant. You never know when they will get you.
Suffocation. Being close is too much, there is no room to breathe.
Being overwhelmed and overpowered, reduced to nothing, or a slave.
I'll never come up to scratch, be what they want.
Losing myself completely.
Losing my independence.
Crying all the time.
'No one could ever be as good to me as . . .'
They will see things about me I hate and want no one to see.
Abuse – sexual, physical or verbal.
It is only a fantasy, and I'll never get near it.

Living through the 'shadow'

Sometimes one way of coping with the early role experiences is to cut off our more fragile child responses and try to live at the parental end. In this way we try and protect the child in us who hurts by looking after it in others, or by hitting out at it in others. It is very hard to acknowledge this in ourselves, because in acknowledging that we have taken on the parental role in our relationships we are admitting that we are behaving like the people who once damaged or hurt us. If we understand how limited our choices have been in acting as we do, and how hooked up we have become acting out these early roles, we can seek help to change. We usually act in both roles in some form, but have greater difficulty with the more negative role. It is hard to face our more negative side – our critical side, the side that secretly enjoys humiliating others, that likes to be possessive, demanding, cruel, taunting or over-controlling. Jung called these darker, trouble-making aspects part of the 'Shadow'. The Shadow contains unknown or little known aspects and qualities of our personality which are not yet in the light.

When these aspects remain unconscious they cause much more trouble and havoc than when they were faced in the light of consciousness. If we have experienced humiliation when young we will fear being in that place and will seek to do anything in our power to avoid it – for example, by living life 'above reproach' or 'beyond criticism'. But the fear will remain, and because we have put it down so firmly in our own lives we will be likely to do the same when it manifests itself in others. Our Shadow will alert itself when we see something in other people which we fear in ourselves. It may present itself in the form of a 'pathetic' old man or woman, someone we see as weak, and out will come our most curling lip and sardonic caustic remark – the very thing we received and fear receiving.

What we do to others we do to ourselves. Those who have been cruelly treated may compensate by being very kind and trying very hard, hoping to redeem the cruelty, but they will expect cruelty and may invoke it by their pleading and appealing niceness. They might actually drag it out of people unconsciously. They may also be drawn to act cruelly to others who take the form of their vulnerable, cruelly treated self. It could be hypothesized that some of the terrible atrocities inflicted upon fragile old pensioners in their own homes are the acting out of an impulse to be cruel and stamp out the frightened, pleading, vulnerable hurt inside the perpetrators, which they see in the cowering posture of their victims' bodies or in the pleading terror in their eyes. In hitting out at others they are re-enacting what has been done to them in actual or symbolic form, and in doing so they are preventing themselves from having to live in the pain of that fragility and vulnerability. This is not to deny that there are people who just decide to allow cruelty or plain evil to dictate their actions.

We may get into a relationship with someone we have idealized and admired and wanted to live up to and please. We may be re-enacting similar aspects of a relationship we had with a parent or other important figure. All might be lovely at first, and then we might find the ugliest dark figure popping up and saying things like, 'You always have to be right'. We might feel resentments at small idiosyncrasies, and be critical of 'feet of clay'. Pulled by our internal restrictions we may explode, bringing forth a demon part of ourselves that we had not known before. We may also be up against incongruities which do not emerge until we are in a relationship. For example, the successful, ambitious young woman, whose hard work and effort have come from a 'parental child' or striving child figure, becomes once again the young, frightened, adaptive child once she's close to a partner. From behind the admired, glossy, confident surface to which the partner was initially attracted steps a small person craving assurance and ready to be pleasing and dependent, whom he does not know or understand.

Dilemmas relating to our relationships with others

All of us feel vulnerable when we are in a dependent position, which inevitably comes about in some form when we have to relate to others. If we have had an early experience (our very first dependency) which was 'good enough', we do not fear dependency and avoid it, or choose it in a negative way. The following dilemmas tend to operate in connection with our relationships with others and determine our choices about how we related to others.

If I care about someone, I have to give in to them or they have to give in to me

When relationships are going well there is give and take on both sides and a feeling of equality. However, when the above dilemma is operating, the way we relate to others feels highly charged and there is no sense of equality. When we care about someone and feel we have to give in to them it tends to be because we want their approval or affection so much that we will do what they want, as in the placation trap (see p. 23). In this choice there is no freedom to be ourselves, and others rule the way in which we respond and act. The 'giving in' is a sign of a need for self-protection, with the assumption that if we do not give in to those we care about something bad will happen and our sense of ourselves will be threatened. This could come from an experience of conditional caring in early life, or from someone who was dominant and demanding.

At the other extreme of this dilemma, we experience our feelings when we care about someone as being quite powerful and demanding. Our sense is that because we feel strongly others must respond and give in to us. We may have internalized the sense of the child who was given free rein or over-protected from an early age, who has become used to their strong feelings being reciprocated in kind and every demand met.

If I depend on someone, I have to give in to them or they have to give in to me

This is a deeper version of the first dilemma, and can form a very important 'B movie' for what goes on unconsciously within a relationship. Our fear of dependency may stem from the fact that we have never actually been given the luxury of dependency when we were small, and thus have never been able to be freely independent from the point of appropriate strength, as Susie Orbach points out in *Understanding Women*. It feels as if when we do allow ourselves to depend on someone, then they are in control and we have to give in to them. We feel powerless and helpless, which can express itself in passivity and sometimes a feeling of emptiness, coupled with a fearfulness of being so much at the mercy of another. We may feel that we come near to being just as helpless and needy as we were when small.

When we establish a relationship with a strong and caring other, it feels as if we can be dependent with nothing to fear. But this may be challenged at some point when we do in fact have to grow and meet our own dependency needs in a positive way. We may accept the giving in, welcome it and grow within this care, and if the other person is flexible to allow this then we can indeed overcome a fear of dependency and allow some interdependency. Others of us, however, may feel we have to give in when we feel dependent, but rage against this somewhere, resenting our powerlessness. If, when we feel dependent, we expect others to give in to us, it's as if we are still at the stage of feeling helpless and needy and that this is the only 'strength' we have – that were it not for our need keeping someone with us, they would not stay.

There is a fearfulness here about 'growing up', as if growing up would make others leave us, and that would not have enough value to stand alone independently. Indeed, this is the actual experience of many people as they grow up: of a mother who found it very difficult to let go of her mothering role and wanted her children to remain as her 'babies'. If we learn that this is our only power or strength we will doubt our ability to grow up and move away independently.

Questionnaire: Caring and depending on someone

If I care for someone, I feel:
self-conscious;
worried;
eager to be seen in the best light;
I must control myself;
I must learn all about the other person and please them;
anxious;
afraid;
vulnerable;

I must give in to them in order that they might care for me;
I seem to withdraw;
passive and helpless;
I expect others to notice me;
I expect others to care equally about me;
I expect others to look after me, meet my needs and demands.

If I depend upon someone, I feel:
afraid;
vulnerable;
frightened of being hurt;
humiliated;
disadvantaged;
I must do what the other wants;
I must give in to the other in dress/manners/behaviour/religion/work/all standards/looks/sex;
helpless and look to others to help me;
I must give over my whole self to the other;
I expect others to be stronger and therefore able to do as I ask;

I expect others to make decisions for me, to do what I want;
in control, as if what I need dominates and makes things happen;
secure that other people know where they stand with me and what I need and will give in to me;
I like to be cosy, knowing what others need and giving it to them and with others knowing my needs.
In this way neither of us needs anyone or anything else;
safe and 'all wrapped up'.

I never depend upon anyone. I do not allow myself to be dependent at any time. I notice this in the following ways:

I do not allow myself to get close to anyone in case I feel dependent.
I never allow myself to get in anyone's 'debt'. If I'm given gifts or paid
compliments I feel terrible and have to give back as soon as possible.
I never let anyone pay for me; I make sure I always pay my own way.
I much prefer to give than receive.
If a woman, I would never let myself get pregnant. If a man, I would never let
myself get married.
I like to be in charge. It's hard for me to be a student, to admit I don't know
things, to share equally with others.
I am afraid of being dependent and will do anything to avoid it.
Secretly I am afraid of being ill or getting old, and my images of these are full
of humiliation, defeat, suffocation or worse.

If you answered 'yes' to any of the above, ask yourself what you fear from
dependency. What gets in the way of your allowing yourself to be in a dependent position? Is it:
pride;
fear (what of);
fierce independence;
rage;
a yet unresolved memory of being let down, suffocated or other?

Spend some time pondering on this. Look at the number of times you
have shied away from any kind of dependent position. Write about this
in your notebook, and let the images or memories stay with you as you
read on through Part 3 'Gathering Information'.

Either involved and hurt, or not involved, in charge, but lonely

This dilemma can operate whether we are in a relationship or not. Our
vulnerability is towards hurt, and our unconscious antennae are quick
to detect it. We have probably been hurt at some time and we therefore
associate all relationships with hurt. We expect to be hurt, and we may
be highly sensitive to words, nuances, actions and hidden meanings
which support us in this belief. To cope with hurt we have learned to
withdraw, either literally or inside ourselves, and this remains our position, unrevised, keeping the dilemma intact. Others may not realize how
we feel, because we don't communicate it directly; all they may know
is that we are hard to get close to. But this is because we are so brittle
and scratchy when we come up against our fear, or because we depart
moodily to nurse the fear on our own.

Many of us cope with this dilemma by not having relationships or by keeping those we do have very limited and superficial. This gives us control over the hurt, but at the cost of our loneliness. For those of us who risk relationships they can seem like a torment because of our fears, and it may take a long time before we overcome this dilemma and learn that we can trust others, and that it is possible to be with someone and not get hurt. Unfortunately when this dilemma operates it's as if we have been waiting for our fear of getting hurt to be activated. And, of course, sooner or later something will happen which bears out our conviction that we have to stay alone to be in charge. Many people do feel lonely, either within relationships, or nursing their hurts alone.

In Chapter 2 we saw that one of Paul's ways of coping with his strong feelings was to bottle them up. His social isolation was also a coping strategy. On a deeper level he had decided that if he got involved, risked feeling close, as he had been with his mother who had died when he was six, he would only get hurt. When we met he felt his depression had been caused by personal hurt from the children of his new love. Before this time he had kept in his 'lonely but in charge' position, and it worked up to a point. On falling in love at forty, however, he risked expressing his deep feelings and being hurt. His ensuing depression followed when, inevitably, the initial intensity and closeness of the relationship began to wane. His adjustment and subsequent change involved working through much of the unrecognized mourning for the loss of his mother, and to understand and feel for the lonely boy who had only had encyclopaedias for company. At the same time, he monitored all the occasions when he felt slighted or got at by others, the times when he fled to his own room after feeling excluded or misunderstood. He tried to establish the reality between his internal terror of hurt, which could be triggered by the smallest nuances, and the reality of what other people were responding to in him. It was a very painful and hard road for him, as he had to get used to what felt like the heartless and thoughtless behaviour of others without withdrawing into his familiar lonely state or having recourse to his sarcasm and pessimism that people just 'weren't up to scratch'.

Exercise

It is important when pondering on this dilemma to realize that the part of you which feels hurt corresponds to when you were a child. The person inside you who feels hurt is the hurt child, and it is he or she who needs your care. When you feel hurt by someone, spend time examining what happened. What was said, referred to, acted out? What was actually said, and what did you hear underneath the words that confirmed your worst fears? Write it down. Try and describe the tone, feeling, image of what happened. Draw it if you can. Notice your eye level when you are pondering this. Are you looking up, or down?

With others I'm either safely wrapped up in bliss or I'm in combat. And if I'm in combat I'm either a bully or a victim

This double dilemma refers to our need to return to the safety or hiding of a womb-like environment when we get close to others. We're either enclosed in the relationship in a 'garden of Eden'-type bliss, or we react aggressively to others, always ready for a fight and adopting either the victim or bullying role.

As you can see, in this dilemma there is no comfortable breathing space in between where we can experience a mutual interdependence. It's as if we have found it hard to learn a model of being with someone which allows for the ebb and flow of energy and difference. We may find that we lurch from one extreme to another: feeling close and all wrapped up one minute, only to swing into combative mode the next. We may have the 'wrapped-up' relationship with one other person and be in combat in all our other relationships.

The dilemma often arises because of our longing for 'perfect care' and fusion with another. This may be the result of an over-close or 'tight' relationship with mother or sibling, or conversely because we have had empty, deprived early beginnings, where it was left to our imagination to provide an ideal model. At the beginning of this chapter we were looking at the reciprocal roles of internalized child self and internalized parent self. This dilemma grows out of the swing between the idealized 'perfect' other, who we hope will meet our every need, and who frequently grows out of our own sense of a restrictive early life, and the child inside us who experienced care as absent or neglectful. So inside ourselves we swing from hope to despair, from clinging to an ideal of how we long for things to be to a position of rage when we are disappointed, at which point we invite a combative situation, bullying others or allowing ourselves to be bullied.

If we can acknowledge this dilemma in our lives and own the origins of its pain, we are half-way to relieving its hold on our lives. It can be hard to accept that our idealization and longing for another who can meet our every need actually gets in the way of our ability to make satisfactory relationships. The fact that no one other mortal person can meet the needs of our deprived inner child can make us depressed. But out of this sense of despair we may begin to find the seeds of giving and receiving care from others that eventually becomes 'good enough'. Likewise, if we have been living a life of combat in relationships, we may need to pause and gather our strengths to begin to take care of the wounded child who moves into combative relationships as the only alternative to 'perfect' care, when underneath it longs for realistic care and attention.

Exercise

Write a story about 'perfect care' or 'perfect revenge'. Make it as dramatic as you wish. Read it aloud to someone you trust. Allow yourself to experience the feelings or longing behind the words, to identify the 'core pain' of the person in the story, and inside you, who wishes to relate to others.

Write another story about how you might care for the child inside whose feelings you have identified in the first story. Use everyday people and objects that have had some reality for you, or invite characters from your imagination who might serve the needs of the child today.

Either I look down on people or they look down on me

This dilemma stings, and furious rage abounds at either pole. How much do we know of our haughty selves who look down our noses, feel compelled to compete when someone is telling us something, have to cap everything with something of our own? And at the other end, how well do we know the self that is looked down upon, humiliated and laughed at, both by ourselves and, we fear, by others? This dilemma is about the world of despising and being despised, and how we deal with

it. Much of the dilemma stems from a particular experience when we felt despised, or were treated contemptuously – by adults when we were small, by admired elders at an impressionable time – and from which we were determined that we are in some part contemptible, laughable, a joke.

Believing this is so painful that we have few options. We can go through life with the false belief that we are all the things we despise and that others will look down on us, whatever we do. In this place we may play the contemptible one, or may block out any feelings by going 'on automatic'. Many compulsive workers – men or women – who become addicted to their work in whatever form do so because they are running from this fear and this place. They fear that if they are not sustained by the admiration of others they admire, they will be exposed and then will have to feel contemptuous or suffer feeling contemptible. In their studies of post-heart-attack patients, *Type A Behaviour and Your Heart*, Meyer Friedman and Ray Rosenman make the following observation:

As the perilous drive continues (to do more and more in less and less time and against greater odds and with increasing aggressiveness and desperation), the Type A person confines his disdain to those persons he is able to control; eventually he begins to entertain less and less regard for himself. It is when this latter process begins that his own spirit starts to wither, and the urge to self-destruct mounts. Much of this occurs in the unconscious, which makes the tragedy no less profound.

We may only sense that there is something inside us which makes us feel miserable and frightened and from which we are aware of running away, but our external adaptation takes up most of our time. We may not know that what we fear is contempt, and we will not know that at times we appear contemptuous. It is usually when our outer adaptation fails that we feel thwarted and fall into the place of contempt or being contemptuous.

Questionnaire: Either I look down on people or they look down on me

I can recognize my own contemptuousness in the following ways:
I feel I have to keep 'one ahead' of others, which makes me competitive. I have to get in my own story, and I am constantly striving to win.

I am judgemental of others who I see as weak and pathetic. I ignore them, or bait them by teasing and provocation over matters on which I know they cannot cope. Or I sneer, am sarcastic, humiliating.

I enjoy others' discomfort when I have 'found them out' or tricked them into falling into their own mess.

I am envious of others' success but cannot bear this feeling, so I repress it and am only aware of it in my difficulty with being 'less than' at any time. I find it very hard to be in a learning position where I have to take from another who I see as being in a superior position to myself and in which I feel inferior.

I feel as if I always have to 'know everything' and be on top, so that I am constantly in a winning position.

I use my contemptuousness in the following ways:
I am very uncomfortable with it, but I use it to drive me on in this world.

I am aware I am envious and competitive, and I use it to get me going, to make sure I keep up and ultimately overcome those in whose company I was made to feel small.

I am revengeful to those whom I feel have put me down. I fantasize about situations in which I am the victor over someone whom I feel has treated me with contempt. I practise very hard so that I can get my revenge.

When things go wrong I am aware of feeling more than usually shattered. It is as if I have fallen from my self-imposed pinnacle, and that the gap between where I now find myself and where I would like to go is huge and insurmountable. I am bitter and disillusioned. I swing from being very angry and bitter towards others, treating them with disdain and contempt, to – when I am left alone, as I frequently am when I'm like this – feeling very miserable and alone, disillusioned, full of self-hatred, self-destructive and suicidal.

I can recognize that I feel others look down on me in the following ways:
I always put myself down, usually jokingly, sending myself up.

I sneer at myself frequently and invite others to do the same.

I try and rise above these feelings by being very intellectual and clever. I use complicated words and sentences that few understand, and I talk in paragraphs in a convoluted way to hide the worm-like feelings I really have.

There is no fight in me. I let others walk all over me, while secretly despising them for it.

I expect others to behave better, but I am not surprised when they don't.

I am bitter. I want others to be better than they are, but I don't give any clues as to how this could be for me. I don't say what I really feel or what I really want, so I allow others to treat me contemptuously and look down on me, and they then take on the other end of the dilemma.

Most of my dialogues with others are in fact in my head. I rarely say what I feel or what I would like to say. I presume that others wouldn't be able to cope with it, and so I don't give them the chance.

Although I do feel 'beyond the pale' and despise myself, I feel that others should know better and do more. I am aware that this makes me incredibly angry, and that I feel angry a lot of the time.

It doesn't take much for people to get through or push me off centre. I do rely on admiration from others to stop me feeling looked down upon.

I rely a lot on having to be in positions of authority or usefulness to stop me feeling the pain of people looking down on me. But even though I achieve those positions – I look after others well, teach others, am my own boss, have a good job with others working for me – I am still on the look out for those who would put me down. *There is nowhere I feel really safe.*

What we have to cope with in this dilemma is the feeling that we are contemptible, and the fear that we will be forced to feel this again as we once did. The way in which we lessen the gap between feeling we have to look down on others and their looking down on us is to submit ourselves to the pain of that despised place. In that place we do indeed get in touch with many of the feelings that arose during our experiences of humiliation as a child. But when we experience them during a programme of self-discovery or therapy we bring to the damaged place another awareness of ourselves: that we are more than the child we once were, even though the feelings we suffer may seem overwhelming. When we allow ourselves to experience the middle place we have to

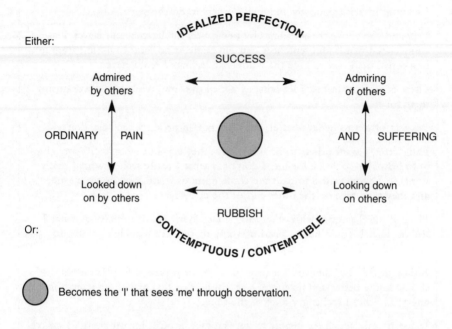

Figure 6 Looking down on others or looking down on me

suffer the pain of disillusionment, sadness, loss and grief for our humiliated self. We may experience simply being ordinary, something that feels terrifying because this meant contempt, and we may have always striven to be beyond contempt or reproach. By being brave enough to stay with this experience of ordinariness and to accept it, we are actually facilitating the healing process.

In Figure 6 we see how this dilemma operates. If we are not living in the top section (admired and admiring) then we inhabit the bottom (contemptuous or contemptible). When we experience 'the fall' from the idealized heights of success, we so fear being humiliated ('beyond the pale') that we turn our fear into a contemptuousness towards others.

Healing by mourning the loss of idealization to become 'real' and 'good enough'

As we become conscious of this dilemma we begin to dilute its power and 'splitting' nature by recognition, and by bearing the 'ordinary' pain and suffering of our core pain. This then gives flexibility for the real self to be more present, after which a change in consciousness can occur in the 'middle' place. Here, ordinary pain and suffering, loss and disillusionment will be experienced as we grieve for the loss of 'idealization'. So healing takes place as we allow ourselves to be ordinary mortals in pain.

Either I'm a brute or I'm a martyr

This dilemma relates to how we cope with our angry and aggressive feelings. If we do get angry and express it we feel like a brute, or we imagine that our anger is brutish. Conversely we get angry but don't say anything. We take on the martyr role, feeling full of self-sacrifice, with all the internal resentment and hostility this evokes. There is no middle place for assertion or appropriately angry responses, and at both ends of the dilemma each position blames the other. For the martyr says, 'I'm not going to get myself involved in anything that's unpleasant or brutish, I am better than that'; while the brute will say, 'It's no good sitting back and letting oneself be slaughtered, it's not worth it. Let's just steamroller over this and get something happening.' Each one serves the other. Each one brings out the opposite, either in another person or within the individual. For everyone who is caught up with the myth of the martyr there will be a brutish side, coming out unexpectedly because of its repression. People who take on the role of martyr are often prone to violent, brutish outbursts, or behave horribly to their animals, children or old people. Many people who appear brutish believe that if they did not act in such a way they would be martyred by others or to some cause in which they do not believe.

We are using the word 'martyr' here in its negative sense and not in the sanctified religious sense. If someone consciously chooses to martyr themselves for a cause they believe in, this is conscious acting from a position of idealism. We may say they are brutish to themselves at the same time, and to those whom they deprive of their full company. The early Christian martyrs set the tone for followers and movements and brought about change.

However, most of us who take up the position of martyr in our everyday lives feel put upon and deprived of our freedom of choice. Thus, we adopt the role resentfully and harbour a good deal of hidden anger. It is this underlying fury which can be quite devastating to others precisely, because it is so unexpected. We feel guilty if we are not serving others or being slaves to the object of our martyrdom, and we tend to look for ways we should be serving this master. We may expect to receive gratitude or thanks from others in reward for our sacrifice. But others may feel enslaved by our martyrdom and unable to go along with it. Martyrdom can be tyrannical and bring out the brute in the best of us! Martyrs can easily become victims, inviting the oppressors in others and thus actualizing and extending the period of martyrdom still further.

Jo experienced his mother as a martyr to his macho brutish father. He had a good bond with his mother and was devastated when she died of a heart attack when he was only eleven. He came into therapy because he was very depressed and phobic about death. Unable to go out to look for a job, obsessed with death and the afterlife, he led a virtually reclusive existence. In asking him to monitor the feelings he experienced during his panic attacks, we discovered that they came on in situations where he feared he might have to be assertive to someone. A man in the shop, on the end of the phone, when out running with his dog. He was terrified of getting into a situation where he would 'boil over in rage like an exploding volcano'.

When we looked at this we discovered that as well as his father's macho image, which Jo felt he could not go along with, the week before his mother had died his father had thrown a lamp at her in a fit of temper. He had associated his father's anger with a brutishness and murderousness, triggering off his mother's death. He had never put these two together before, but his unconscious had, preventing him from expressing any kind of anger in case it came out in the same way. He had blocked off assertiveness, frightened that it might turn into anger and aggressiveness. When he could see how this dilemma had ruled his life he could begin to learn to be more assertive, to choose his own way of being angry. Then he could begin to go back into the world less afraid, and free himself from the unconscious ties that had deprived him of his own life.

Questionnaire: Either I'm a brute or a martyr

Why am I am martyr? What makes me take up this position?

Because I believe it is the only way I can receive gratitude and thanks from others?

Because I believe it is the only way I can be?

Because I don't believe in my freedom and right to a full independent life?

Is it for me a form of love?

Did I learn it and am now copying it without revision?

Am I caught up in a centuries-old woman-as-martyr-to-men complex?

Name the martyrs in your family, in your experience – from literature, the Bible, films, stories. Do you identify with one of them? Do you fear being identified as a martyr, and so adopt a brutish role?

In what way do I express my hidden 'brutishness':
against myself;
against my animals;
in fantasy;
in sudden outbursts of temper directed against others?

If I am a 'brute' is it because:
It's the only way I've learned to be from (i) family, (ii) others?
If I'm not a brute I'll be a martyr (like someone I know)?
It's the only way I can keep on top and avoid victimization?
I enjoy the power and letting others live out the martyr role?
It limits my life, as I have to keep it up, and sometimes I'd like to relax?
Brutes also have feelings. What are they?

The male/female dilemma: as a woman I have to do what others want; as a man I can't have any feelings

As a woman, I have to do what others want, even though it makes me cross, because there is a powerful myth which says it's not feminine to express yourself as you'd really like. Others don't like it, and it spoils relationships.

Are we breaking with these myths today? We are trying to, but it's often surprising how much they live on and unconsciously inform what we do and how we behave. They are under revision, but we tend to slip back into them when things get difficult or we try out new ways of expressing ourselves that are misunderstood. The old myths seem to be as follows: women are passive and they serve others; they yield to men and the masculine way; they are the givers of the world; they give out and they give in. Representing the power within relationships and the family, this should remain their domain, and they should not venture outside to compete with men in the world of men.

For generations women have felt suppressed by men and the masculine ideology, by the force of patriarchy. Although there have always been pioneers such as Mary Wollstonecraft or Marian Evans (George Eliot) to show that the female spirit was still alive, all reflection of women has predominantly come through men. Since gaining much more independence economically, sociologically and biologically, women have still had to go through the masculine channels to receive recognition, often having to steel themselves and work much harder than men in order to achieve this.

In the midst of this transition in women's roles, relationships are suffering. One in three marriages ends in divorce. Many women are leaving it until later to get married, and then have difficulty finding a partner who meets them in terms of standards, expectations and equality. Many women feel very torn at this point. They want independence to work and express themselves, but they still feel there is a substantial cost involved and that it poses a threat to relationships. Alice, a successful architect with two children, is aware of this tension in her own life:

'At work my role is very clearly defined and I am respected for it. I say my piece and it is heard and acted upon. I experienced myself as being free and powerful in a creative sense. It is stimulating and exciting and I love the work I'm doing and the feeling of expansiveness and generosity it gives me. But when at home something else seems to take over. I am not boss in my own home, and I fear being seen as such as I see it as a basic threat to the safety of my relationship. So I become somewhat tremulous, giving in reluctantly to my partner's whims and wishes without being able to say what I really think and believe in. It's as if I feel that were I to bring in some of my more assertive self he would see me as strident and demanding, and in fact he has said several times, "Oh I'm not one of your office minions . . . you can't behave like you do in the office here." I don't feel I can answer because I feel he's right, that somehow I've got to find a way of being more submissive in my private life to make up for "getting away with it" elsewhere. I know

I'm resentful, and I often get headaches at the weekends and feel unbearably tired when I get home. I associate that with my confusion, not knowing what to do, and a general weariness and lack of clarity about the whole thing.'

Many women have received the old myths from their mothers and grandmothers, and the picture of the submissive 'feminine' woman as being still what men want does live on. Some women will find this role suits them, and are drawn to a man who will encourage it. Indeed, it may work well, but perhaps it represents a rather limited role example for the next generation of daughters. Some women actually sacrifice their own views and voice when they marry or enter a relationship, and upon having children. And for some it is a relief to do so – not to have to fight or struggle any more, but be content with the age-old passive role of serving home, husband and children. And, indeed, within this role there are many modes of expression. But to give up one's own voice because of a fear of not being feminine causes only conflict and struggle, and leads resentments and angers to build up underneath.

Somewhere in this transition of male and female expressions lies the hope for the emergence of a way of being a woman that forcefully brings into the light of consciousness the most positive qualities of the feminine principle:

• Receptive, rather than passive.
• Empowering, rather than selflessly giving to others.
• Flexible, adaptable, yielding and creative, rather than submissive with 'no mind of her own'.
• Centred in body and emotions and unafraid of each, rather than over-emotional, flighty, frivolous, self-conscious.
• Sexual and sensual, rather than seductive, flirty, posing.
• Nurturing, rather than manipulatively feeding and devouring.
• Containing, rather than possessive.
• Holding close and letting go appropriately, rather than emasculating (men and women) and over-controlling.

From a central womb of womanhood a woman could then express her masculine side. This would be ancillary to her feminine being, not instead of or to compensate for the negative sides listed above. Such women are rare, but perhaps to be found in the future?

As a man, I have to be a 'proper' man, which means not expressing anything to do with feelings.

This dilemma will remain unrevised if men can find both work and relationships that avoid the need to get into anything of a feeling nature. If women are still living out the need to define being feminine as not being assertive or having independent views, the men with whom they are involved will be able to dictate the tone of the relationship and look to women to contain the feeling side of things. Many men do in fact manage to avoid having anything to do with feelings, until something happens that hits them personally on that level – their partner leaves them, they get ill and become dependent on others, they fall in love, they lose someone whom they had never realized was important to them.

With the change in the role of women in society, relationships between men and women are having to adapt radically, and men are finding that they must deal with their feeling side earlier than in previous generations. For many men who have been brought up in a traditionally 'macho' environment, there is little or no developed language for expressing feeling or emotion. The myth seems to be that a man must be the hunter and striver in the outside world where his rational, focused side is uppermost, and that the convoluted, diffuse world of the emotions would only impede progress and draw a dangerous veil over the masculine purpose. When men cut off their feeling side because they are afraid of being overpowered by it, they become lopsided. They can get stuck at the extreme end of the masculine principle. They tend to become lonely and are unable to relate to others, their work or the world. They can become depressed because they think they are supposed to act like an automaton, so rejecting a major aspect of themselves and appearing brittle and unfeeling, strident and fixed.

The old myths about men and masculinity persist: tough, macho, in charge and command, driven, strict, controlled, focused, unyielding, unable to compromise. Any show of softness is seen as a weakness. Although a man may have strong feeling instincts and a strong feminine side, he may have been discouraged from using or expressing this aspect of himself because of the powerful taboos that exist against it. There are a hundred little injunctions – 'boys don't cry', mother's boy, cissy, hiding in a woman's skirts, floppy, spineless, weedy, wet, impotent, foppish – and most of the terms are derogatory, linking the feminine side with negativity.

Questionnaire: The male/female dilemma

What do I feel are the important qualities of being a woman, a man? How much do I include these in my own life?

In what way am I lopsided in my use of masculine and feminine?
I expect men to:

be strong;   not be bossed or affected by a woman;
make all the decisions;   have the most important role;
not to be fazed or bothered   not give in to any weakness.
by anything;
be able to take liquor;
have exclusive male company;

I expect women to:
be kind and gentle;   be good housewives;
have warm feelings;   be the peacemaker;
care about children and relation-   have a special 'women's' world;
ships;   never be aggressive or masculine.
keep themselves looking nice;

I expect men and women to share:
strong ideas;   an understanding of each other's
strong feelings;   'no-go' areas;
decision-making;   tears and sadness;
assertiveness at all times, and to be   anger;
aggressive when appropriate;   other.

We may not yet have incorporated the strength of a feeling heart into masculine judgement, but we always know when these two attributes have come together something wise and wonderful happens. A wise leader, judge or company head will be able both to relate in a heartfelt way and make hard decisions. Betty Friedan, in her book *Woman: Her Changing Image,* writes about her visit to West Point military academy to meet the first new women officers. Would they be 'grotesque female imitations of the bloodthirty male stereotype, with the feminine values – sensitivity, tenderness, intuition, cherishing – deadened and drilled away by the brutal cadences of military command'? Instead, however, she met a group of women who had endured physical testing and emotional battering, to emerge with a new sense of sureness about being women . . . their commitment to the moral questions . . . the values and interests of family life, survival not machismo, and the qualities of being they brought with them meshed with the wisest of the men as they all struggled to answer questions of survival . . . the realization being that this, in military and civilian life, depended upon qualities previously devalued as 'feminine'.

Although the feminine principle has been in the dark for centuries, it seems to be re-emerging to be valued afresh and with vital implications for our ecological survival as well as for our use of aggression, weaponry and technology. When it is more fully integrated into the psyche of both men and women it allows the masculine focus to be used more appropriately.

Chapter 4

Snags and self-sabotage

'Yes, but . . . if only'

Snags seem to operate when part of us is saying, 'I'd like things to be different'. 'I'd really like things to be better, but . . .' Or when we say, 'Oh well, I could never have a life like that', or gaze very enviously at others and say, 'It's all very well for them'. We may also start to reminisce in such a way as, 'If only I'd done this, but of course . . . if I hadn't had the childhood I had or the schooling I had . . .' So the overall effect is to make us feel that our life has actually been snagged in some almost magical way. Part of us has the desire to lead a fuller life, to have better relationships, to feel freer, to feel better about ourselves, be more successful, to be more imaginative.

Part of us is saying, 'Oh wouldn't it be lovely . . . if only . . .' While the others part of us counters with 'But I couldn't . . . I'm not lucky . . . it couldn't happen to me . . . other people wouldn't like it . . . I've never had the chance others had . . .', and so on.

Family myths

Sometimes this sense of 'yes . . . but' comes from the strong ideas and images about our role that we pick up from powerful people in our early lives: 'She was always such a good child', 'Such a clever boy', 'She was the one that kept the family together'. These can be very powerful myths and often prove difficult for us to challenge. It's hard to throw off the idea that these myths actually are the real us. We may be helpful and good and kind, but it may not be the sum total of who we are. We may also want to be fun, frivolous, exciting, naughty, cross, and so on.

Another powerful injunction may come from the family myths themselves: 'People in our family never . . . smoke a pipe . . . wear loud
clothes . . . shout a lot . . . go into that kind of business . . . marry
outside their kind'. This means that hanging over us, imperceptibly
(because we may not have realized it), is this idea that 'I'm not entitled
to be anything other than what my family has made me'. Under this
guise we put down or repress any kind of otherness or ways of expressing ourselves which don't seem to fit in with what is expected of our
families. One girl said to me years ago that although she had been going
through a difficult patch in her marriage she had never, never considered divorce, because no one in her family had ever been divorced. It
was a completely alien concept.

Our attitude to work, friends, religion, health, ways of proceeding are governed by our early family and what the family accepts. Obviously all have an impact upon us. For many of us they may suit us well, but when we find that we are snagging ourselves as we've described above, it may be that the way the family would have us live is actually inappropriate and we need to look at it afresh.

Families may also make judgements: people who think too much about themselves are self-indulgent . . . people who don't have a proper religion and don't go to church don't have moral fibre . . . you'll never get on in the world if you let anyone see what you really feel . . . don't let anyone see you when you're down, they'll only take advantage . . .' See if you can start making a list of the myths and some of the ideas that abound in your own family about behaviour, about ways of proceeding, from the smaller concerns like dress and appearance to the more major questions of politics, religion and relationships.

It may also be that the snags in our life develop because important people close to us actually do not want us to change. This may not be obvious, but remain hidden within a relationship. Ask yourself if the 'yes . . . but' in your life is related to what you anticipate from others. Sometimes we think that if we were to improve ourselves, become more successful, happier or healthier the people around us might not know how to deal with it. They may oppose it, because they feel unable to cope with what our changing means to them.

An example of this might be when one person in a relationship begins to enjoy success, while the other – parent, husband or wife, for example – becomes ill or depressed. It's as if they can only thrive when the other person isn't feeling so good. Thus, we may have become unconsciously caught up in the life patterns of another. What maintains the relationship is the interdependency of this imbalance, where one partner thrives because, and at the expense, of the other. It is as if there would not be enough 'wellness' or 'goodness' to go around for both people. This is a difficult situation to deal with, and in the chapter on relationships we will be looking at this more fully. Try now to outline how much or how often the snag of 'yes . . . but' operates in your life, and become reasonably clear about the nature of the snag.

You may not be consciously aware of snags because they are held in the unconscious but, having read this section and completed the questionnaire, allow the concept of being snagged to be part of your thoughts, so that if you are actually snagged you can become aware of it.

Questionnaire: Snags

I recognize that I 'snag' myself in the following ways:
Every day I say, 'Yes . . . but' or 'If . . . only'.

I always feel that others are:
luckier;
more successful;
happier;
more attractive;
better than I am.

Name the past obstacles that you feel have got in the way, causing a snag in your life and preventing you from being successful or happy:
If it weren't for . . . I would be . . . now.
My parents never let me . . .
I never had the chance to . . .
If only I'd been allowed to . . . I would be . . . now.
Other.

Look at these snags honestly and ask yourself: How have I contributed to making these events or occurrences into more than appropriately damaging or negating beliefs about my life and success?
By unrevised resentment, bitterness, anger, laziness.
By using the occurrences as excuses or reasons why I have not, or do not, take up opportunities.
By not trying to do what I really would like, if I could overcome a resentment or anger, to achieve in alternative ways.

How much do family myths about how to be and what is allowed live on and influence your choices, forming a snag? For example:
'There's never been a divorce in our family'; 'No one from this family has ever gone on the stage'; 'We never wash our dirty linen in public' (i.e. talk about our feelings to others).

Do snags operate because you believe that if you make your own free choice of how to be, someone important to you won't like it, or an unrevised, important family value will be challenged? For example: 'If I am assertive my marriage won't survive'; 'If I leave the job I hate and train to be a teacher my wife won't cope'.

Self-sabotage

Other evidence of a snag operating is when we seem to arrange to avoid pleasure or success. Or, if we are successful and happy we have to pay, either by depression or illness or our ability to spoil things. When success is within our grasp, we find we are not able to claim it. We may have achieved high marks in an exam, we may have got that important interview, we may have lost the weight we wanted, but we don't allow ourselves to fully have it – we miss the appointment, we immediately put the weight back on, we mess up the next paper of the exam – thus actually wiping out the good event that we were about to take part in.

'Magical guilt'

Sometimes what lies behind this spoiling behaviour is a sense of being 'magically guilty' for something that happened early on in the family, or for somebody else's life. I use the word 'magically' guilty because it's a guilt for something we couldn't possibly have taken responsibility for or feel guilty about. Magical guilt can have a very powerful undermining effect on our lives. It usually comes about because in our families we felt more privileged than one of our siblings, or even one of our parents. We might be cleverer than them, or healthier. This is often exaggerated when a member of the family is ill or depressed or if someone dies when we are small. We may feel inside ourselves that this has something to do with our luck or strength.

This is not a conscious thought, but a powerful undermining and unconscious process which can catch us like the undertow in an apparently smooth river. We then develop the unconscious, mistaken belief that 'I am strong at the expense of my brother or sister or my aunt, my grandmother, my mother or my father's weakness. I am healthy at the expense of their illness. I am well and fit and happy at the expense of their bad feelings and depression. I am not entitled to my good fortune or my good luck. My talent is at the expense of their misery.'

Because early on in life we want to be attached to those figures who are important to us, it's actually very difficult to come to terms with these ideas in any reasonable way when we're small. We unconsciously take on the burden, and begin to live life as if we were not fully entitled to, but were magically guilty in some way for our successes or happinesses. Our only way to cope with that is to deny them in some way, to deprive ourselves of them subtly – we may reach the point of claiming a lovely friendship, a good career, or a marvellous travelling experience, and we suddenly spoil it at the last minute. We either miss the boat, or we get ill or depressed or we do something quite extraordinary which prevents us taking it up.

Envy

This particular snag may also come about because we've experienced envy from one of our siblings or a parent for our perceived good fortune, good looks, strength, sense of fun, freedom, abilities and skills. This may not be obvious. Very few of us are comfortable about actually acknowledging this. If you cast your mind back you may recall comments like, 'I don't expect you to be able to do things like that', or, 'A great girl like you! I would have thought you'd do a better job', or, 'Trust you to do the most difficult thing there is', or, 'I suppose with your skills you can have anything you want'. Such remarks are said in a slightly hurt, slightly belligerent way by people whose favours we want to keep. We then begin a process of learning to hide the skills and gifts we have, to jeopardize them rather than risk the wrath and the envy of those people whose love we crave.

It can be quite upsetting when we eventually realize how much we are snagging ourselves in our lives and acting as if really we aren't allowed to take up our gifts and skills, and it can be really quite painful to realize that this actually comes from being actively envied in our early lives. We can only free ourselves from this pattern by making all the instances and all the realizations conscious. Once we can see the situation clearly, we can then start to free ourselves from it. We can actually stop the pattern of self-negation and snagging.

Sometimes this is a hard task, because if we have incorporated into our being the idea that we really weren't entitled to very much, it's quite difficult to start to claim to have something. When we do begin this journey of claiming our lives we will feel the heaviness of guilt and the conviction that something really bad will happen. We wake the previously unconscious fear that we will be rejected because we are taking up our lives for ourselves. And some of those old voices that made us feel bad about our gifts will come back from the past: 'You're completely selfish', or, 'You're a ruthless man', or, 'No one wants somebody like that', or, 'You give no time to other people' – all the kinds of accusations that tend to come from those who feel they're not free to take up their own gifts and skills.

But once you have embarked on this journey and the realizations are becoming clearer to you, you can also begin to understand how important it is to free yourself from them. Because they are magical injunctions: *It is not true* that we are responsible for the depressed, miserable, negative, unhappy lives of those who have gone before us. It *is* possible to claim one's gifts without feeling guilty for them. As we embark on this journey we can only become wiser, more fulfilled and more comfortable in what we are doing, and able to summon up the energy needed. Able also to inhabit a space where we can look back on what's happened, and particularly on how we've been caught up in these magical guilt processes of the past. We can free ourselves and other people from being involved in them. As we take this journey up we are, of course, facing these magical guilts from a different place, because we're that much older and the defences with which we had to protect ourselves from the harsh words or the harsh judgements of those around us are much less.

Realizing how much we have snagged our lives or stopped ourselves being happy may be rather a depressing task at first. It's important to remember, however, that the process we've been engaged in is not stupid or bad, but something we've been caught up in because it was the only way we were able to manage. This is what we learned when we were younger, this was the only way we could cope with what we were up against. But having recognized what we've been doing it's vital to understand that we don't have to keep on doing it.

By changing our behaviour we can not only learn to control our own behaviour but we can also change the way other people behave towards us. Once we have dared to confront what we feared most, we face the ghost and the ghost is never so frightening again. One we have learned to consolidate what's inside us, then we learn to stand up to those who, because of their own difficulties, would not want us to change. Something quite important happens when we stand up consistently for who we are, and in many cases this has a transformatory effect on the other person. It sometimes seems that others do resist the changes that we want for ourselves, particularly those who are closest to us. They might say things like, 'You're not as you were', or, 'All this psychotherapy is making you too inward', or, 'I don't like what it's doing to you', or 'I think it's dangerous'. We often underestimate them. If we're firm about our right to change, those who care for us will usually accept it. If they

---

Questionnaire: Self-sabotage

Make a list now of the times and ways in which you feel you sabotage yourself.

I fear the response of others if I:
do well;
look good;
win anything.

I fear most the response from . . . (name the person or persons).

Because of my fear of others' envy through their (a) disapproval, (b) withdrawal, (c) sharp words, (d) criticism, (e) saying, 'It's all very well for you . . .', I play down what I know and what I can do (a) all the time (b) in certain situations (name them).

I feel I'm not entitled to:
success;   love;
nice things;   freedom;
happiness;   a good job.

I feel that if I get things others will be worse off and suffer. Who will? Where does this feeling come from?

If something good happens for me I feel:
It's just luck;   I could never create it for myself;
I don't deserve it;   I could never keep it going.
It won't last;

---

cannot accept, however, then we often do have to make a painful choice. Having completed this section, name those people in your life who wish you well. Begin to allow yourself an equal freedom and to allow yourself to claim your own life freely.

Chapter 5

Core pain and core
pain statements

So far we have been trying to name our problems by identifying the traps, dilemmas and snags in which our thinking about ourselves becomes caught. Don't be alarmed if you identify with a number of traps and dilemmas, and if your notebook seems to be getting full. All the information you gather about yourself will be used to construct your life story in a way which reformulates the way things have been for you in the past in a creative and useful way.

In this next section we are going to try to establish the nature of our core pain. Core pain and core pain statements tend to become so entrenched in our ways of thinking about ourselves that we take them for granted. We then see life through a lens coloured by these attitudes. In order to inspect the lens we need to identify its nature and to then ask ourselves whether it is still appropriate. The traps, dilemmas or snags we have identified in the other chapters all stem from our core pain. When we are ready we can begin to find ways of challenging the limitations such a lens may be having upon our life. Read through the following chapter and see if you recognize your way of assuming things about your life that needs examination and healing. As you complete each of the exercises, see also if you can identify, in reciprocal role terms, the part of you whose role incites or maintains your core pain.

'Everything has to be difficult, whatever I do'

This is the traditional 'yes . . . but' mode that was linked with snags in Chapter 4. But is also a way of thinking and being in which we experience everything we do as half-baked – the classic depressed position, which feels joyless no matter what improvements are made. The core pain feelings are connected to depression, anxiety, emptiness and worth-lessness. These may be maintained by a 'stern coper' or 'harsh judge' reciprocal role self. If you recognize that your thinking goes like this and there is always a 'yes . . . but' at the end of your sentences and in your attitude to life, consider the following:

It's got to be difficult, because I need a struggle. If I don't have a struggle I might be more depressed.

If things weren't difficult and I was happy with my life I would be asking for trouble, pushing my luck.

My struggle is how I identify myself – that whatever happens to me, at least I've worked hard, struggled against the odds, kept on going.

I need to be admired for my ability to struggle.

I need the process of struggle and the sense of a heroic quest to over-come. If I didn't have this I would be a wimp.

I am by nature a pessimist. After all, what has been easy for me, ever?

Mother/Father said, 'Don't count your chickens before they're hatched' – so I never take anything for granted, I prepare for the worst all the time. Whenever I've looked on the bright side I've always been disappointed, so I gave it up.

Do you feel any of the above are linked to the following statements:
My fragility with myself and life.
I've got to have a cause or quest.
My discomfort with life – I'd rather fly away and float somewhere.
Everyday life is hard and mundane.
I feel easily trapped and oppressed by the everyday. I'd like to be free again and not pinned down.
Life for adults is hard and full of responsibilities.

If you have identified that you are on a quest in your life and that you find the difficulties associated with your quest stimulating and satis-fying, you may decide that your internal assumption that things have to be difficult has a purpose and is worthwhile. If, on the other hand, you can identify that your presumption is connected with a fear of being pinned down, depressed or being seen as weak, you may view your struggle as being similar to the myth of Sisyphus, doomed endlessly to push a boulder up a hill, only to watch it roll down again. In Part 3 we will be gathering information about our early lives and about how we came to possess the attitudes we have. You may find yourself much enlightened by understanding the nature of your own boulder (which may not be yours in fact!). Pause here though, and ponder or fantasize on what it would be like if the boulder, or difficulty, were not there. What would it be like if you could change the lens that makes things difficult? As you begin to recognize the times when this lens colours the way you do things, experiment with leaving this assumption to one side, and moving into things with an open mind.

'No one ever helps me. I have to do everything myself. If I didn't, nothing would happen'

This tends to be a core pain statement that grows out of an early environment where we had to do most things for ourselves; where it was hard to ask for help, or if we did, it was met with, 'I'm too busy' or 'Can't you do it yourself?'. Or it may be that there were specific, perhaps hidden, payoffs for doing things for oneself, especially before one's time. The harassed single mother or busy parent with a lot to do may well express a great deal of pleasure at a child who shows he or she can manage well, and these may be the only attributes that are rewarded. In families where parents were ill or absent for long periods, for example, or in the case of children who were moved from one foster home to another, the art of self-sufficiency may be well developed and the only means of survival. It may have been difficult to bear the helplessness or inadequacy of a parent, and so we get on and manage not just ourselves but parents and siblings as well. The core pain is helplessness, hopelessness, fear and loneliness.

In some people this assumption is so well developed that they have no concept of their own needs and feelings whatsoever, and survive by their independence, 'gutting it' through many of life's crises without apparent difficulty. The problems come when this assumption is dominant. We find it impossible to relax and let others help us, and sooner or later we become exhausted. If we cannot let go we may, without realizing it, prove exacting company to be with, demanding that others meet our standards. We may develop a cynicism and bitterness in our belief that we are the only people who do anything, and even snarl at people who try to help us or to live up to these standards. Underneath we just do not believe we can actually trust a soul. And the terror of letting go enough to allow someone else to help, and perhaps make a mess of it, seems difficult to overcome.

Exercise: 'No one ever helps me . . .'

Make a list of all the tasks you do (a) at home, and (b) at work which would really benefit from being shared.

Monitor the number of items you think to yourself, 'I always have to do it', 'It's always just up to me', or the times when you feel put upon or grumpily resigned to having to do things for yourself. Do this for a week. At the end of the week look and see how much this assumption operates in your every-day life. Start questioning it. Need it be so, every time?

Experiment with putting off tasks for as long as you can bear and note the feelings that come up.

Note how much the presumption that things will not get done unless you do them actually heightens the anxiety and the determination of the self-fulfilling prophecy.

Talk about what you feel to someone. Explain how difficult it is for you to leave things to others, but how you would like to do this more.

Can you live with what feels like others' inadequacy?

How serious would the consequences be if things were not always done to your standard?

Can you identify the 'role' within that maintains your difficulty?

I personally carried on under this assumption for many years. I found it hard to work in a team at first, because I was always going off and doing things either on my own or without consulting the others. The rest of the team saw me variously as arrogant, bolshie or insensitive, a 'know it all', wanted to be the star turn. Of course it was all of these things, but I didn't know it. When I began to realize this, and to under-stand that people cared about it, that they wanted me as part of a team, and that being in such a place was actually a relief from the isolation and fierce independence of going it alone all the time, I was very grate-ful indeed. I learned a lot, grew a lot, and know now how to catch myself before I go off on my 'got to do it all' stand. I've also found that

I can trust others to do what they feel like doing for me. Whatever the result, I appreciate the effort, and now I actually recognize it!

If we can give up this position without losing our drive to get things done when needed, and without fearing that we will lose control or standards, which would be depleting or anxiety-making, we are free to have a much more varied and relaxed life.

When we come to Chapter 7 on problems and aims you might want to make this task a prime aim and work towards changing the substance and the hold of this particular assumption.

'Always feeling bad inside'

We're not always aware of how bad we feel inside until we reflect upon it. It might manifest itself, for example, in feeling bad about other people, therefore projecting our internal bad feelings onto others. We then feel people are against us, life is against us, events go wrong for us. What usually happens is that we feel the badness is all outside, reflected in external events and other people. When reflecting on it, however, we actually find that those bad feelings are inside us, and one of the reasons we appear to experience them in others and in world events is because they are the most intolerable things we have to deal with.

Feeling bad inside might also reflect itself in terms of the kind of relationships we make. If we only feel free to make relationships with people we don't like very much or don't admire, whose reputation is not very pleasant, this may also be a reflection of what we're feeling inside. We feel so bad that we can only make relationships with people who on some level might be worse than us. We don't feel free to have relationships or friendships with people we like or are attracted to, or who have a reputation for being nice. The result of all this is that we feel depressed most of the time – that thin veil of depression or, in more severe cases, deeper levels of depression from which we feel we're never going to be freed. We somehow manage to carry on under this veil, automatically doing things we feel we must do, but never really experiencing pleasure or happiness in any form.

Sometimes these bad inner feelings can manifest themselves in physical form – nausea, heaviness in the legs, tension in the neck and shoulders – as if what we experience as badness is somehow located and expressed by the body in graphic form. Feeling bad inside may also lead us to what I call 'displacement behaviours' – overeating or starving, harming ourselves in some way, taking provocative risks, driving too fast, drinking too much, smoking to excess, taking up daring sports, flying too high. There may be times when we spend too much money, or money we don't have, and buy things we don't need. Or we may associate with people or groups of people with whom we really have nothing in common. You may want to add to this list, but all these things are possibly an attempt to get away from the feelings we're plagued with internally.

Sometimes in our early lives we are actually told we are bad and that 'nobody loves a bad girl or bad boy'. Sometimes the word 'bad' is actually used; more often it is disguised in various subtle forms and we pick up messages about what we then interpret to be our badness. It may be that we don't come up to the standard that is required of us. Perhaps our parents' view of us is that we don't give enough, therefore we're selfish. We might enjoy doing things that the rest of the family doesn't, so we're labelled odd or difficult. We may find ourselves in the grip of rather difficult feelings in our early life – fury, a desire to hit out, a sense of entrapment and persecution. We might be the subject of actual perceived cruelty on a mental or a physical level. When there is nowhere for these feelings to go, no outlet for their expression, no one we can talk to about them, we're made to feel even worse if we do start to express our feelings out of this place.

These feelings tend to stay inside and, rather like a boil, they can fester, sometimes for years. So we carry around this simmering emotion, often somewhere in the body, or in this rather veiled depression we talked about earlier, and it isn't until we have to ponder on it or somebody actually asks us that we start to realize to what extent we've harboured this myth that we're bad inside ourselves. Although we may not actually feel we're bad, we may sense that the feelings we are carrying around are, and so we feel bad inside. We are aware that something in our core isn't quite right, that there's something wrong with us, something unpleasant and difficult. But when we don't understand why we feel like that or where it's coming from, we often try to hide it, which is why those bad feelings are often projected onto other people and situations, or we carry them around like a great burden day after day.

Questionnaire: 'Always feeling bad inside'

If you recognize that you feel like this, just spend a few moments quietly inside yourself. See if you can get some sort of graphic image for the way you feel. Start with the phrase 'It is like . . .' and let your imaginative level, your unconscious level, speak to you in the form of a picture, colour, shape or image. It doesn't matter what comes to you, just stay with whatever emerges. Ponder on it. See if there is anything more this image wants to tell you. When you feel you have grasped this particular state of being, this always feeling bad inside, anchor that image, or sense or actual picture of what it feels like to be you inside most of the time.

I recognize I always feel bad inside by;
a heavy weight in my body;
feeling sick;
my depressed mood.

I always think the worst about myself.

Sometimes I believe I am evil.

I tend to move with a 'bad' crowd.

I feel that people always end up hating me.

Whatever good thing happens I always return to the feeling I was never wanted in this world.

If something good comes my way I can only spoil it.

Because I never do anything good, I must be bad.

However many of the above you tick, you need to allow yourself to grapple with the idea that you actually *are not bad*. You may have absorbed this idea about yourself from your early life and it may press very heavily on you. It might be pressing so heavily that it's ruining your chances of proving to yourself it's not true by winding you around in its trap. *But it is a very old message and belongs to the past.* Try and find someone to talk to about it; share it if you can. This particular assumption is greatly helped by sharing, because it's an assumption that's based on hurt and pain. Get some help to begin to lift yourself out of it. Look at the things about yourself that are not 'bad' however small or little. You've read this page. That indicates that part of you is searching for answers – that's not bad but positive. Believe in that, that you have it in you to embrace something different from the old messages and the harsh judgement of 'I am bad' that has directed you so far. How often do you say that of others? How many others do you consider 'bad'?

In my experience people who consider they are 'bad' have so many other attributes they've worked hard to develop because of their presumption, but these attributes are unrecognized.

Not having feelings

Sometimes when I ask, 'How does it feel?' (that now most cliched question of the psychological professional), people look at me in puzzlement and say, 'I think . . .'. They are not in touch with the world of feelings at all, and may not have any language for it. I once had to write a list of 'feeling' words for someone who for years had simply not used any kind of feeling expression. In Chapter 2 on dilemmas we looked at the 'bottled-up or burst-open' dilemma, and described how feelings can be neglected or rejected early in life, because they are misunderstood or just plain frightening. Some people presume that they do not have feelings, when in fact they are so bottled up that not a glimpse of them comes out. When feelings have been as firmly shut away as this, a coldness can come over people. They tell of horrific events without expression; they appear unaffected by the most devastating news; they seem controlled and unfeeling when personally challenged. What has happened to the feeling level? It may be hiding, to be triggered off when something does get through; it may be waiting for the 'right' time in terms of development. (I know a man whose bottled-up feelings came pouring out when he was forty-five and had a 'mid-life crisis'. He surprised everyone who thought he was a cold, unfeeling schemer until that point.) Perhaps we may wait for a 'safe' environment for feelings to come out – a long-term relationship, a satisfactory job of work, for example.

If feelings have been so damaged and battered, or if no satisfactory release for them is found, they may get completely split off. But this is unusual, and is frequently part of a more serious illness. Feelings may, however, be split off into different aspects of ourselves – the body, for example. We may have physical symptoms instead of feelings – the symptoms have the feeling 'for' us. We may try to contain our feelings by choosing a profession that will force us to operate only in our heads, in the rational and logical avenues. We may act out instead of expressing feeling, by driving fast, drinking too much, taking drugs, taking up dangerous sports and activities, gambling, fighting, stealing. Whereas all these things may be merely a matter of personal choice, if we feel we recognize this assumption as belonging to us, it is worth considering how many of these displacement activities are in fact our way of expressing the feelings we presume we do not have.

Every one of us has a feeling nature. Some have larger or more dominant ones than others. But feeling is an important function in terms of our sensing, valuing, and sensitively judging situations, as well as being one of the ways of expressing emotion. We can use feeling without being 'emotional'. We use feeling when we appreciate something beautiful; hear a wonderful sound; notice the first crocus. Feeling needs the slowness of time. It is much slower than thinking, which is quick and immediate.

The void

Sometimes people say they have a 'black hole' or void inside them. They fear this place, because they believe it will swallow them up. If we iden-

Exercise

If you recognize that you are suffering from not having feelings, ask yourself when was the last time that you 'felt' something inside? Where did you feel it in your body? What was that feeling? When did it occur? What was happening at that time?

If your answer to the last question was a long time ago (more than two years), what was the result of your recognition of feeling? Did you express it, and if so how? How did others respond? Did something happen to make you decide you would not express feeling again?

If you have been unable to answer the first two questions because you cannot recognize the expression 'felt', cast your mind's eye over the last week. What is the most unpredictable thing that happened? Describe it, and what was happening.

Talk to someone about not having feelings. Begin to explore what feelings are and how other people express them. Become a 'student' of feelings.

Look through the section 'What Makes Us Tick?' in Part 3 and see if you can identify how your current sense of not having feelings came about.

In beginning to let yourself experience feeling, take your time. Choose music and poetry or descriptive writing to express feelings, before words.

If you are seeking to bring back a feeling level into your life, begin to value feeling positively rather than resenting it or seeing it as an expression of failure.

If you recognize that not having feelings is the result of some past trauma, talk to someone about this. Begin to analyse what happened to you, and allow the process of mourning, grieving and healing to take its course.

When feeling re-emerges it is like the thawing process after a big freeze. It hurts. Take it slowly and try not to be afraid of the pain. See the pain as glad evidence that your feeling nature is still alive and needs your help at containment and nourishment. Let it thaw out and flow and flourish. Trust in it.

---

tify with this we may try our best to avoid this place, keeping very busy all the time, never allowing any 'void' qualities to well up in us. We may fill our void with people, work, food, drugs, activity – anything external. We do not trust ourselves inside, because inside us feels as if it all leads back to the void.

For Alistair, the void, once he was brave enough to explore it, was a 'can of worms' containing everything he feared and loathed about his past and about some of his current feelings. In Chapter 6 on writing our life story and working on our diagram, we will see how Alistair is currently working to cope with his particular void. In exploring his 'can of worms' we met snakes who would come up and bite him in the form of negative judgements such as, 'You'll never stay in the fast lane', and strong feelings such as 'I'm unhappy', both of which he suppressed as quickly as possible. Alistair first realized his particular 'void' when one day he caught himself thinking, as he rushed from one appointment to another, 'I wonder if taking drugs would help?' He believed that if he allowed himself to stop, he would fall victim to the vacuum and emptiness which he associated with the void. All his life he had coped with this feeling by being incredibly busy. We met when his body had begun throwing up symptoms – duodenal ulcer, anal fistula, chest pain – and he had become phobic about illness and death. One of his first tasks was to allow himself half an hour each day for reflection. He found this very hard to keep up!

Sometimes the void can be explored through visualization, through drawing. Often life itself plunges us into the void, and we have to face it the hard way – through a serious illness, accident, breakdown, or being left alone and isolated.

Exercise

How do you recognize a void inside you?
I feel as if everything happens to me as if it's behind glass.
I see other people doing things, but I don't belong.
It's like another planet.
I keep very busy with friends, relationships, work, eating, drinking, chaos, 'things', duties, etc., because I know that if I stopped, I would fall in the void.
Inside I feel very lonely. Few people, if any, know this.

In recognizing the void you can try and not avoid its presence by feeling into this place more fully, and finding a language to express the void through:
drawing or painting it;
using images – 'it is like . . .';
telling someone you trust about it.
You may need help in coping with living with the void – for example, co-counselling, therapy, sharing with another. Allow yourself to consider this possibility.

Part 3
Gathering Information

Where do we start?

Hopefully you have by now got a full notebook of ideas about the difficulties you are having, some of which may go back a long way in time. Perhaps you are ready to ask, 'Why do I feel like this? Why do I get myself into traps and dilemmas? 'Where do these conflicts come from?'

Remember the concept of the individual as a seed who comes into the world carrying his or her own potential for life. Our basic seed is good and sound. If our seed contains an apple pip nothing can prevent that seed from growing into an apple tree. It may produce some strange fruit and its growth may be stunted or gnarled, but nothing can stop the 'appleness' trying to emerge. As you read this next section remember to look for signs of your own appleness or seed nature, which may have been eclipsed, distorted or disturbed by your environmental history. Use this section in the way that you would flick through a photograph album. Try and keep hold of that sense of your own inner nature or seed. Focus on what appeals to you, feels right for you. PUSH WHERE IT MOVES!

Before you start, sit quietly somewhere by yourself and ask: What gives me joy? What has brought me through the dark times?

Opening boxes

In this section we are going to be opening a few boxes. Some of them might be painful and difficult. Psychotherapy is not easy, but it does bring relief if you stick with it and keep your eye on the point of it all. We are going to use everything that you find out about yourself through this book. Everything from this section is going to go towards writing your own life story. We need to know exactly where the difficulties are rooted so that we can understand them. We need accurate description so that we can build accurate problem charts and aims for change. These are the aims that you will be monitoring each week, to see how you are doing. If you have decided to embark on this book in a co-counselling way, then you will be able to share this process with another person throughout the book. If you are concerned about dragging up old ghosts and someone is willing to share, go ahead.

Subpersonalities

As you read through this book and begin gathering information about your own life, you will probably realize that there are many parts to your personality. Every person has different aspects or facets; some of these are dominant during different phases of life, and some seem to remain hidden, or just on the edge of our conscious personality. Each of these aspects is called a subpersonality. This does not mean that we are split, divided or schizophrenic, although a lot of people do worry about this when they realize they are made up of a variety of different parts. Knowing and understanding our different aspects is an important part of helping our life to change.

If part of our being is a small child for example, we need to know the nature of that child – the sex, age, attitude, feeling and experience – in order to encompass him or her into the wholeness of our being. The child may have some specific need – to be looked after, or he or she may need to be helped to grow up. We may have more than one child-like part inside us. Some people resonate easily to the idea that they have a 'boss' inside them who tells them what to do. This 'boss' figure may come from a dominant parent or teacher, and may appear as a police-man, or army sergeant, even a Hitler figure. When we name and confront this part of ourselves, either through active imagination or drawing, we become more in charge. We may then recognize when this part of ourselves is uppermost, and we may wish to curtail its power, and most certainly we would wish to question its authority. We need a part of us that helps us get things done, but not if it is so bossy and demanding that it restricts the rest of our life.

Other figures that people find as subpersonalities include animals, birds, sea creatures, rocks, unformed images, even just blobs or jellies. Also, all of us carry at least one contrasexual subpersonality within us, and these are important figures in helping us to understand the masculine or feminine side of our nature. If, during your journeying in this book you find that your masculine or feminine nature is represented by only a faint, deformed or locked-away figure, you might like to begin by claiming that figure, helping it to have more room in your life and more say in how things are. Even if we don't much like the figures we come to recognize as part of us, we need to allow them space, because they are present for some reason and once embraced they are never so unlikeable or frightening as we at first presume. Not everyone will respond to the idea of using images to describe how parts of themselves feel. If you do, however, and would like to use this way of working, make a drawing in your notebook, and watch how the image changes or grows as you become more aware of its presence and qualities.

The child within

Understanding where our conflicts are rooted helps us to see how very powerful fears, often unconscious, act to keep us behaving 'as if' the circumstances which produced the original problem are still in full force. Although over the years we have grown to be competent adults, inside us there is a small person who has not yet learned that the new outside circumstances are prevailing. He or she still behaves as if unless he pleases, avoids, cuts off or acts in a particular way, his mortal and emotional life will be seriously threatened. The child within carries our core pain.

We are looking here at the consciousness of a child, infant or small person. The part of us that took on board the realities of early life and coped as best we could is still in this early stage. Memories thus evoke feelings that are fresh, as if they happened yesterday. Examining the world of our childhood, together with the feelings and images of our present, is an important part of the change process. We are now going actively to give a life to a part of ourselves that may never have seen the light of day, because it was too afraid, too rejected, too damaged. This is not easy, because these same fears still prevail, but this time we are bringing to our exploration an openness, kindness and willingness to listen in a different way, all of which are new.

The purpose is to relieve the small part of us from isolation and rejection, fear and limitation. We are bringing a listening ear and a caring heart to the places that hurt. This work is done in psychotherapy all the time. No book can hope to step into the place of a living person met each week in the privacy of the same room and time. But these pages may offer a beginning for the safe exploration of our misunderstood self, challenging old assumptions and messages, and facilitating the discovery of previously hidden parts of us that we will come to value.

A useful framework

Another reason for exploring how our life has been so far is that we need a useful framework in which to place what has happened to us and how we feel now. By examining the past we can see patterns that we have learned that are no longer useful and need to be given up; and in their place we learn to see another pattern, the pattern of our 'seed' self whose colours have been blurred by survival. The path that this self follows may not be as well trodden as our survival self, but the tracks will always be there. Our task is to look for them. By peeling back who we have had to become in order to survive, we find who we really are underneath.

And as well as looking at the unhelpful patterns remember to ask yourself: 'What makes my heart sing? What brings me joy?' Start listening to your own note, your own heartbeat.

Am I odd?

The third reason for looking into the past is that we often take what we feel for granted. Many people say to me, 'Doesn't everyone feel like this?' or, 'Surely this is a common experience?', as if they were trying to find what was 'normal'. I think that this is a very basic concern when someone embarks on a path of self-discovery. Am I odd? Am I commonplace? Should I be making a fuss or thinking there is anything different about me just because I feel as I do? Freud tells a story of a young man who visited him early in his career. When Freud asked him to describe what he did each day, he said, 'Same as everyone else . . . get up, throw up into the toilet, dress, go to work . . .'

Each of us needs to know that everything that happens to us has its distinct flavour. There may be similarities between oneself and others, and this is always heartening, but our experience is uniquely our own. Claiming that uniqueness is part of allowing ourselves to be real, but we need to recognize it first. We may also need someone to help us do this, and to put our experience into some kind of context. When I suggested to Freda that it sounded as if she had had to grow up quickly and become a 'little mother' when her brother was born and her mother became depressed, she responded with a good deal of feeling. Suddenly something helped to explain why she felt responsible for everything. For the first time she could see how it fitted, and she was very relieved. She had placed something, made sense of her experience and could, if she chose, not have to take the path of responsibility again except out of free choice.

The next section is like one long questionnaire. Give yourself time to reminisce about your early life, and make notes and drawings as you go along.

What makes us tick?

Prebirth

As our understanding grows we become more and more aware that interuterine conditions do affect the growing infant to a greater degree than was perhaps previously considered, and that the effects are not all physical. The womb is our first container, our first contact with sound, space, warmth, movement. Georg Groddeck writes in *The Meaning of Illness*:

In the mother's womb the child is made for nine months; it lives, grows, and develops in the womb. Never again in his life does the human being have relations as intimate as those he entertains with his mother during pregnancy. The extent to which we harbour the wish to be loved and to love is conditioned by this period of intimate togetherness. The idea of 'mother' dominates our emotional life with regard to our relations with other people; the longing for the kind of togetherness we once had continues and determines the choice of friends and work colleagues, makes us desire women (or men), helps us choose a partner to marry and gives us a union with another person for a few seconds in the embrace. The 'It' in us retains a memory of a state of perfect togetherness and urges and seeks a repetition, breaks up the unified love of the child into a thousand ever-changing parts which are forever being transferred to people, animals, plants, dead and living objects, ideas and creations, and now and then they produce larger emotional complexes.

Self-forming properties

The womb has properties which begin that definition of 'self'. These go on throughout life, but are formed most specifically and acutely in the early years after birth. The concept of 'self' is linked to the seed with which we are born – who we uniquely are – and differs from the ego, which is the centre of conscious personality mediating conscious life and the everyday. The self is concerned with growth, meaning, journeying; it connects us with spirit, our uniqueness and the collective self which is connected to all. What is often viewed as Fate is an act of the self pushing us into actualizing our real self or urging us to seek change.

The properties needed for the forming of the self are rest, being alone, rhythm, warmth, containment and safety. When we become ill or experience difficulties later on in life we tend to be drawn back into these womb-like properties for healing. During times of rapid growth and change, during transition times, it is useful to remember the very first qualities of environment that helped us grow safely. For example, our need for rest lives on in the practice of sleep, usually in the dark and in a safe, warm place. It is also an opportunity to return to unconsciousness and to allow its communication through dreams and images. Our need for rhythm, first experienced with the mother's heartbeat and swishing of digestive fluids, lives on in our need for music, poetry, dance and the rhythm of regular breathing. All these are necessary precursors to creativity, and when we feel depressed and cut off from life we talk about being 'out of step', 'out of rhythm'.

Birth experience

The womb is also the place which we struggle to get out of, and many people believe that the kind of birth experience we had does shape the way our lives go. My sense is that the kind of birth and the early months tend to go together in terms of what we absorb from mother, or whoever is mother. What we are told about our birth naturally depicts how we have been received. 'Your birth was the most terrible thing . . . it went on for days', may be said with the kind of horror and disgust that can make us feel quite a liability.

The following questionnaire is designed to help you ponder on the nature of your own birth and the atmosphere into which you were born.

Birth stories and reciprocal roles

Psychotherapist Angela Wilton has made a study of birth stories – the actual birth as well as the earliest postnatal experience – and their link with the reciprocal role procedures we were looking at in Chapter 3. She asked people to tell the story of their birth and its impact on the family, using any anecdote, story or image from any source – parents, siblings, doctors, midwives – that added to the picture. She included jokes, myths or catch-phrases, as well as any actual memory of the birth itself.

As she worked with different birth stories she began to notice how the atmosphere around the birth story was often mirrored in the person's ways of relating to others. For example, a mother exhausted and angered by a long, arduous labour might be less able to bond with her baby than a mother who found giving birth exhilarating. This birth

---

Questionnaire: Birth and prebirth

Our time in the womb is our first experience of unconditional being. How much time do you allow for *being* rather than *doing*? Weekends only, evenings, two hours per day, only holidays, never?

How does your need for containment – a house, room, building – reflect itself in your life? Does the place you live in suit you? What is it like? Describe it, and see how much of it is an extension of your original container, offering retreat, safety, protection. If you find it does not offer these properties, where can you go to get in touch with them? For all-round good health all of us need safe and appropriate containment (many are happy with caravans, campers, small spaces) every day for a period of hours.

How much sleep do you allow yourself – enough, too little, too much? Are there restrictions against sleep in your life (internal voices telling you to get up and not sleep)? Look back over your life and see how you have used sleep, whether it has been allowed or not in your life. Babies and teenagers require a lot of sleep, as if they needed to balance the enormous growth in consciousness and physical change with darkness and rest more than at other times. (Groddeck believed that during the years from fourteen to thirty he had about fourteen hours of sleep each day, and that this was in preparation for his interest in the unconscious.)

How much care do you take of yourself – warmth, safety, protection?

Do you allow rhythm into your life – music, dance, sound? When was the last time you felt in touch with the rhythms of life and felt you were part of it – today, yesterday, last week/month/year? Where did you feel in touch most? By the sea? In the country watching the seasonal changes? How much do you allow this to affect you positively – all the time, partially, not enough, never?

How much do you know of your actual birth? Was it a natural birth, forceps delivery or Caesarean? Was it easy or difficult? Were you breast-fed or bottle-fed?

---

story would carry an atmosphere of pain and struggle, inducing possible hidden and 'magical guilt' in the child. These feelings might well be carried over into other relationships. Parents who hope for a certain sex of child may have difficulty covering up their disappointment when their baby turns out to be a boy rather than girl, or vice versa. This disappointment may give rise to the person feeling worthless, especially when they get close to others, and to the belief that they have to strive to justify their presence.

Sometimes when a baby is born after a bereavement or loss, he or she becomes associated with this rather than being greeted in their own right. As a result, the person grows up believing that they were 'born under a shadow'.

Over half of the people in Wilton's study felt they had damaged and hurt their mother during the birth, so burdening them with the reciprocal roles of either *hurt* one or *damaging* one (as if to be alive is to damage others), evoking guilt and a need to make compensation. Another theme was 'just we two', where an easy birth was followed by close and uninterrupted bonding between mother and child, with the father absent. The stories tended to emphasize an idealized central and perfect position in relationships, from which there could be, in reality, a long fall! Relationships in adult life with the 'just we two' emphasis could be over-close and dependent, mutually admiring, with a tendency to overidealization; or, if this was not met, a crash into feeling rubbished or, conversely, rubbishing anything too 'ordinary'. (See Figure 6 page 92)

The 'unwanted' theme was also prominent, leaving the person with a sense of ambivalence about commitment and an anticipation of rejection: the rejected/rejecting reciprocal role.

Sadly, there seem to be fewer stories where a sense of *joy* is evident. Perhaps as mothers and fathers now take part together and have some control in the nature of the birth experience of their child, this could change. It's also important to emphasize that even when births are long and arduous, the reward of a live and healthy child frequently overcomes any painful memory.

The reason for examining your own birth story as part of gathering information about your life is to bring in the lesser-known areas which may still be in the dark for you. Sometimes when we hear these stories they make sense of events that have remained a puzzle. I have found that when people begin to ask friends and relatives about their birth or their early life, many new realizations come to light. It also offers an opportunity for corresponding or meeting relatives who may have been scattered over the world, as well as those who in the past had been scapegoated or labelled as black sheep.

For some people these times of gathering also afford the opportunity for forgiveness: of a mother or father who one learns was immature or ill, suffering from hardships we can only imagine, given little or no help, dominated by others, and living in poor and inadequate housing. While it's important to experience fully those feelings that have become blocked or split off by our need to survive earlier life events (and this may mean expressing rage and fury at what appears the unfairness of our lot), part of moving on into maturity is to let go of our feelings about the past. When we are ready.

For some people the atmosphere of their birth seems to accompany them on other transitions. For example, a long difficult birth can be seen as a reluctance to come into the world, and other transitions or 'rebirths' into new jobs, houses, or relationships can seem to take on that similar feeling of difficulty. People who have had premature births sometimes feel impatient, they can't wait to get on. Some people describe their lives as being like 'waiting in a passage', 'feeling stuck', as if they were stuck in the birth canal on some level, still waiting to be delivered. If we've been born with the cord around our necks, do we often feel a constriction in the throat, particularly at times of transition, or when we are being asked to push on to make a move?

The atmosphere of our birth will not necessarily dominate our lives, for many people overcome difficult or protracted births naturally. But if you feel there is a link between the flavour of your birth and the kind of physical experiences you have while undergoing change or transition, it is worth going through the process of your birth in some detail, especially if there is still someone you can ask. Even if there isn't, your symptoms and intuition will be enough to let you know what to concentrate upon. Perhaps those of us who had slow and difficult births need to recognize that this may be the way we go into new things, and accept it for what it is. In knowing it consciously we can choose whether to get help to push ourselves on a bit, or whether to let the slow difficult way take its own time.

Multiple births

This means that several lives share the same space right from conception. Sometimes this creates rivalry and a keen competition for space and attention. Sometimes there is a complex mixture of strong feelings: those of intense love and bonding to the person with whom you have shared your whole life; and intense hatred and jealousy for when the other or others would seem to be favoured, and you feel your already slender share of the goodies is threatened. Multiple-birth children are actually deprived maternally, however hard the mother works: it's built in, because those moments of being alone and special to Mum are rare. But even short regular moments of uniqueness throughout a life can help to consolidate our sense of 'self'.

Many multiple births also include deaths, especially today with the new in vitro fertilization techniques where several embryos are fertilized but do not survive. When one child or more is born, and one or more has died, there can be a tendency for medical staff to be so pleased that there are any survivors at all that they can overlook the impact of the deaths of those who have perished. If you have been in the womb with another, at some level you will know this. If that person has perished but not been accorded his or her due recognition, there will be an uneasy gap somewhere, and perhaps even a sense of guilt. Do you ask yourself, 'Why did I survive and not the other? Was I greedy, did I take more than my share?' These feelings and thoughts are probably not conscious, but survive unconsciously, perhaps subtly undermining our freedom to get on with life as we might.

Adoption

In adoption we are carried by one woman and then nurtured by another, or many others, during our first years. We come to each one as a stranger with whom bonding has to be achieved and new signals learned. We are now much more aware of the importance of the early years to our development. People who have had many fosterings, many different 'mothers' and many moves seem to suffer the most in terms of insecurity and lack of self-esteem. But sometimes, if there has been one central kind of influence, even the most deprived early backgrounds can be compensated. During the process of self-exploration, people who have been mainly in touch with the negative side of their backgrounds do often unearth the memory of someone who was kind and helpful, someone who showed care and introduced the person to something of value in themselves.

One man I know who had had several difficult fosterings before living in a reasonable children's home for several years, kept his life very ordered and unadventurous, not making many friends and not risking relationships. He had a fine sense of colour. He would wear coloured socks and have an attractive tie and handkerchief. When I commented on this he looked startled and embarrassed. Teased for his 'foppishness', he'd tended to repress this side of himself. But on exploring it further he did acknowledge his love of colour and design, and his attraction to beautiful things. He liked to frequent the London street markets and pick out small objects like glass and silver, and it seemed he did have a knack for this kind of thing. But he felt it to be 'wrong' in some way. The source of his understanding for these objects was an old lady he used to visit as a punishment during his early fostering days. (It seems a strange concept having to visit the old as a punishment.) At first he had hated it, and was angry to be associated with the 'cast-offs' of society – babies and old people who weren't wanted. But this old lady had a room that resembled an Aladdin's Cave, and when he showed an interest (which he had in him naturally) she encouraged it. It was the only concentrated attention and appreciation he received during his early years. The memory of it was buried underneath years of basic survival in a difficult competitive world that revolved around who was going to get the best parents or foster parents. It was a moving moment when he realized how much kindness he had received for himself and who he was, and it raised his self-esteem. He started to value his appreciation of colour and shape and took it seriously enough to begin an evening course in design.

Many people who are adopted carry the sense of rejection all through their lives, and that burning quest, 'Why wasn't I wanted, or good enough?' In an interview with Anne de Courcey in the *Evening Standard*, the writer John Trenhaile explained that many adopted children are overachievers, struggling to compensate for some sin they are not even aware of having committed:

The feeling that you have failed a test you didn't even know you'd been set . . . In my case I felt I had done something so unspeakably wrong that my own mother gave me away. But it took a long, long time to realize this.

Sometimes people who have been adopted feel resentful, angry and rejected underneath their everyday thinking. This can express itself through low self-esteem, feeling that you are just not good enough, or a terror of being abandoned, which in turn may lead to an obsessional interest in security, being attached to objects or rituals of checking, or a need to transcend life completely. Some people split their biological and adoptive parents into good/bad or ideal/second best. Biological parents may be idealized, and the split between the two sets of mothers or parents may be reflected in relationships, or form a 'snag'. For example, people who 'allow' themselves a 'second-best' relationship while yearning for the unattainable idealized 'real'. Now that adopted children can search for their biological mothers/parents this split has a chance to be healed, both by the reality of finding actual parents less than ideal, as well as healing through self-exploration or therapy.

It is useful to know and understand the source of these attitudes, and to find ways of releasing our feelings about this event. There is nothing we can do about it. We have to find ways of accepting it and not letting negative attitudes narrow our options. The atmosphere and event of our birth can live on unconsciously, sometimes seriously affecting our attitudes to ourselves and to others. Once we have got hold of it, we can look at it and see that we have been living 'as if . . .'. Do you recognize that any of the following underlie your feelings about yourself: I unconsciously behave as if I'm about to be: (a) given away; (b) abandoned; (c) teased by being given life but nothing else; (d) rejected?

It is possible to find ways to release ourselves from this hold and to give ourselves the proper, full, accepted life that our biological mother felt unable to do. Many people who have been successfully adopted, and who are tremendously grateful to their adoptive parents, also carry some of the intense feelings that less successful adoptees carry, but feel guilty about expressing them. They feel they should be grateful and give all their loyalty and self-expression to these parents, and that it would hurt or harm them if they were to know of the suffering. The cost of gratitude may feel as if it damages the 'real' parent or image, thus spoiling hope or longing. Consequently, it is often only in later life that people feel able to look at their past and their attitudes in a fresh way.

Questionnaire: Our first reception

Were you expected; wanted? Did it matter if you were a boy or a girl?

How long had your parents been married when you were born?

Where did you come in the family: eldest, only, middle, youngest, etc? (See Figure 7, page 139.)

Were there any miscarriages, stillbirths, other children who died but were perhaps rarely referred to?

Were you welcomed with open arms and smiling faces?

Was much expected of your presence, for example as the first:
boy;
girl;
grandchild;
child for generations;
heir to title, fortune, family business?

Was your birth an attempt to redeem:
lost other lives;
disappointment?

Was there an unwritten hope that you would:
carry on a tradition;
break with tradition?
(Many upwardly mobile parents, or parents whose own lives may have been deprived and difficult, want their children to have a life which is completely different, and this has its own restrictions.)

In what tone is your birth talked about:
today;
as you first remember it . . . by mother, aunts, uncles, grandparents, father, siblings?
Ask around and find out what you can of the way in which you were first received into life.

Development of seed and survival self

Infancy

In Chapter 3 on the problems and dilemmas of relationships we saw that our infant experience shapes many of our internal attitudes to ourselves, and at a time before we have started to form thoughts about anything. Our infant world is experienced mainly through our bodies –

hot, cold, wet, soiled and uncomfortable, hungry, empty, full; held gently, firmly, roughly, not held at all; stroked gently, soothingly, lovingly, roughly, angrily, harshly, or not at all. There are other experiences: like the fear of falling, and of falling for ever because we have no mechanism to provide the thought of a boundary or end; being left to cry and to feel abandoned because we have no experience of not being abandoned until someone comes; being teased and taunted by something we want which is placed just in front of us and then whisked away; being played with like a toy and the pressure to amuse; being centre stage, a source of entertainment. Because we are so dependent and vulnerable when we are infants we experience a great deal of anxiety if what we have known as consistently keeping us safe is threatened in any way. Dr D. W. Winnicott uses the term 'primitive agonies' to describe these unbearable anxieties of the infant.

When our early infant life is adequately provided for, our fears are allayed and our anxieties do not get out of proportion. We learn to trust that what or whoever goes away will come back; that it is safe to know love and being loved, and to know and love oneself; and that there are parts of us we can trust to be safe and to where we can retreat. We form appropriate boundaries between ourselves and others as we grow from infancy into childhood, a process which takes from the time of birth to between two and three years.

When the soil isn't quite right for our growth, however, and it becomes non-nurturing, neglectful, hostile or inadequate, our development is thwarted and we learn to bend the shoots of what would be our natural growth in order to accommodate the experiences we undergo. In the infant years, before thought process, and before we have separated what belongs to ourselves and what is the property of others, our only defence against what is experienced as a hostile outside is to shut off and withdraw. This might be the end of a process that has been preceded by a lot of crying and screaming, which, if it goes unheard, unresponded to, means that we give up, become despondent and in despair turn inward into ourselves. We may also split off the things that are unpleasant and experienced as 'bad' from the good experiences, so that later on in life things appear as either good or bad, but it is impossible to put the two together.

For example, it could become difficult, if not impossible, to be angry and love someone at the same time, or to receive someone's anger without feeling intense hate and cut off from them. When we split off in this way we often carry the negative forms as 'projections' and find that we attribute to others all the unresolved 'bad' parts we have been unable to cope with internally. This might come up in relationships where we experience the other as bad or against us, as chaotic or hateful, and these feelings can get transposed onto our employers, friends or relatives, who we then invite to live out for us the unresolved difficulties or rejected parts from our early life.

From birth to about the age of seven the ego is developed against the background we have just described. In order for the ego to grow healthily and be of use to us as a lens through which we see and operate in the world, we need a 'good enough' background. We need to feel that we are loved and therefore lovable; liked and therefore likeable; accepted and therefore acceptable. We need to know that however 'bad' we are, we will not be rejected.

From the early continuum of the womb, we need to feel that our bodies, our shape, our desires, are acceptable, and that from being touched we can freely experience sensuality and prepare for later sexual development; that our bodily functions are normal and part of an important rhythm which serves us rather than something which should be hidden.

If our early years are accompanied by what we called a 'too tight' environment, where a parent or guardian is too attentive and protective, we get little experience of the outside world and therefore lack the tools to cope with adult life. We tend to grow up to be afraid of life and our instincts, unwilling to take any risks, avoiding challenge and thus isolating ourselves. Conversely, if there has been too little interest, too loose a soil, we feel ungrounded and 'dropped', which can emerge later in depression and a lack of ego strength or self-esteem, a sense that we inhabit a 'nowhere world'.

Recollecting early life and influences

Make a family map or family tree. Use different colours for different people and different shapes. Alongside each person put their date of birth, occupation, style, personality traits and any other description you feel is significant. See Figure 7 for help.

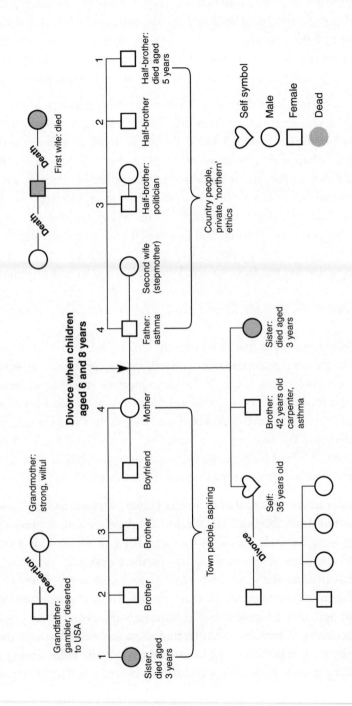

Figure 7 A family map

Spend a few moments with your eyes closed, and feel into the type of early childhood you had and the type of early environment. Did it feel (a) too tight and enclosed, or (b) too loose? See if you can get an image of your mother, or whoever was mother for you, the feel of that person. Where are they in relation to you? What does the image tell you about your early life and the child you once were?

Many people have few or no early memories, although sometimes early memories start to come back during therapy or self-questioning. What is your earliest memory? Picture it, in all its colours and shades. What is happening, with whom, who is there? Set the scene for yourself down to the tiniest detail – what everyone is wearing, the texture of the cloth, smells around you, sounds. Again, closing your eyes, feel into your own place in the recollection. What are you wearing? Feel your feet on the ground, feel how small you were, actually become yourself as a small person in that picture. Write down what is happening, and what the feelings are. When you look at it now, what do you make of it in terms of the child you were then, what were you having to deal with, decide, accept? How were you received, treated, talked to?

When you have got this memory, anchor it by writing or drawing. Make another picture inside yourself, of the early life you would like to have had, using some of the same ingredients or none, painting in all the feelings, objects, ideas, atmosphere you would have liked as a small person to have had. See if you can, from this exercise, begin to understand the world you inhabited as a child, and the kind of choices you had to make in terms of survival. Make a note of the parts of you that went underground or unnoticed and undeveloped.

Ponder about where you fit in the family network and on how this position has influenced you. Eldest children are said to have similar beginnings as only children: they are 'King or Queen' for a day, or until a small sibling comes along. As the eldest you had 'new' parents, inexperienced at the art of parenting. Sometimes the eldest or only children are expected to be more 'grown up' that is appropriate for their age, and are given responsibilities way beyond their years.

Second children are often treated more leniently, because parents are by now experienced and more relaxed. If the elder sibling is making a success of things and fitting in with the family network, a second child may feel they have to keep up. Or, if the eldest has in some way disappointed parents and family expectations, the second (and this can apply to any children who come afterwards) can take on the position of the eldest, making the eldest feel redundant and a failure.

If the second or fourth child become a middle child then there is a sense of their having to 'jockey for position' in a family, and they can easily feel in between or in a 'no place', close to neither side. Sometimes the third child is the 'sunshine child' who has it easy, with few expectations or demands. Sibling often divide into pairs, as families with two parents and two children can become two pairs. Pairs are comfortable, but threes make complicated triangles.

All this may happen without our realizing it. We may just know that we didn't feel we really belonged in our family and wondered why. Youngest children often have a lot of freedom, but can also be neglected or taken for granted. Sometimes they are babied longer than is appropriate because they are the last to leave the nest. Often spoiled and cosseted, they may find it difficult to grow up and lead their own independent lives.

Were you allowed to play as a child, and if so, what kind of play or toys did you have? Spend some time reminiscing about this.

Use the following list of questions to help build a sense of the different experiences of your own childhood.

Exercise

Spend a few moments looking at your own position in the family. Include stepbrothers and sisters, mothers and fathers. You might like to have some fun by gathering a number of objects – for example, shells, stones, plates, glass – that might depict your family members. Choose a favourite object for yourself and place this on the floor first. Then assemble around you all the other family members, including steps, fosters, halfs, and any animals and neighbours if they were part of the family life. Look at your pattern and how the people relate to each other. Move the objects around to indicates times of change. For example, if one parent left or died, when you went to school, when siblings were born or other people joined the family. Moves are useful points that help us to remember times and places. We can often remember something happening in a certain house, but not how old we may have been.

Qualities of father and mother

Describe the one or two main people in your early life. If you had a father and a mother, divide the page into two columns with the headings 'Mother' and 'Father', and list underneath the main qualities of each: their likes and dislikes; their sayings and ambitions.

Mealtimes

What were mealtimes like?
Did you eat:
together;
separately?

What kind of atmosphere was there:
silent;
formal;
informal;
tense;
happy;
chatty?

Were there rituals about food such as washing hands, saying grace, 'father always carves', 'I always sit here'? Were there special subjects for conversation?

Recall your favourite and least favourite foods. What was the difference?

What were the rules? For example, were you made to clean your plates or sit until you had finished all your food?

Who did:
the talking;
laying table;
preparation;
clearing up?

What habits, fears, difficulties, pleasures, have come out of your experience of family meals?

Celebrations

Name and remember one good and one not so good celebration, a birthday perhaps, or Christmas.

Recall your memories of any of the following:

feeling;	being dressed up;
anticipation;	bringing in the neighbours and
festivity;	friends;
poverty;	who was allowed in;
worry;	who was allowed to see us;
rows;	details about food and presents;
atmosphere;	decorations;
feeling spoilt or neglected;	fuss.

Relatives

Who were they? (Go back to your family tree)

How were they received?

Who spoke to whom?

Family feuds: what was their nature? What was the history, story, mythology? How did it live on? Who perpetuated it?

Were the older members of the family treated kindly, so encouraging you to do the same ('Help your Nan, she's slow on her feet')? Or was there shame and impatience for the old and infirm ('Here she is again, dragging her feet as usual!')?

Were those who were a bit slow treated equally and well, or secretly laughed at, ridiculed and ignored?

In cases of great social or financial change, how were relatives who had not 'made it' treated:
slighted;
with shame;
ostracized;
looked down upon;
kindly;
generously;
willingly?

Religion

What was your father's, mother's or other relative's or important person's religion or belief system?

How did it manifest itself?
church every Sunday?
fierce rejection of anything 'funny' or irrational?
any other memories?

Was religion talked about in a free way?

Were you allowed to have your own view as you were growing up?

Was religion important to you – the Bible stories, the idea of God, Jesus, Allah, Siva? Was it:
frightening;
reassuring;
wonderful?

What lives on today from your early experience with religion and religious ideas? The concept of:
sin;
guilt;
love;
discipline;
wonder;
awe;
belief?

School

Take either primary or secondary school or both

What was your first day at school like? Perhaps you went to a playgroup or nursery school first. Do you have memories of this, or, at age five your first experience of the outside world?

How were you told about it? Was it billed as 'big school'? How were you:
prepared;
not prepared?

Who took you? How did you react to:
teachers;
other children;
the classroom;
tasks?

What lives on in you today that comes from early schooldays?

How did you cope with:
lessons;
seeing the board;
the playground;
other children;
teachers?

Did you ever run away or want to come home?

How did your parents cope with talking to teachers about anything to do with school and school meetings?

Did you have school dinners or take your own lunch?

Did you feel different from other children? If so, why? Was it:
clothes;
hair;
hygiene;
parents;
where you lived;
colour of skin;
religion;
being clever;
being not so clever;
speaking in a different language;
not understanding others?

Were you bigger or smaller than others? Did this matter?

Did you follow in brother or sister's footsteps?

Did you have to keep up an image of:
your older sibling;
family standards that differed from school;

a way of talking (posh or not posh accents);
behaviour;
church;
hairstyle;
what parents' occupation was;
car;
house;
dress?

Did Mum help with school or was it Dad?

Did you get rewarded for achievements, or did no one notice or seem to care what you did? What were the rewards?

Did you travel on your own or with others?

Did you have to care for a younger sibling? Did you mind?

If things went wrong at school – bullying, fights, teasing, taunting, unfair treatment by staff – who did you talk to?

If things went wrong at home, was there someone at school to whom you could turn?

How did it feel to come home after school?

Draw or paint any of the feelings or memories that come to you.

Friendships

1. Were you allowed to bring friends home?

2. How were they:
   received;
   treated?

3. Did your parents' morals and ethics become judgements on your friends? What was this like for you? Did you:
   remain divided in loyalty;
   continue the friendship anyway, but secretly;
   give in to your parents and drop the friends?

4. Were you allowed out in gangs or groups? How early?

5. Were there restrictions on timing and where you were allowed to go?

Money

1. Did you know how much money your parents earned?

2. Was money shared around, or were you given pocket money?

3. Were you encouraged to, or did you have to earn your own money?

4. Was money important for:
   saving;
   buying things;
   having power?

5. What were the myths about money in your family?
   'filthy lucre';
   good for investment, not to be spent frivolously;
   never talked about;
   worshipped;
   everything was priced or referred to in relation to its cost?

6. Did you have money, and if so were you and your parents comfortable with it, or did you dislike being different from your peers or others?

7. Was there hidden guilt about money, especially inherited money or money that was 'won'?

8. Were you hard up or poor, and how was this:
   like everyone else;
   sad;
   a disgrace;
   humiliating;
   painful?

9. Was money used as bribery:
   for passing exams or doing things well;
   for being 'good';
   for keeping out of the way;
   for looking after brothers and sisters?

10. Did money get involved in class distinctions. Was it divided into:
    'common' money;
    vulgar money;
    nice money?

11. What did you learn about value systems from the family's attitude and handling of money:
    spendthrift;
    money goes through hands like water;
    skinflint;
    mean;
    hoarding;
    spending it all on cars/booze, etc?

Spend some time looking at your own attitude to money and how you may have used money over the years:
Do you feel you have to hold on to it?
Are you afraid of it?
Does it burn a hole in your pocket?
Are you obsessed by it?
Do you never have enough, however much you earn or are given?
Do you hate and despise it?
Are you embarrassed about talking about it and cannot discuss money matters?
Are you comfortable with money matters?

Authority figures and heroes

1. Who were the great authorities of your day? policemen; the Army; the firm; the factory bosses; the director; the government; Prime Minister; the church priest, vicar, minister or other religious teacher? dead authority figures such as Winston Churchill; Joan of Arc; Mountbatten; Mrs Pankhurst; Nye Bevan; Gandhi, Florence Nightingale? film stars, authors, adventurers, sports heroes?

2. How were they spoken of?

3. What did this reveal about your parents' character:
   they like them;
   they aspired to become like them?

4. Were these heroes useful to you?

5. Did you develop your own different heroes and heroines?

6. Who were they at different periods of your first twelve years – perhaps they came from television, books, history, the Bible, films, actual life, sport?

7. Is there today a flavour of the hero or heroine in your own life from the past, from your parents?
8. Does it suit you or has it become a 'standard' or ideal to aspire to which is inappropriate for your needs and your own individual ways of doing things?
9. If you had to choose a 'hero' today, who would it be?

Social position

1. Was your family socially conscious:
   not wanting to be different from the neighbours and 'show ourselves up; or
   did they aspire to leave the 'class' of origin and be different?
   The class system is very powerful in the UK, as is the money system of the USA. In India a person's caste can never be changed in one lifetime, and has to be accepted and endured with the hope of a higher caste in a new incarnation. But in the Western world there is a lot of movement between classes and upbringings, largely brought about by opportunities in education, training, money growth, private enterprise, travel and communications.

2. What were the traditions in your family to do with social position and social mores, and/or seeking other 'better' positions?

Talents and gifts

Encouragement for one's abilities can be rare in families. It is as if families feel that to encourage or praise a child for their skills will make them big-headed. Many people grow up not knowing that they are really good at something, that they have a skill with people. In Chapter 4, 'Snags and self-sabotage' we looked at the effect of envy upon someone whose skills or gifts were more developed or extended than those of a parent or other family member. Some families feel 'shown up' by a family member who betters themselves or shows unusual talent in a certain direction. We can be made to feel guilty for our talent and hide it or leave it undeveloped. Only later, when perhaps we are able to succeed, can we begin fully to claim this part of ourselves. But sadly some people do feel very crippled by their guilt about having gifts that they never develop, and remain thwarted in some way, envious of others' successes, frustrated and living out only half of their capacity.

149

1. Make a list of the gifts you feel you have. If appropriate include things like communication, good listening, good with people, patience, kindness, ability to analyse or put things together, intuition, as well as being good at sport, writing, science, selling, making things, colour, reading, storytelling.

2. How did the family remark on your gifts:
   kindly;
   fully;
   proudly;
   encouragingly;
   took no notice at all;
   denied them;
   called you names when you did something well – 'Don't let it go to your head', 'Show off';
   compared you with others, themselves or their ancestors.

   The things we are good at may also not be properly understood by our parents. They may appear to discourage our talent because they don't understand it and they can't see where it will all lead. A report by a schoolmaster about Barry Sheene, the champion motorcycle racer, read, 'Barry has got to learn that fiddling with motor cycles won't get him through life!' We may have been good at butterfly and insect collecting when our parents were mechanically minded. We may have loved the ballet and music, when our parents were only interested in the house and garden.

3. Go back to the time of your early growing-up period – four to twelve – and see what your own interests were then. Write them down. Include the ones you might be tempted to dismiss – car number collecting, train spotting, bird watching, getting up early to watch the dawn rise, walking. (I was heavily penalized for wanting to walk on my own when I was eight or nine. My mother found it definitely odd behaviour and I felt ashamed for my 'oddness'. I can see now that it was the time I collected myself, my dreams and thoughts, and it served as an important precursor to writing and therapy. Some people could say that to accommodate it I chose a conveniently 'odd' profession.')

4. Make a list and see how many of the things you were drawn towards are still part of your life today.

5. How do they live on?

6. Have they been driven underground?

7. Can you resurrect any of them – in part, or in spirit or in whole?

8. Was the opposite true in your family – that talent was overemphasized and looked for even when it wasn't there? Did you feel you had to oblige and come up with something to please and gratify your parents' desire? Sometimes parents who have a particularly strong talent hope it will come out in their children. Or parents hope that their children will do the things they were unable to do, living out their own unfulfilled life. I know a young man who is naturally quite introverted and shy, and whose mother is the same. She dislikes her shyness but has never done anything about changing it, and she projects the extrovert person she would like to be onto her poor son. As a result, he is bullied into joining things that do not suit him and wearing clothes that are loud and fashionable. She tells false stories of his daring deeds, which make him curl up with embarrassment. He tries to oblige her by having a go at the more extrovert tasks, overcoming quite a lot of fear on the way and aligning himself with friends who expect him to be always full of bravado and loud jokes. It is killing his spirit.

9. Did you feel that you had to work hard to be what you are not in order to please your parents' fantasy of what they wanted from a son or daughter?

10. Are you still having to live up to that today?

11. Does it suit you?

12. Do you want to change it?

Sexuality

This still taboo subject, much discussed but never really understood, can dominate one's early life whether obvious or not. Have a look at how your sexuality was formed against the background of your family.

1. Was touching:
    allowed;

encouraged;

not allowed;

allowed too much so you weren't sure of the boundaries between what was acceptable and what was not?

2. Was sex alluded to via:

jokes;

other people;

animals;

pets;

television?

3. Did sex mean one thing if you were female and another if you were male?

4. Write down some of the myths you received about sex as you were growing up. For example, 'All men need sex; women don't, they have to put up with it.' Sex is often alluded to as going on 'down below' like a time bomb, so it becomes dangerous and mysterious.

5. Were you told about sex:

at school;

at home,

via a brother or sister;

other relative?

What did you make of it?

6. Were you helped to feel good about your body or were you ashamed of it?

7. At what age did you first become sexually aware?

8. Could you talk freely about sex in your family? Did you want to? If not, what did you feel? That it had no place in the family; that you'd rather discover it for yourself, for others?

9. Did you feel that sex always meant sexual intercourse, or were you aware of the other forms sex could take?

10. Did you grow up recognizing that sensuality and sexuality were different?

11. Was homosexuality talked about and, if so, in what way? What feelings did you have about it for yourself; for others?

12. Many people find sexual matters difficult to talk about without embarrassment. Have you found this? At what times and in what way?

13. Are there still questions you'd like to ask about your own or another's sexuality? Are there things you don't understand? Make a list of them.

14. Freud believed that the sexual urge was prime in human beings, that it was behind many different expressions of power, whether physical, political, financial or creative, and that when our sexual energy is blocked we become neurotic and disturbed. How much do you agree with this view in terms of your own life or the life of your family? If you do not have an active sexual life at present, can you see ways in which the sexual urge is expressing itself, for example, through the energy you put into things, the language you use? Or perhaps you have transcended your sexual urges in some way, like the practitioners of tantric Buddhism and other spiritual groups who recognize the power of sexuality but do not feel the need to act it out with others?

15. A lot of people say, 'I feel very screwed up about sex.' Can you identify with this? If so, make a list of things that bother you about yourself and sexuality:
messy;
laughable;
unnecessary;
never works with others;
always ends in a row;
makes me feel great/other person feel great/both feel great, feel closer;
embarrassing;
fraught with emotion;
humiliating;
gets in the way;
overrated;
causes anger and disappointment;
it makes me fearful (of what?).

Spend some time looking at the mixed messages you have received about your sexuality and about sex generally. Usually most of us need more information about sex and permission to seek that information. On one sheet of paper, or in your notebook, write down your own mix of old messages about sex and sexuality. In a separate column make a note about what you would like to unravel, sort out or feel better about.

16. If you were sexually abused as a child, how does this affect you now:
by denying any intimacy;
being very angry underneath;
feelings of shame affecting self-esteem;
self-abusive behaviour such as drinking to excess, not valuing life;
allowing others to abuse me by taking me for granted, hitting me, hurting me, depriving me;
in an almost paralysing sense of guilt?
There are now many special agencies to help survivors of incest and sexual abuse. You may wish to contact one of these. You may prefer to find a counsellor or therapist who will help you with your journey of healing this most difficult and painful of wounds, a person who will treat your story with care, confidence and compassion. Beware of any therapist or other professional who implies that you are in any way to 'blame' for past sexual abuses. A guide to choosing a therapist appears on p. 252.

Illness

Did illness or ill health affect your family much? Was one family member, yourself perhaps, ill more than the others?

Make a list of all the ill health within your family, with dates and the length of the illnesses and any periods of hospitalization.

Make a list of all your own periods of ill health, with dates and kinds of experience.

How was illness referred to:
(a) with fear and reverence for operations, pills and doctors;
(b) with a more cavalier approach, where it was left to nannies, grandparents or neighbours to look in or visit?

If you were ill, who looked after you? How was your illness handled, how much did you know about what was happening to you?

Look carefully at the number of separations caused by illness, and see if you can get in touch with the feelings of these items. Who, if anyone, did you play with? What kinds of ideas or fantasies did you have during these times about where your parents were, or who they were? (When small children are admitted to hospital they sometimes 'forget' who their real parents are and attach themselves to nurses or other staff members as a way of protecting themselves from the pain of grief.)

What were you told about your illness? Were you shown sympathy and kindness, looked after in the traditional way, given warmth, comfort, succour, shelter, cosseted until you were well?

Were you believed (sometimes parents do not believe us when we have a pain, and this can be very hurtful)? Or were you treated crossly as if your illness was a nuisance, an inconvenience that upset the routine? In many one-parent families where the parent is the sole breadwinner, and going to work means the difference between eating or not, the onset of a child's illness can be a frightening prospect, and may be treated with fear and denial, before time and energy sees the situation accommodated.

Parent's illness

What did you know of them? Or were they mysterious, not referred to, hushed up?

Did they become barriers to your being with your parents and having fun with them? Children often come to fear 'Dad's heart' or 'Mum's wheezes', and can be made to feel that they will make the problem worse by their behaviour. They mustn't laugh too loud, be rowdy, indulge in rough and tumble, play tricks, roll about in bed with parents first thing in the morning, in case they cause deterioration, or worse, death. I have known many people who said, 'I felt I couldn't raise my voice beyond a whisper in case Mum fell down dead'. And many people as children have, directly or indirectly, been made to feel responsible for their parents' poor health or indeed their death.

What was the nature of parents' or grandparents' or other family members' illnesses? So often what we retain of childhood impressions – smells, bandages, potions, creams, prostheses, coughs, wheezes, noises, dark clothing – remains like a pastiche, on the level we received it, and there may be many mysteries about of the nature of illnesses. Many old wives' tales about health and sickness spring from these times when things were not explained to us or made clear, but only hinted at, and left to our imaginations or to the tell-tale evidence of smell, bandage or groan.

Ponder this for a while. You might like to include grandparents or other family members who may have been ill. How much has your experience of other people's illness affected your own attitude to health, sickness, to control or feeling out of control, to life and death?

Accidents

These often stand out in the memory during childhood, or where memory lives on unconsciously to be triggered off by a sudden fear of a place for no known reason, or by a news item or accident to a friend. Accidents such as burning, scalding, falling, bumping heads or knees, grazes, stings, swallowing foreign bodies, being bitten, etc. can carry with their memory a clear imprint of the time, feeling, priorities, action of the day, and these events can prove powerful in terms of the way we subsequently take care of ourselves. We may become overcautious or, in defiance, reckless. Childhood accidents are often accompanied by parental anger and blame – 'I told you not to take your bike on that road/play with the neighbour's dog' – and the association of fear, danger, pain and panic with blame, disapproval or rejection can actually convince us that we are bad or foolish and that we mustn't try anything unusual or difficult or exciting, or we may put acceptance at risk.

Some children are punished for getting dirty or tearing their clothes, long before they are mature enough to look after themselves and take responsibility for such adult ways. One girl I knew, who had had a number of hospital admissions for various illnesses and accidents, subsequently became very depressed and was unable to communicate properly. After some months we did come across the memory of her experience of being twice scalded badly enough to go into hospital for several weeks when she was under ten years old. The most powerful memory for her in her revisitation of the image of these events was her mother's fear and worry, and her overwhelming sense of being burdened by a large number of children and now a child suffering from burns. The daughter vowed inside herself that she would never complain about anything, that whatever happened to her would be her own fault, and she must not burden anyone with her feelings. When she did become unwell later in life she returned to these feelings, and was so overwhelmed by them that she turned inwards into depression.

Write down the accidents and the attitudes that accompanied them within your own family.

Death

Were there any deaths in your family before you were twelve, or after this time, during adolescence, which made a big impact upon you?

Write something about the person or people you lost, what you lost most at the time, what you most missed. Write something about what you learned from them about the world and about yourself. There might be negative things as well as positive.

How was the event of death handled in your family? Was it talked about?
How soon after the death did you know the person had died?
Were you told how they died and where?
Were you allowed to go the funeral, hold flowers, take part?
Could you talk about the death, did you feel free to express what you felt, ask questions, or were you told to be quiet or made to feel you had upset someone too much?

As you flick back the memory album, see yourself as a small person in whose family someone has just died. Imagine yourself, dressed and standing or sitting in a room in your house. Get as strong a picture as you can of that small person and then sit beside them in adult form. See if you can feel into your child of that time. Did you:
withdraw;
go silent;
go off your food;
throw things around;
scream and yell;
have nightmares;

find it difficult to sleep;
find yourself clinging to another adult or a soft toy;
find yourself being drawn to one particular place;
become ill in any way yourself;
have fantasies or dreams about the dead person, hear their voice, see them as if they'd come back to life?

In the years following the death, how was the person spoken of:
never again;
never without tears and upset;
were you told off for talking about them;
were anniversaries remembered, did you take part in them;
and today, how much do these deaths live on in your memory, or have they been blanked out?

Sometimes when a death occurs early in our life, and we are not allowed to discuss it or mourn, it can produce 'magical guilt' in the young person, which may unconsciously undermine their later life. It's as if when very small, we take responsibility for the death (and also for things like the serious illness or miserable life of, for example, a parent or sibling). There are two ways in which this can work. We may have had some negative thoughts about the person who dies, and because we are small and our thinking is not sophisticated we presume that these negative thoughts had something to do with their death, that they contributed to it in some way. We may carry this magical guilt (magical because we couldn't possibly be guilty) unconsciously for years, until we reconsider it and decide to free ourselves from it.

We may also develop a sense of magical guilt because of our own survival: someone close to us died and we did not. Why should we survive and they not? Do we deserve it? Sometimes we think not. This undermining idea may also develop if there is a damaged or very ill parent or sibling in the family. We feel as if our health and wellbeing, or success and happiness, is at their expense, that if we grow up and claim our lives fully it will mean a rejection of the other's life, and that somehow instead we should be limited, damaged and as ill as they were. It's a very uncomfortable idea that our happiness has only been achieved at the expense of someone else's unhappy life. And so it lives on unconsciously inside us, coming out as self-jeopardy, self-sabotage, arranging things so that we do not fulfil our potential or really embrace fully what we can do. In the process of change we have to face those feelings of terror and guilt when we want to carry something through fully for ourselves, but the rewards in terms of self-acceptance and a wider sense of personal horizons are vast.

If you have lost a parent how has this been for you? Has it affected the way in which you relate to people of that parent's sex? Sometimes, if a parent dies when we are very small (under eight), we feel guilty about it – especially if we have favoured the living parent and thus feel disturbed about 'gaining' anything from the death (the Oedipus complex describes this dilemma). We may then cover our 'magical guilt' by idealization or hero worship of the dead parent.

Loss of a father

Men who have lost a father early in life do sometimes have difficulty relating to other men, particularly older men, and this is more so if there were no other good male figures after the father's death. Sometimes men can grow into adulthood feeling that their masculinity is 'on hold', not yet formed. One man said to me, 'It's as if I'm waiting to grow into a man . . . still I feel like this and I'm forty-five.' Some men feel they have to overcompensate for not having had a father, by being more in charge, powerful, strong and successful to make up for the loss. This is often encouraged by the widowed mother, who may view her son as a replacement husband. This means inevitably that the sons grow up way before their time, trying to fit into dead men's shoes that they cannot possibly ever fill. Left behind is the 'fatherless boy' inside them. Unless he is claimed properly, later in life he will still be there – lonely, sad, cut off from a possible mentor, champion, friend, example and mate – possibly dominating the inner life of the man, and preventing him from fully claiming his manliness. Getting in touch with this fatherless boy is an important part of mourning for the loss, which may never have been accomplished. When the father is mourned for by the boy who has become a man outside, but wants to feel one more fully inside, something important happens to the growth process.

A girl who loses her father early in life may later on have difficulty relating to men freely, because of fear of losing them. Sometimes people who have died are made into heroes irrespective of what they were like in life. It may then be difficult for a woman to find a man who lives up to the hero her father has become. In her idealism, no man may match up to him. She may find herself searching for the 'perfect' man only to feel more and more disappointed, but without realizing why.

A parent's death may also cut a child off from that side of the family, their values and lifestyle. I have known many people who knew nothing of their father or mother's family because they had died early on. The remaining spouse either could not bear to be reminded of their deceased partner in any form and did not keep up with the family, or they remarried and lost touch. Sometimes in rediscovering what a dead parent was really like, by using old photographs or writing to anyone who knew them, people reclaim the character and flavour of their lost parent and can also claim that part of themselves. The individuality of the dead parent may have been forgotten, or hidden, and the child left may be quite like their lost parent but not realise it and feel odd or different.

At forty-eight, Alice discovered a whole host of relations in Russia whom she had never met because her mother had lost contact after her father's death. She found they shared her love of music and dancing, of colour and melancholy verse, qualities her mother had criticized in her and which she had come to feel were undesirable, extrovert, and pretentious. Finding that she did indeed carry some of the essence of her father was a real gift to her.

During therapy, Anne brought many old photographs of herself as a child with her parents. Her father had killed himself when she was three, and the subject was never referred to. He was made out to be a 'bad lot', unstable and generally no good. She was convinced that not only was there a poor quality running in her blood, but that her father hadn't cared enough about her to stick around. By writing to one of his friends, whom she had discovered quite by accident, she was able to piece together her father's last few days, when he was hospitalized and suffering from shell-shock during the war. He had believed he was responsible for killings in Germany and France which his conscience could not tolerate, and in a frenzy of self-hate and acute misery he had leaped out of an eighth-floor window. This friend went on to describe to Anne some of the horrors of war and the lack of help available to people, such as her father, who were sensitive and conscious of what they were being asked to do. Anne was herself a pacifist, and this realization changed her given view of her father's character. One day she brought some old photographs (discovered in the drawer of her aunt's desk) of her father holding her as a small child. Her arm was firmly round his neck and she was smiling radiantly. He was the image of a proud Dad, holding her as if she were the most precious thing on earth. Suddenly tears welled up in her eyes: 'I feel as if I was loved by him,' she said, 'even though I didn't have very long with him!' This realization made a profound difference to her, and although she had to work through her ever-present fears of rejection from men, and her habit of reading rejection into everything that happened, she had begun the process of building a more solid core to herself, upon which could be built other profound experiences.

Loss of a mother

When a small child loses their mother it is an extremely sad day. As we said in the chapter about relationships, mother, or whoever is mother for us, is the earth into which we were planted. We share her unconscious for the first two years, and she represents our link with care and nourishment, the nursery years. She is the person who makes our emotional and physical world safe. When we lose a mother our most basic world is shattered and we feel frightened, alone and very vulnerable. Although others may take her place and give us mothering, we have lost our link with someone who, whether liked or disliked, was the centre of our world. As she is often the actual centre, family life is seriously disrupted when a mother dies and children may be fostered or farmed out to other families while help is found.

The loss of a mother may live on throughout the following years like a yawning gap. Part of us may stay 'on hold' internally from the time of our mother's death. Our instinctual, emotional and intuitional life may remain undeveloped as we struggle to survive in what to us is an alien world. Later we may look for 'mothering' influences to allow us to complete the unfinished work of our development. We may seek quickly to become mothers ourselves, or conversely, avoid mothering, because we know the excruciating pain of loss.

A man who loses his mother early on may be deprived of a feminine influence, thus not developing the feminine side of himself and finding it awkward to make relationships with women. Whatever the way of compensation, the wound inside will be deep and the need for appropriate mourning and release of sadness is important, as well as looking at ways in which we have overcompensated for the loss in our personality.

How old were you when your mother died?

Describe your world until that point if you can – where you lived, your own room, toys, playtime, school, atmosphere.

What is your most lasting memory of your mother? Paint this picture if you can, with all the details you can manage.

Do you feel you have properly mourned the death of your mother? Is the mourning process held up in some way:
by the lack of knowledge of the facts of her death – time, date, where she is buried, nature of her death;
by not talking enough about her, about how you felt for her, what you miss about her;
because part of you has not let her go, not accepted that she is dead?

How does she live on in you:
by how you live;
the nature of your work, family, ideas, religion, ambition?

Are you still carrying a candle for her:
appropriately, having accepted her death and now remembering her lovingly;
inappropriately by trying to live as she would have, or as she wanted you to?

Does she have an unconscious presence in your life:
through dreams;
through ideas of how to 'be';
through magical guilt;
as a force which drives you which is not your own?

Do you feel you have to compensate for her death?

If you feel you have lost out on mothering, how does this manifest itself in your life?

If someone else took on the mothering after your mother's death what is your relationship with that person or people now:

grateful;
happy;
satisfied;
resentful;
angry?

Take a fresh page in your notebook and write down the positive and negative aspects of the mothering you received after your mother's death.

How much have you been able to take on 'mothering' or looking after yourself? Are you:
kind;
gentle;
encouraging to yourself; or
harsh;
neglectful;
demanding?
Can you change this if needs be?

Parents' relationship

Were your parents happy together? If not, do you know why?

What was the atmosphere like:
when they were together;
when father or mother came home and one of them was already there?

How long were they married before you were born?

How did they meet?

What were their fantasies about each other – Marilyn Monroe or Clark Gable . . .?

Did they agree how you should be brought up, or did you got to one parent for some things and the other for others?

Did they have a good physical relationship? Did they touch and hug each other? Did you reckon they were active sexually? Does this idea seem repellent and if so, could you never imagine your parents making love?

Have you wanted to keep them as 'Mum and Dad' and not as ordinary human beings?

Did you prefer one to the other? How did this affect family life?

Did you feel your parents stayed together 'because of the children'?

Did you feel you had to intervene on behalf of one of them, to protect each from the other?

Many of these acts, although not conscious, may have been automatically taken on board. In defining ourselves alongside one parent we may be unconsciously rejecting what it is the other parent stands for. Many children of an alcoholic parent try and take on a role that will protect the non-alcoholic parent or the whole family from stigma, only to find later on in life that they partner an addictive-type person or become at risk themselves from addiction. Again, it is as if the psyche is trying to restore balance and to ask us to claim what it is we have rejected.

Divorce and separation

Children always suffer when there is a marriage or partnership failure. Parents are the small person's rock and security. To have this threatened is devastating. The effects of divorce can be lessened by the way in which parents act afterwards, and how much they each help the children not to feel guilty, or to feel that they have taken sides. Although a parent may say, 'It's your mother I'm leaving, not you', the rejection is no less absolute.

For a girl whose father leaves the family in her early adolescence, there is the additional blow of feeling rejected as a growing woman at the beginning of her maturity. A son whose father leaves the family may feel pulled between mother and father – wanting to see his father, and aware of a new role as surrogate father with his mother. Younger children may feel pulled from one place to another as they have to adapt to new places and faces, and to weekend fathers or mothers.

When a mother leaves a relationship and children, we experience the same feeling of rejection, or a sense that she left because we weren't good enough. If the mother has been the centre of family life it may feel as if the heart has gone out of it, that our world is a very cold, unforgiving place. If parents divorce or separate when a child is very young, there may be no memory of the actual event, but what will be absorbed is the atmosphere and emotions of those undergoing the separation.

If your parents divorced or separated:

How old were you at the time?

Who told you what was going to happen?

How did you feel?

What were your first thoughts, fears? Did you voice them? Did you get heard?

How much did your life change at this point – at home, at school, with friends?

Did you carry on seeing both parents?

Was there a difficult atmosphere or competition between parents for your attention?

Did you feel you had to take sides? Did other family members approach you?

Did you miss the parent you saw least? What was it you missed most?

Did you feel angry inside? Perhaps you did not express it, but do you think now that it came out in some other form – angry outbursts, tantrums, breaking things, banging your head, shouting, spitting, etc? Do you still feel angry now?

Do you feel it was anyone's fault?

Did you blame yourself?

Could you talk to anyone about it – brothers, sisters or family members?

If you grew up with only one parent, what were your fantasies about the absent parent? What kind of relationship, if any, did you have with them? How was the absent parent referred to:
lovingly;
adoringly;
disparagingly;
with a curse;

critically;
as a hero/heroine?
What effect has this had upon your attitude to, and relationship with, members of the opposite sex, and with members of the sex of the parent you grew up with?

What do you feel about being the child of a single parent:
different;
deprived;
hostile;
ashamed;
embarrassed;
odd;
it was good fun;
it was an adventure;
it was special?
Note what it was that your feelings were specifically attached to.

If either parent remarried, how did this affect you? Did it change your relationship with your parent? If so, how? What did you lose or gain? Were there new family members, step- or half-siblings? How did you feel your place in the family changed?

What effect has the experience of separation and divorce had on you? Has it made you nervous of relationships or a commitment? Has it not made any difference at all?

Part 4
Making the Change

Chapter 6

Writing our life story

By now you have a notebook with lots of writing, some pictures, and some ideas of how your life has been so far. You probably feel as if we had been opening a lot of boxes, some of which may have been tightly shut for a long time. You may be feeling a bit worried or alarmed at the number of factors about your life which are painful and of which you may not have been aware. Do not be alarmed if there seems to be a lot. Stay with your 'seed' self. Believe that it is there. This next stage of the book shows ways in which we will use all that you have been through and put it together in a useful and, we hope, creative way. We are writing out how things have been for you and how you have coped in the only way you knew how.

Some people protest that they could never write anything about themselves, and are so daunted at the prospect that they don't even begin. It really is amazing how this fear (inbred, I believe, from school, where what we write is always judged) simply melts away when we allow ourselves to get involved in our own creative process. This next section is for no one but yourself. You need not show it to anyone. No one will be dishing out stars or dunce's caps. Once you allow the ideas, images and metaphors to inform you, the sentences will form themselves.

How to start

Get one large sheet of paper or several small index cards. Take your notebooks and flick through, casting your eyes down the pages. Take the words, shapes, images, forms or phrases that leap out at you, or any particular words you seem to have used a great deal. Don't worry about being dramatic or self-conscious. The simpler the phrases you can find to describe something the clearer will be the picture of your life and development, and the more powerfully will the images stay in your mind as you begin the process of change. Some of the phrases that come up in the following five examples of life-story writing are:

Special when close – Feelings bottled up – Special family – Sitting on a volcano – Death waiting at my shoulder – Wild Janet and Controlled Janet – Black hole – Ostrich attitude – Can of worms – Stolen child – Wide-eyed eldest child – Child behind the chair – anxiously skidding away – Puppy dog – 'What . . . little me?' – On the treadmill – Scared rigid – On automatic

Take your own examples and either brainstorm them onto the large sheet of paper, or write each one on a card.
When you feel you have enough, begin elaborating upon each phrase or image. For example, 'I grew up in a family where . . .' or, 'All my life I have felt that . . .' or, 'Early on I remember feeling that I was . . .' or, 'I have few conscious memories of my early life, but having begun to question how things are in my life I can guess that I took on the position of . . . early on'. Give as much detail as you can. Facts, memories, realizations.

When you feel you have the important experiences and facts you would like, put on your 'observer' hat (or ask your co-counsellor), and analyse what effect your early environment and your attitude to this has had on your thinking about yourself, and on the way you act in the world. The process needs to go something like this: because of 'a' and 'b' I believed that I had to be 'x' and 'y'. This has led me to having an 'e' attitude to others and to behave as if 'j', 'h' and 'l'. Your story might then begin something like this:

Most of my life I've been afraid of other people thinking I was stupid. This seems to go back to the time when I was very small and the youngest of several brothers who were all very clever. They used to call me 'dolly dope' and 'slow coach' . . . I felt helpless and upset. I tried to keep up by running after them and pleading with them to let me come on their outings, but they only laughed and said they could never have girls around. Both my parents were out at work all day and were too tired to listen to my complaints about my brothers, yet they expected my brothers to take care of me when they weren't there. I feel these experiences have contributed to a pretty low self-esteem inside me, which I fight by being quite aggressive and macho. I give as good as I get. I play the toughie and tell crude jokes, but inside I am hurt and sad and I wish someone would notice. But things don't happen by magic and I have to learn a decent way of being with others, especially men, where I don't have to appear so tough. I would like to risk taking off my tough mask from time to time and just seeing what came out. It's a risk, but I've got to get something to change how things are or I will remain on my own, the butt of others' jokes. I drink far more than is good for me, and I know this is related.

The final process is to end your story by writing something about what changes you would like to make and how you might begin to achieve them. This will involve changes in self-perception, in 'faulty' thinking and in false beliefs. Or they will be changes in patterns of traps such as avoidance or pleasing, isolation or thinking negatively. The latter will involve facing fear. This might be the only change needed. In the case of dilemmas, we must change from living lopsid-edly to being more balanced, again embracing the things we have learned to fear, and reframing our experience by challenging the 'as ifs' that live on from the past.

You may wish to write your story in prose form, or you may prefer to illustrate it with sketches, drawings, cartoons or colour paintings. Alternatively, you may like to write verse or rhyme, poetry or a stream of consciousness. Another way is to use a flow chart or tree, showing the passage of your life from roots to branches, with images or words to illustrate what has happened during growth.

Writing the story of our life is always a powerful experience. It can be very moving. When we write the stories and then read them out loud during a therapy session, something very special happens. Usually it is the first time we have heard exactly how life has been for us, and how our early formed attitudes to ourselves and others have contributed to our present difficulties. And we begin to understand how, by changing these attitudes, we can move away from what we may have believed were indelible footprints or entrenched habits over which we had no

control. It may be the first time we have a glimpse that we can be in control of our life. Writing our story also helps to sort out confusion, and to give us a clear vision of how things are and how they have been, rather than our muddling on any old how and hoping for the wind to blow in another direction.

Six examples of story-writing

The following are six different examples of life stories taken, with their permission, from people working in therapy. Names and professions have been changed to protect identities. You will see how varied they are and how completely individual. They may help you to get more ideas about how to write your own story.

Sylvia

I grew up as the *wide-eyed eldest child*, taking everything in and not always sure that things were right for me. I felt special love from my father – when he was home – and from Grandma – when she was allowed to show it to me. But otherwise I don't remember there being a readily available lap or someone to pick me up when I fell. I felt like *the child behind the chair*. It seems my mother was not very enamoured about having children, and perhaps we were a hindrance.

Because now feeling things deeply is very painful for me, and because

I didn't have a safe framework in which to express feelings, I have developed ways of keeping feelings at bay. I do this either by *showing off* intellectually, observing and commentating, often very astutely and with flair, but in the head, or by *controlling things rigidly*. This control also extends to relationships, when I sometimes feel anxious and threatened and prone to angry outbursts unless I am in control. I feel as if something is holding me back from claiming my life fully for myself. Perhaps the *child behind the chair*, who represents my deeper and more painful feelings, is wanting recognition, and I perhaps need to relinquish some of my tactics for keeping feelings at bay, even if experiencing feelings is painful. Then I can be more rounded and integrated as a person and move forwards to claim my life, without *anxiously skidding away* from real feelings.

Janet

I grew up in a lovely family where I was the youngest and felt *special*. We were very close and I feel upset when anything happens to break that closeness. When I broke out to 'do my own thing' it hurt my family and I feel really guilty about it. I feel God is punishing me for it my letting bad things happen to me.

I live now as if I have to keep my *feelings bottled up* and bend over backwards to please people and be a good mother, wife and daughter, so I don't hurt people. I feel that if I make trouble, they might stop talking to me, and that is terrifying for me. It reminds me of when I was seven years old in hospital after I had my tonsils out, and when my sisters weren't allowed to see me. I can remember how lonely and frightening that felt, and perhaps that is why the panic attacks I get now often feel as though something is stuck in my throat (like the pain after the tonsils were removed). Sometimes it is as though anger and strong feelings, which I'm frightened to express, get stuck in my throat too. But I daren't let them out because they would hurt people.

In the past two years a number of things have happened that have threatened the safety of my *special family*: my mum's illness, Mike's [husband] dad's death, and the dog biting Shân [daughter]. This has shaken my security and I feel 'anything could happen', as though I am *sitting on a volcano*, or as though *Death is waiting at my shoulder*. I'm very frightened that something bad might happen and that I might die. This probably causes me to have panic attacks (sometimes sparked off by outside events like the boy getting hurt in the playground). At times I have experienced a sort of *black hole*, feeling there's nothing there, as though the anxiety and fear are so great that it makes me cut off from the world around me.

Perhaps I also have this fear of death because I feel my life is passing by and that I'm missing out. Although I like being a good mum, etc., I don't really do anything for *me*. Perhaps deep down I feel if I do what I want it will hurt others, and that I don't deserve to put myself first. But I also believe that there are parts of Janet that want to come out and express themselves. I have tried to blot out *Wild Janet*, but perhaps I need to feel that it's OK to be my full self, and accept all of me, to like myself and express my feelings. And I need to realize that, by doing these things I won't be hurting people and the world won't come to an end.

Stephanie

I was born into a family where I somehow seemed to be carrying the pain of generations. My father was born twenty years after a 'black sheep', his father died when he was eight and his mother died in front of him when he was fourteen. My mother came from a family who avoided conflict. Like my father, she was the only graduate of the siblings, and her older brother and sister died young, so she may have had to make up for them in some way.

In our family, Barry my brother and Jennifer my sister had special places. Barry is the boy and the oldest and he is like the prodigal son who returned from the threshold of death. Jennifer is special because she is the youngest and there was a belief that everyone must be nice to her because she is fat.

I am in the middle, and it feels as though the bad fairy at my birth wished that, no matter what I did, I would never be good enough. Spilling the orange juice as a very little child is still an unexpiated crime for which I cannot gain forgiveness, no matter how hard I try. I was labelled clumsy when I was six and that label has stuck – as 'exotic', 'difficult', etc. Since then, I have always felt that I'm treading carefully, trying to negotiate a minefield laid by my father. I'm aware of this little bright face, eager to live, eager for approval, always being knocked down, bouncing back, but somehow being left behind. So it feels that I have never been able to flourish: I am the shrivelled bud of my poem, who has never been nurtured or allowed to grow properly.

As a result of this, I have become caught in a trap of 'trying to be perfect'. In order to be acceptable, I aim at perfection. I never feel good enough, but still try to please, and eventually feel let down and out of control, which reinforces my sense of worthlessness. So I try again, even harder.

Another way I have of coping is by taking all the knocks on the chin, trying to bounce back no matter how much I've been knocked down, keeping the face bright, even if bits of me are left behind. But in this cycle, I come – more and more – to expect to be hurt, and I have begun to believe that I don't deserve anything good.

In some ways, this is what happens in my relationships. With men, it seems that I recruit those who fulfil the '*prophecy*' of my never being good enough, of deserving nothing for myself and of expecting to get hurt and abused. Getting herpes is like a physical manifestation of this, an emblem of the transaction where I try to give everything that's good and joyful and get back an increasingly more threatening sexual disease. They leave me, and that's my legacy – so now I feel completely diseased. It's the same feeling as I exposed in the 'letter' to my father: 'I tried to think of an image to describe how it felt to be your daughter. What came to mind was that when I was small, over a period of time you slit me open, placed a box of maggots between my heart and my stomach and slowly and deliberately sewed the scar away. Your living legacy was that I could never again feel peace, goodness, satisfactions; just rotten-ness at the core . . .' (See p. 211).

In my relationships with women, it sometimes feels that, in the give-and-take equation, the only part available to me is the giving, and I have learned to interpret this as being as valuable as actually receiving. I have the image of me as a plant that grows legs and moves out of the range of any nurture that may be intended for me – so convinced am I that I don't deserve to receive. Perhaps therapy is an opportunity to change this pattern. With a few women, it feels that they are strong enough to force me to receive, although then I feel controlled and trapped as if medicine were being forced down my throat.

One of the family sayings is, 'Stephanie has only one problem and that's Stephanie.' And I have come to believe it in some way, as though

I am eternally snagged in trying to be fully myself. I have the feeling that I have never been heard and that I therefore have never been really connected with someone. Deep down I am still the deprived, needy child craving recognition, warmth and acceptance for who I really am. But I daren't show this neediness, so I try and behave well and please and give, treading carefully and thinking before I speak, terrified that the neediness will seep out and make a dreadful mess and doom me to more verdicts that I am clumsy and impossible. I wanted to star in the play, but ended up being cast as the ugly, grunting troll.

I often intellectualize my feelings – carefully releasing words so that I don't overwhelm people. But I am entitled to experience my feelings fully, even if they are very painful. And I do have some profound self-knowledge, as, for example, expressed in my poetry. There are some good bits on which I can begin to build the full, real, lovely Stephanie: my closeness to Barry; the warm, creative and admirable part of my mother which doesn't seem to judge me and is also close and very special to me; and the newly acquired sense that I have an *'angelic overview'* of the minefield – as an allegorical picture of a Tuscan field, with my father laying mines as I fly above, unseen, blowing raspberries at him!

I need to believe in the shrivelled bud – that it is good and valuable at heart, that it will and can grow, that *I* am the one who can nurture it and allow it to flower, and that I don't need to find ways of being special other than as the 'fortunate victim'.

I need to start learning to take as well as to give, without feeling I need to spit out the goodness. I need to feel I can stand tall; the little, bright face can become the full, bright Stephanie.

Alistair

I have very few memories of my early life, and it's possible that much of my feelings from that time have had to be buried under my urgent need for control. I saw my father as a strict authoritarian, a hard-working research scientist who was rarely at home. My mother seemed to spend most of the time in bed depressed, and was always trying to leave. I followed my very clever brother to boarding school and felt the pressure of expectations to follow in his footsteps. Just before boarding school, at eight years old, I had a frightening experience of racing in the school playground with another boy – the fastest boy – and slipping and hitting my head so badly against a brick wall that I was hospitalized for two weeks and at home afterwards for several months. I have no memory of my parents visiting me during that time, only an overwhelming sense of loneliness and fear of being made to go to school. The one positive element was my nanny, who waited to get married until I went away to boarding school so that she could look after me.

I can conjecture that the early part of my life was quite deprived emotionally, with the feelings of the child I was at the time unexpressed and unexplored. The natural range of feelings of suffering and deprivation and rejection are feeling hurt, angry, abandoned, needy, jealous, vindictive and destructive. There was no place for these feelings and the only way I could cope was to learn strong patterns of control over everything to do with feelings, and the only way I would hope to receive anything for myself was by constantly trying to win. Mother said, 'Let feelings out,' but I didn't believe it. Father said, 'Chin up, son.'

I felt in control and good about myself later on at school, because I could do things well and be in charge. Life at home was extremely difficult, because I was trying to keep my parents together during their increased threats to divorce. And again I felt alone and lonely, and took responsibility for the adults, missing out on getting help for myself over the choice of career.

All this has led me to have an *ostrich attitude* to my inner feelings and needs. I feel that I have to strive constantly to win, that if I stop I have failed. And even when I do win I don't feel satisfaction or pleasure, but the despair of feeling I have to go on winning. I have tied my life up in such a way that I have to stay *on the treadmill*. There is little room for self-reflection, for connecting with the imaginative artist in me, or the creative dreamer. This self-deprivation has resulted in my being terrified of illness, loss and death, as if this were a metaphor for my own creative, free life being snuffed out by the desperate need to control my own life and win. I feel that if I let go it will all go wrong, or be a dead end like the brick wall. I was recently intensely moved by a piece of music. I found out it was called 'The Stolen Child'.

I would like to be able slowly to get in touch with some of the pain of my early childhood feelings, allow them space and air, through therapy, talking or through drawing and painting. I would like to make this vulnerable area within me less anxious and afraid, less the *can of worms* I fear it to be. In doing so I realize I may have to face the fear and sadness and lose some of my more controlling side for a while, until a more appropriate balance is restored and I feel freer to make more comfortable choices for myself as a whole. I would like to be brave enough to open the can of worms, rather than spend my life trying to run away from it and putting myself at risk of exhaustion and ill health.

Freda

I was the elder of two girls in a family who were very keen to get on in the world and achieve both social and material success. My father was an immigrant from South Africa and my mother had a northern background. Both had quite strong accents which made them self-conscious of how they spoke, and each struggled to overcome this. My sister and I were sent to elocution classes when we were six. We had to practise our vowels on every car journey and to practise reading aloud. We were harshly scolded if we got things wrong, and mealtimes are full of bitter memories of being corrected over the way we pronounced things.

In between my sister and me there had been a brother who lived only a few days. I think my mother never got over it and she was always depressed and looked sad. My father often said, 'Oh don't go on about it. What will be, will be,' and she would shut up and tears would roll down her face. I think they both would have liked a boy, and my sister and I reacted to this in different ways. My way was to try and be as pleasing as I could, do what they wanted, be the person they wanted me to be. My sister was actually very clever, but never felt she got the encouragement she needed. She felt they were always expecting her to make up for not being a boy, and although she was clever she always spoiled it somehow. She would go in for the exams and mess them up, and she left college in the middle of her training and went into a job that didn't really satisfy her.

I don't remember Mum losing my brother directly, but I remember a lot of muttering and whispering, and that certain things were never referred to. She dinned it into us that having a baby was the worst pain of all, and always went into big emotional silences whenever someone was expecting. It seems as if, looking back on it, Mum did have the exclusive use of the emotional realm. Somehow I always felt that whatever I felt it could never be as bad as her – losing a baby and all that. So I grew up used to putting the lid on what I felt, and later on not being aware I felt anything really. I did somewhere inside me, but it was very deep.

When I was about seven my sister started her illnesses. She used to be ill most of the time, and no one ever knew what was the matter with her. She got labelled a hypochondriac. When she was fourteen she stopped eating and the school sent for my mum and dad, and we all had to go to see a psychiatrist. It was awful. Mum was crying and saying to Lyn, 'Why do you do this to me?' Dad was saying, 'After all we've done for you!' I think I tried very hard to make things better. I tried to keep the peace, to listen to everyone, and it was around this time I began to be expected to be the one who coped. Until then I had been quite clever too, and good at sports, and much was expected of me, that I would bring honour to the family, but I didn't. One of the reasons for this was that I started to put on a great deal of weight. I couldn't stop eating. I was very ashamed and tried diets and running it off, but it just made me eat more. Now my parents had two children they were ashamed of and our holidays were pretty miserable. I tried to escape into books and reading, but was called selfish and ungrateful. My mother really wanted me to sit with her most of the day and entertain her; my father was quite pleased if I did this as I took her off his hands, and he was pleased if I tried to encourage my sister to eat. But other than that he had really given up on me, because I was nothing to be proud of.

What I have realized is that I have never really been a small child. I don't think I've had much freedom or fun. I've always had to be very grown up, and this has left me not really capable of letting go. I appear serious and I'm over-conscientious. I take on much more than my share of tasks and become a general dogsbody. I'm beginning to see that I've used eating as a way to fill up the emptiness inside, which is related to feeling basically I'm nothing unless I'm serving or giving out to others. The eating takes on a self-punishing role, because I fill myself up when I'm bothered – usually when I'm cross with my husband or I'm taken for granted by others – and then when I'm full up I feel so guilty and disgusted with myself I go for long runs and also take laxatives to try and get rid of the food.

I married a man who is a mixture of the negatives of both my parents – a depressed bully in other words – whom I try to please and serve and long for a few crumbs. My *puppy dog* attitude brings out the bully in him, and my overeagerness to look after him, which I believe will make him love me, almost pushed him into depressions, which I then feel I have to take care of. I take menial jobs because I haven't dared believe that I can do anything better, or that I'm entitled to, and I often catch myself thinking, '*What . . . little me?*' in a *martyrish* way, when I really know inside that I could do something better for myself.

I envy others their success and long to be free, but it's as if something pulls me back. I would like to find out what there is inside me that was there before my little brother died, because it feels as if something of me was put on hold or even died at the same time. I would like to give up believing I have to please others all the time in order to gain approval and love. I would like to feel what there is of the real me inside instead of the groaning emptiness that gets dumped with food and then punished for it. I would like to free myself from the guilt about not being a boy, about my mother's depression, about my sister's anorexia and at not being able to make these things better. I would like to give myself permission to be angry sometimes, and to know when I feel angry and outraged and to learn a language for it. I would like to be free enough to have a good belly laugh.

Martin

It seems as if in my early years I was the centre of my mother's life. My parents married late and I was an only child. My father was away travelling for much of my childhood, and when he was around took little interest in me, and has remained to this day a difficult and uncommunicative man. My mother felt he wasn't intellectual enough and often ridiculed what he said and did. It feels as if she looked to me to fulfil her ideals of what a man should be, in her eyes. I was forced to be centre stage, feeling unconsciously that I must conform and be hard-working and good, perhaps to make up for my mother's disappointment in her husband, perhaps to ensure that I was loved and accepted. As a result, I was often lonely and anxious, but there was no place for these feelings to be expressed other than in nail-biting and in the agony of intense boredom, both of which made me feel very ashamed. There was no place for negative or angry feelings, and I learned early on the habit of pushing away anything negative that might come into my head. I learned to be vigilant about all my actions, to judge myself constantly and to fear things that came into my mind that did not conform to the image I believed was mine to live up to and upon which my survival was placed.

It seems as if in some way I have remained on the *treadmill* developed out of my early life through my professional training, repeating the pattern of trying to live up to what I believed was my lot through excessive hard work. I have believed that I must be all things to all people in order to be a good, caring professional. It seems as if I have felt it necessary to provide what is expected of me from others or I will not be recognized and valued.

Since my mother died, the pattern of things in my life has begun to change. The feelings I have never allowed to the surface have made themselves known, and the natural resentment at having to live my life entirely for others in order to be recognized has made its point. I am frightened by my angry and negative feelings; they seem to rock and threaten my entire equilibrium. I find I cannot control my thoughts, which swing from one thing to another. I can understand that many of these feelings are ones which have been repressed since childhood – they are natural and ordinary feelings. But because they were not allowed earlier on, they still carry with them potency and fear. I find I desperately want to gain control of what is happening to me inside. Some days I want a 'magical cure', when I will wake up and it will all be over; other days I feel despairing and hopeless and am plagued with guilt about what is happening to me, and seek reassurance that all will be well.

Some days it is very difficult for me to acknowledge what is happening to me and that I can have an active part in the transition from survival self, which was very restricting, to being more my real self with a wider range of choices, both intellectually and emotionally. I need to believe more in my own capacity to make change, to use my own insight, to listen more directly to the voice inside which allows stillness. 'Be still . . . and know . . .' One of my biggest hurdles is to get over feeling bad and guilty when I am angry, envious, cross or impatient with anyone. Rather to have the feeling, acknowledge it, and feel free to express it, or not, as is my choice. I would like a more active relationship with everything that is happening to me, so that I may use some freedom of choice and get to know sides of myself previously in eclipse. I need to believe that I can emerge stronger and more myself, and not have to take refuge in the helplessness which at times overwhelms me and makes me fear for the future. And that the strength I have is not from will-power and putting it through for others *on automatic*, but something of my own which is flexible and not dependent on others.

You will see that everyone's story is quite different, that the images, phrases and what each made of the different experiences was highly individual. Your story is your own and you need to claim it as your own story and place on the journey so far. It should contain enough of the essence of what you feel now and something of an understanding of how that has come to pass, even if you have to hypothesize because you cannot know all the facts. (Even when facts are known everyone will make something different even of the same life events.) Include in the story both how you feel things have come to be as they are in your life, and something about what you hope to be relieved of and what you would like in the future.

Chapter 7

Targeting the procedures which create problems and deciding on aims for change

We saw in Part 2 how we learn to manage our core pain by developing a core pain statement. For example: 'Only if I behave in a certain way (please others, avoid action) will I survive'. Although necessary at the time, these statements that shape our everyday procedures can restrict our choices. This chapter is devoted to naming these restricting procedures that we take for granted and setting realistic goals for change. We will look at how Sylvia, Freda, Janet and Alistair made charts of their problem procedures and developed their aims for change. In Chapter 8 we will see how Alistair, Martin and Freda also made use of diagrams to reveal the way their procedures grew into the sequences that eventually lead to problems and back into core pain.

You may choose to make either a chart for rating procedures and aims for change, or a diagram of the sequences as you recognise them. Once created it is useful to carry these diagrams or charts around with you, so that you can turn to them when you feel stuck, or feel the old responses and problems coming on. Recognising where we are in our learned sequences is the beginning of change, however far down the sequence we have travelled. It is never too late to stop, revise and reverse! When you have read Chapters 7 and 8, choose the best way for you to set about focusing on the areas in your life story which need revision and change. Don't be overambitious. Be realistic. Once we begin to change even the simplest thing, other changes follow, like the ripple effect of a stone on water. Start small.

It is important to remember that what we seek to change are the learned procedures, the core pain statements that have created the traps, dilemmas and snags that limit our life and cause problems. It is essential to focus upon the learned procedures rather than the problems the

procedures create. For example, our problem may be an eating disorder, but the procedure underlying it may be that we bottle up feelings for fear of making a mess, or we stuff down anger for fear of being rejected. It is the procedure we need to address and change. And in time the ripples of change will alter the way we use food.

Sylvia

Sylvia decided to look at her life when she began to have angry outbursts with people at work. She had also been aware for some

Sylvia's target problems and aims.

Problem: *Either* in touch with the child and feeling and being in pain; *or* using my telescope to avoid.

Aim: To feel safe enough to let the child come out from behind the chair and be part of adult Sylvia.

Problem: The 'Telescope': a 'performance trap'.

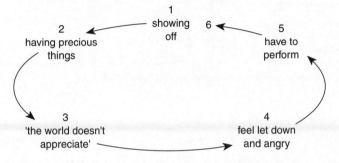

Aim: To value and love my whole self and listen to myself, first.

Problem: *Either* controlling by being rigidly intolerant and tough on people; *or* being controlled and feeling I'm having my hair pulled.

Aim: To be aware of and trust my own strength, and not to take the wrong things too seriously.

Figure 8 Sylvia's diagram of her problem procedures

time of feeling depressed and sad, and of a sense of meaninglessness in her life. As she worked with her life story and the reformulation of her problems she became aware of her inner creative spirit, her 'tiger'. Being in touch every day with her tiger has helped Sylvia to feel more 'whole', to become less depressed and to give up her 'performance' self. She has been much less frustrated and is less likely to burst out angrily.

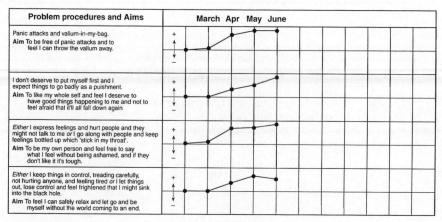

Problem procedures and Aims	March Apr May June
Panic attacks and valium-in-my-bag. **Aim** To be free of panic attacks and to feel I can throw the valium away.	
I don't deserve to put myself first and I expect things to go badly as a puishment. **Aim** To like my whole self and feel I deserve to have good things happening to me and not to feel afraid that it'll all fall down again	
Either I express feelings and hurt people and they might not talk to me *or* I go along with people and keep feelings bottled up which 'stick in my throat'. **Aim** To be my own person and feel free to say what I feel without being ashamed, and if they don't like it it's tough.	
Either I keep things in control, treading carefully, not hurting anyone, and feeling tired *or* I let things out, lose control and feel frightened that I might sink into the black hole. **Aim** To feel I can safely relax and let go and be myself without the world coming to an end.	

Figure 9 Janet's chart of her target problem procedures and aims

Janet

Janet's diagram targets her problem procedures and aims as shown in Figure 9. She monitored them over a period of a few weeks and they all changed dramatically. Janet had sought help from her GP because of her panic attacks, and was referred for short-term therapy. She identified with the 'doing what others want' trap and the 'I'm bound to do things badly' trap, also with the keeping things bottled up or making a mess dilemma. She also identified with intense, extreme and uncontrollable emotions and with swinging into emotional blankness.

After four months of working with her story and her target procedures and aims Janet was able to do without her valium! Her focused therapy helped to free her from the guilt which had led to her fear of death and panic attacks. In her final 'goodbye' letter to her therapist she wrote that she 'had a bad day now and again' but was always able to say what she felt and was enjoying the release and freedom after years of never having her say.

Freda's target problem procedures and aims

Freda came into therapy because of her depression. Her eating problem only emerged later, as she had been ashamed of it. Also she had failed to see it as a 'problem', even though she had never eaten with her family or her friends. She was eating only a very limited diet and taking a great many laxatives which were seriously affecting her digestion. Her target problem procedures and aims were as follows:

Problem: Depression.

Procedure: I feel I've never been me or been able to let myself go. I don't think much of myself and get into the 'I'll do this badly' and 'worthless' trap. There doesn't seem much in life for me so far, because others' needs have always been more pressing.

Aim: To monitor everyday negative and depressed thoughts such as those outlined above. In keeping a record of the weeks, to look at the negative image I reinforce by my thinking. To challenge this thinking, because it has been learned and is related to a 'false' idea of myself. In letting go of the 'false' self I am making room for the 'seed' me to emerge. To develop more time for the things and occasions that put me in touch with the 'seed' self – music, certain friends, being in the country – and to do these things with the child who once loved them in mind.

Problem: Placation trap, 'doing what others want'.

Procedure: I have always felt worthless and that others' ways are better and more successful, so I give in to anyone, and then feel cross with myself and anxious. People can easily tyrannize me, and I tyrannize myself by judging myself harshly.

Aim: To be aware of the times when I placate or create tyrants. To bring my awareness into the moment and take the choice to risk saying 'no' or having a different view when that is what I feel. To trust what it is I feel I want to do much more thoroughly, even if sometimes I am wrong about my decision.

Problem: Eating compulsively, then starving and bingeing.

Procedure: I long to be 'full' but feel bad if I have anything, so I have to get rid of it.

Aim: To monitor feelings prior to, during and after eating compulsions and binges. To recognize the links between internal emotions and feelings of 'longing to be full'. To write out, speak out or paint out some colour, shape or image for these feelings, however unformed, difficult or 'odd'. To give permission for the feelings to be 'born', authentic and not judged. Ultimately to find other ways of expressing needs emotionally other than by eating displacement.

Problem/   Self-sabotage due to irrational guilt about dead brother and
Procedure: mother's depressed life.

Aim: To be aware when I 'sell myself short' or put myself down when what I say is not true about myself. To be aware when I let others 'win', or take a back seat when I know inside I could take part and be creative in my own right. To take the risk of expressing myself more assertively sometimes, to claim my right to my own life, however successful or different from my family, and not to carry the myth of the family's disappointment and misery. When I really want to do something with the spark I feel inside instead of feeling guilty, to say, 'I AM ALLOWED.'

Freda took up her journal-keeping enthusiastically, like a thirsty woman who has longed for tea and only had water. She said it was like having 'permission to live properly, even if only inside a notebook'. After a few weeks her depression began to lift. She did stop placating, and as she did so her eating problems got worse. They now took the full brunt of all the feelings that had been hidden in the depression and were swallowed up in placation. As the eating difficulties increased so did Freda's images about eating and being full. When she allowed herself to stop placating she could express the images. A colourful language emerged, linking early life memories with her current need to starve herself in order to experience control.

Freda found visualization and drawing particularly helpful. (We will look at how to do this in detail in Chapter 9 'Techniques for working through the process of change'.) During one particularly moving session she got in touch with the feelings she had experienced when her mother came home after the death of Freda's brother at the age of six days. There was a strange mixture of awareness of mother's flat stomach, her profound despair, the intensity of her weeping (which she showed only to Freda, not to friends), and the insatiability of her mother's need and hunger for something to fill the space left by the dead baby.

Freda described how she felt 'eaten up' by her mother's needs and demands, which returned later when her sister developed anorexia and Freda was once again expected to fill an empty space. As a child her own inner emptiness and confusion increased. One of her drawings depicted a huge open mouth that was being shovelled with tiny fish by a thin witch with a child's broken-handled spade. In one of her dreams her right hand was being bitten by a wolf. She drew a picture of the wolf, and came to associate this animal with her hunger and need, her 'wolfishness', which would nip her from time to time to remind her both of the level of hunger she was experiencing (for something which she needed to name) and of the devouring quality of her experience of her mother's neediness, from which she was struggling to free herself. (This neediness appeared in many other people – husband, sister, children, family – and until she began to claim her own life it appeared as powerful and wolfish as her early experience of being a child with her very needy mother.)

Having had some moderate success with freeing herself from the placation trap, Freda was encouraged to try more changes. She was also encouraged by friends' new respect for her holding on to her own ground. Two key phrases – 'selling myself short' and 'I am allowed' – helped her to have the courage to keep up her own note with people, especially difficult people like her mother to whom she felt duty-bound and very unfree.

Freda dreamed a great deal and was interested in her dreams, and so she began reading about them, and about myths and fairy tales. A number of animal motifs appeared in her dreams, and she became especially fond of a fawn and a frog. She saw that these creatures had been thought of negatively, and had been banished to the darkness of her unconscious because they represented aspects of herself that she presumed were 'jelly-like, slobs, pathetic, losers'. When she could recognize the value of these creatures, she began to take them more seriously.

She began to like their simplicity, their instinctive nature: they knew how to live naturally. She was able to see how much value they had to offer, and she began to integrate them into her own being, as part of her own wholeness. In the beginning the animals were images for her to ponder on. Later she became drawn to dancing, to expressing herself in writing, and she felt most content and 'in herself' when outside in the countryside. Once she had connected with the instinctive, free-flowing nature of these creatures, the urge to binge diminished, and she felt much more fulfilled in her life.

Alistair's target problems and aims

Alistair's target problems and aims were as follows:

Problem: High blood pressure and exhaustion.

Procedure: Overwork to stave off anxiety, fear, illness, death, causing no time for myself and anxiety to leak out.

Aim: Make space for some anxiety and fragility to take care of these feelings.

Problem: Eternal tread wheel and depression.

Procedure: Constantly striving in order to win, to cope with feelings of failure and inadequacy.

Aim: (a) To recognize 'can of worms'. Recognize when activity is accelerated in order to cope with 'can of worms'.
(b) to find a container for these feelings (therapy).

Problem/ Can't let go and relax in any way.
Procedure:

Aim: Take half an hour every day for reflection.

Alistair also made a diagram for himself which describes his main traps. His story is recounted on page 176.

When you have worked out your own three or four target problem procedures and aims over the next few months, make a chart like the one in Figure 10. Each week mark on the chart how you feel you have fared according to the *aim*. Remember the aim may be simply to be more aware of the procedure itself, or it may be just to give yourself

Rate each problem

Describe problem:	Describe aim:	Aim achieved No change Much worse										
Placation trap	*To recognize trap and learn to be assertive*											
Describe problem:	Describe aim:	Aim achieved No change Much worse										
Describe problem:	Describe aim:	Aim achieved No change Much worse										
Describe problem:	Describe aim:	Aim achieved No change Much worse										
			1st week	2nd week	3rd week							

Figure 10 Rating chart for your problem procedures and aims. Keep the chart in your diary or pocket book and look at it every day. Mark your progress each week at the same time.

half an hour a day for self-reflection. Once you have accomplished the aim, you may wish to move on to the second stage of aiming for something more ambitiously connected to your problem or difficulty (Figure 10). Alistair is aiming to move from his half-hour a day reflection to allowing the experience of the feelings he's never had time for. His next step will be to use them in his everyday life, and ultimately to live more harmoniously with them.

Chapter 8

Making diagrams of the way you cope with inner conflicts

Having written about your life it is very useful to create a working diagram of exactly how you have learned to cope with difficult feelings and inner core pain.

To make the diagram we need to find words to express what we consider our core state pain to be, bearing in mind our history and what we know we are still carrying around and feeling. Freda's core state pain went like this:

Deprived: She had no unconditional love from either parent and very early on took the position of the 'parental child', taking responsibility for her mother's loss and depression.

Guilty: Irrational and 'magical guilt' for the whole family's disappointments.

Depressed: No vehicle for self-expression or love for real self.

Angry: Hidden, turned against self.

To find words for your core pain you need to feel into what inside you is your greatest fear and your most overwhelming feeling of pain. If you imagine again the world of the small child, when we have to begin to cope with the core pain, you might envisage the kind of experiences your child self would most seek to be rid of. These might involve feeling:

afraid, terrified, lost, abandoned, forgotten, deprived, abused, left, rejected, lonely, in pain (physical, mental and emotional), angry, furious, in a rage, spitting, shrieking, yelling, crying, screaming, dropped, teased, tantalized, longing, waiting (to be held, loved again, picked up, nurtured, for Mum/Dad/other) hungry, starving, empty, needy, intense.

Spend your time feeling into which of these states could apply to what you feel inside. There will be other words you will wish to add to describe how you feel. If this does not come easily to you, ponder on this page and its ideas, and let your unconscious inform you of how to address your core pain. An image, word or dream may come to you. Or you may just come across the word you need by keeping in touch with the feelings you have and by letting them indicate the right description. Sometimes we are able to describe the nature of our core pain by outlining the learned reciprocal roles that maintain it. For example, a demanding perfectionist role may be our way of coping with, but also maintaining, a harshly judged self, where core pain is experienced as worthlessness.

The next stage in making your diagram is to describe the procedures you have used to cope with the core pain, with arrows leading to them. The self-survival procedures tend to loop back again to the core pain. Thus for Freda we would have Figure 11. Freda coped with her inner pain first by pleasing others, and later by overeating when the core state feelings made her feel bad. The diagram shows how each of her coping tactics, while useful when she was small, in adult life trapped her. Each old coping pattern ultimately led her back to her inner pain.

Freda could see how the 'doing as others want' trap led to the perpetuation of her depression and restricted her own life. By using the diagram every day she could see exactly where she was at a time of difficulty or conflict. The eating to cope with the emptiness and feeling 'bad' made her guilty, for which she was self-punishing, and then felt alone. She 'snagged' her life in a way that deprived her of using her own creative skills. Her way out of the map, the *exit* point, was through recognizing her ability to be able to cope, as she had done all her life. But instead of using it in a placatory way for others for survival, she began looking at it as a natural skill that could be used to help create a better framework for her attitude to herself and for her life practically.

There are two more diagrams in this section – from Martin and Alistair. Diagrams can be as simple or complex as suits us individually. To begin with, keep your diagram simple. If you recognize that you avoid things, work out the feelings you are trying to avoid and mark in the avoidance, as shown in Figure 12.

Alistair is currently working on his life story and diagram (see Figure

DILEMMA

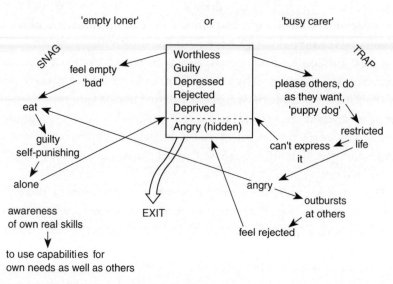

Figure 11 Freda's diagram: coping with core pain

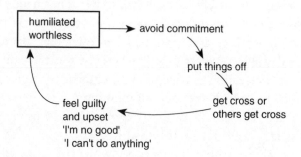

Figure 12 Martin's avoidance diagram

13). Because he has organized his life through excessive striving and control he has had no time for reflection, for letting his natural, spontaneous thoughts come to the surface, or for following his ideas. He had to suppress all of his vulnerability early on in life, mainly because of a very tense family situation and because both his parents were largely absent. He had a very clever older brother, and he picked up early on that if he did not strive to win he would be left behind and regarded a 'failure'. Thus, any feeling of which he was not in strict control has come

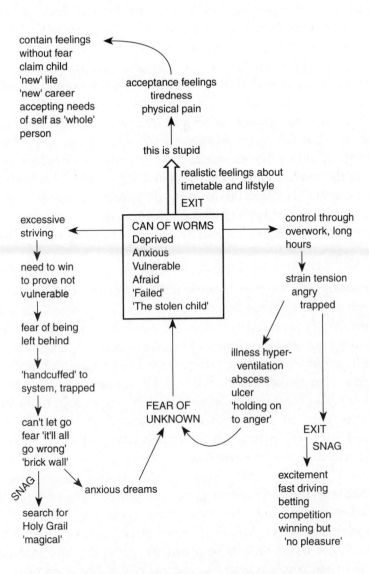

contain feelings
without fear
claim child
'new' life
'new' career
accepting needs
of self as 'whole'
person

acceptance feelings
tiredness
physical pain

this is stupid

realistic feelings about
timetable and lifstyle

EXIT

excessive
striving

CAN OF WORMS
Deprived
Anxious
Vulnerable
Afraid
'Failed'
'The stolen child'

control through
overwork, long
hours

need to win
to prove not
vulnerable

strain tension
angry
    trapped

fear of being
left behind

'handcuffed' to
system, trapped

illness hyper-
    ventilation
abscess
ulcer
'holding on
to anger'

can't let go
fear 'it'll all
go wrong'
'brick wall'

FEAR OF
UNKNOWN

EXIT

SNAG

SNAG

anxious dreams

search for
Holy Grail
'magical'

excitement
fast driving
betting
competition
winning but
    'no pleasure'

Until revised, Alistair hoped for relief from his core state pain through exits which were snagged – the 'Holy Grail' and high excitement. The more realistic exit at the top offers a wide open space for him to reconnect with his 'seed self' and feel the excitement of real creativity which is not snagged.

Figure 13 Alistair's life story diagram

to be seen as a failure. When we met he was so afraid of the out-of-control feelings that he had shut them off completely. They would 'leak' out through 'odd' thoughts, dreams, irrational fears for his own health and a great flood of fear when two close friends died suddenly.

Alistair is now able to acknowledge how unhappy he has been and to look at what this means in terms of his life. This acknowledgement alone has allowed him to review the job he does (he works a fourteen-hour day every day, starting at 5 a.m.). Previously he had been 'on automatic', and his internal needs had reflected themselves in health problems such as a duodenal ulcer and abscesses, although he could not allow himself proper time to take care of these matters, or to look holistically at the implications of his symptoms for his general stress level. Had he continued to deny his needs and difficulties, he may have developed a health crisis before he was able to look at his lifestyle and in what way his lopsided living maintained by his way of thinking about himself and its causes.

Martin's diagram (Figure 14) is the most complex so far, but it was of particular value for him because of the extent of his agitation. He had great difficulty with swings of mood and with obsessional thoughts, in particular his preoccupation with the word 'baptism'. He had been baptized a year before the onset of his depression, but he had always felt guilty about it because he believed it went against the wishes of both his wife and his mother. His chart shows how his survival-self mode was either to please others he considered 'perfect' and strong, or to work excessively hard to meet 'perfect' standards. Both survival modes restricted his own natural 'seed' development and contributed to making him dangerously exhausted. He was caught between his desire to become his own 'seed' person and the guilt he felt when this conflicted with the two most important and powerful people in his life, his mother and his wife. The most intense period of his depression began after his mother died, as if he was at last allowed to be free of her very tight hold, but felt both panicky about this and guilty for wanting it. Much of the guilt was unconscious and his map helped to make it consciously realized. He felt very guilty for every negative thought about anything or anyone, and every time he had the tiniest negative thought he would punish himself with feeling bad or by tormenting himself with the word 'baptism'.

One of the most wonderful experiences about people's traumas is that

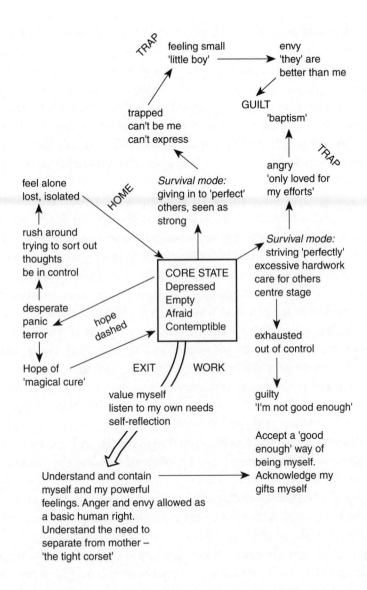

Figure 14 Martin's survival diagram

the trauma itself contains the key to the answer and the way out. Although the word 'baptism' could be used obsessively and as a punishment for not being 'good enough', Martin also needed to be 'reborn' into his real self and initiated into the adult freedom of choice about feelings in full range.

Martin has managed to contain more fully the extremes of his mood swings, and has been able to explore with his wife ways in which he restricts himself within their relationship and projects onto her the more stifling aspects of his mother. These both make him feel contained and safe, and he panics when he is apart with nothing to do; but they also make him feel enraged at the restrictions and he once again becomes the 'little boy'. He needs time to process and hold his now wide range of feelings and to accept this as part of himself, to understand that he does not have to be 'perfect' or centre stage in order for life to be meaningful.

The following is an example of working with a diagram made for Karen, who was recommended for focused therapy after a number of overdoses. She had a pattern of making intense and immediate relationships with men which ended explosively after just a few weeks, when she would then make an attempt on her life. Karen was only eighteen, but had had five admissions to casualty over the previous two years. Her family background was unsettled. She had been fostered at age four, then adopted by a couple who split up when she was eight. She was 'parcelled round' to family and friends, but never settled anywhere. Two 'uncles' had sexually abused her and she had also developed a pattern of bingeing and starving as a way of trying to control her confused feelings. As a result, by the time she began secondary school, and all her peer group were pairing off, she felt worthless, unlovable and that no one really wanted or loved her. All she could identify with were stories from romantic novels or an idealized longing for what we called 'perfect care'.

A diagram (Figure 15) helped her to see the pattern of her responses to relationships which had led to her overdoses. This gave her a certain degree of stability, so that she could see why and how the patterns had emerged and begin the work of receiving 'good enough' care for herself. This diagram helped Karen see what patterns were involved in her starving/bingeing routines. What she began to work through in her therapy was how her idealization had become a substitute for her grief at the

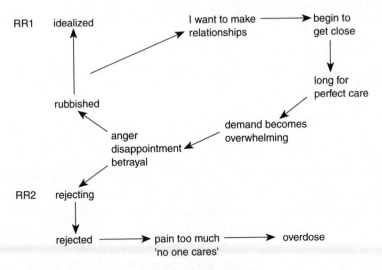

Figure 15 Karen's diagram: two reciprocal role patterns

loss and deprivation of her early life, and how it prevented her from receiving something that was 'good enough' for her needs.

Go over each of the diagrams again and see if you can follow them clearly. Each stage should result in the next one by following the arrow. In a trap, the way of coping leads back to the core state, sometimes after quite a detour. A dilemma (the either/or, or if/then) results in a lopsidedness that also causes a return to the core state; and a snag tends to keep the core state as it is all the time. The *exit point* is found when the way we act results in self-expression and communication that is direct and assertive and leads us where we need to go. The exit point allows us time and space for self-reflection, for getting in touch with our real seed self and where it wants to go in life.

Chapter 9

Techniques for working through the process of change

So far, we have described how to write the story of your life and how to make a chart of problems and aims for change; and we have looked at how to make a diagram that you can use each day to help monitor where you are in terms of the way you operate. What we need to look at next is how we process the change we are looking for. How do we actually go about making change when some of our habits are lifelong and pretty determined? Please be encouraged by the knowledge that the psyche is devoted to maintaining movement and balance, and will do anything it can to prod, push or catapult you into action to prevent you becoming rigid, stuck or lopsided.

Perhaps you have had your jolt and this is why you are reading this page; perhaps the book itself will act as a jolt. Perhaps it will work by confirming what you already knew somewhere but hadn't put into words. If you are seeking change and the change is the way of your real self, this self will help you. So often we get bewitched by the fear of change and what others think: Will I be liked for this?' 'Will this bring me success?'

There are many different ways of bringing about changes and shifts in consciousness, and there are many therapeutic styles which can assist in this. In this chapter we will look at a number of these, and you may be drawn more to one than another. There is no one way of working, the best way is the one that works for you.

Self-monitoring

We have mentioned the method of self-monitoring throughout these chapters as a way to help us develop an awareness of our different patterns. It is best to choose something specific to monitor, like depressed or negative thinking, or the 'doing as others want' trap. Buy a small notebook that you can carry around and refer to easily. When you recognize the trap or dilemma write down the time of day, place, who if anyone you are with, what else is happening and WHAT YOU ARE THINKING AND FEELING. Keep this notebook for a week before looking at your entries. Sometimes we have to keep up the monitoring for three or four weeks before we can see any kind of pattern emerging.

The main purpose of self-monitoring is to increase your awareness of your own patterns and tendencies. With increased awareness you can become more astute about how one thing leads to another in terms of your own and others' reactions, and in time you can halt or change the process, once you have understood how it operates.

What do you monitor? Unwanted thoughts; strange sentences; odd feelings; obsessional words or acts; physical symptoms such as headaches, tinnitus, chest pain, feelings of nausea; forgetfulness; depersonalization (feeling I am no one . . . losing my sense of self); anxiety; fearfulness; not wanting to go out; ways of eating. These can all be monitored so that you can look at this aspect of yourself more clearly.

When you have your notebook with its entries, read through and select one or more words or phrases that you use frequently, and identify a repeated theme, person, time or place that links the monitorings. For example, through self-monitoring one man learned that his tinnitus grew worse whenever he was unable to be assertive. It became like a call or reminder that he needed to express himself and not be passive or placatory.

Journal-keeping

Use a larger notebook or perhaps a special kind of notebook or hardback exercise book in which to write your thoughts, dreams and ideas. In this way you are keeping a record of your inner life, what you are feeling and experiencing, what kind of thoughts you are having, what happens to you as you journey to know yourself more fully. You may like to keep your journal each day, or just for when you feel things strongly or have an idea about something.

At times of personal investigation or assessments, and particularly in times of crisis and despair, we often find that something in us tries to express itself in the form of symbol, metaphor or image. Some of us are drawn to write poems or pieces of prose; some write streams of consciousness with no particular process in mind, just letting what comes out flow; some like to doodle or draw, paint or colour what is happening to them.

Whatever form it takes and however bizarre it may seem, don't be put off, but let whatever wants to find form inside your journal. You may not understand it fully at first, but as time goes on, and certainly when you look back on it, it will give you a vital link with your inner world and to whatever meaning you might be seeking.

Working with the imagination

Imaging, visualization, active imagination and body drama

There is no situation to which the creative use of your imagination cannot be applied. We all have this capacity, even though so many people say, 'I can never imagine anything' or, 'I've got no imagination'. To test yourself out, close your eyes for a few minutes and lean back in your chair. Imagine yourself picking up a lemon from your fruit bowl. Place the lemon on a board and take out of your drawer a sharp knife. With the knife cut the lemon in half. Pick up one of the halves and put it in your mouth. Notice what is happening. Is your mouth watering, are your eyes tightening or squinting, is your tongue curling? If it is, and it most probably is, then you have just imagined yourself eating a lemon with full body reaction. There is no lemon in sight, so where did that reaction come from? Imagination!

We have seen throughout this book how negative thinking about ourselves produces negative feelings. We may cope by bottling up our feelings, by avoiding or withdrawal, or by feeling we have to please others all the time. Although we may have many solid environmental reasons for believing the negative image of ourselves (if we were actually told negative things or there was much evidence around for us to believe the negative), such negative thoughts and damaging internal views are perpetuated by our powers of imagination. In the cases of phobic disturbance and anxiety the most infectious negative thought is that 'It will happen again'. This idea is kept in place by the imagination.

Many people who are fearful and seek to avoid their fears have very vivid imaginations. They will tell you, 'Oh I can't do that . . . I'll be sick . . . I'll fall off . . . someone will come after me'. These ideas will often be accompanied by vivid images and pictures of what might happen. The range of our imaginings can be from the fearfulness of school-children taking exams and imagining the worst possible questions to the pathologically jealous husband. Imagination will support our fears and thoughts, however 'faulty' and unrevised.

I think there is also a case for saying that if we do not use our imagination helpfully and creatively it will use us! If we don't value and use the energy force in us it has nowhere to go, and it becomes like the genie in the bottle, bursting out uncontrollably when we least expect or want it. It will rage against restrictions.

I am a great fan of the imagination, which has a poor press except in the world of the arts and music where it is revered and admired. But in terms of everyday human expression people tend to dismiss its potential usefulness and say, 'It's *only* imagination . . . '. Some people even think that it is dangerous and, because it's non-scientific, has no place in medicine or psychology. However, the creative use of harnessing the powers of the imagination for healing body and mind are now being realized through pioneering work with cancer and other serious illnesses.

Let us think again about imagination. It has the power to hold images from years ago which lie hidden, returning only when something triggers them. We have seen how imagining a lemon can make us salivate, we have seen that imagination can recapture the original fear of agoraphobia or the terror of a panic attack. If imagination can do all these things it can also work extremely positively. Mostly, however, we forget to use it because we haven't learned to consider it as a resource, or a technique for replacing negative images with positives ones.

How to develop the powers of the imagination

Take your notebooks and look at the number of images and descriptive words you have used, the number of times you have written, 'I feel like a . . .' or, 'It is like a . . .'. You have created images and are already in the world of the imagination. Allow yourself more of this. When you are out walking, let yourself look at the shapes of the landscape rather than seeking to name trees and plants or count the number of bird species. When people are talking to you, whether on the television or in your life, see if you can find an image for them – something they remind you of, or a shape or colour. When you listen to music, lie on the floor and let the music conjure up images. When you are reading, read fiction, romance, poetry, fairy tales, children's stories, texts that are fun and full of simple wonder, that make you laugh. Getting into the realm of the imagination means getting out of the rational, logical, over-focused way of thinking. When you go to sleep at night, ask yourself for a dream.

How to use the powers of the imagination

Reframing problems through visualization

You will already have used your imagination to create your life story and your diagrams. Choose now one or more of the difficulties you have. If you have identified with the 'doing as others want' trap, imagine yourself in a situation with someone you have always felt you had to please, and imagine yourself saying 'no' to them. Set the scene for yourself – a room, a place – and decorate it in your mind, giving it colour and shape. Choose here and how you will stand or sit, what you will wear. Watch what you do with your hands and feet. Place the other person where you can see their eyes. Make sure that your eye level is either equal or that yours is slightly above. (If we've found earlier that we tend to be always looking up at others, it might be that we always place others above us and ourselves in an inferior position.) Have an easy conversation with this person, speak to them as if you were in charge: say the things you would really like to say, rather than waiting to respond to their needs or questions. Then visualize that they ask you to do something you do not want to do. Smile at them and say, 'I'd love to be able to help out but I really can't at the moment.' Practise it out loud. Say it several times. There will doubtless be many other versions of things you would like to say which you can bring in here. Watch the other person's face. Notice what kind of look or gesture would normally trigger off your placatory response. Say 'no' to this gesture and look. Say it again. Practise it with a real person.

If you identify with the 'I'd rather be on my own' trap, imagine the most fearful situation you can create. Be the observer in this image and take note of all the ingredients. Who is in the image, where it is, what is the nature of the frightening quality, what is going on? Add to it as much as you want. Draw it in your mind with full colour and horror. Remember you are a fly on the wall. When you feel you have understood the full reality of the image from your observer position, prepare yourself to enter the frightening space. Choose a friend or special object, a 'talisman', to accompany you if you wish. Dress yourself for such a fearful journey (some people choose armour, skins, fancy dress, the dress of heroes) or find images for the qualities you would like to have – courage perhaps, or attractiveness, relaxation, humour. Imagine yourself dressed or armed with these attributes, and visualize how you would look. When ready, go forth in the changed image. Remember you are dressed appropriately for the encounter. Let yourself into the part. Do what you have to do. Experience what would be the most useful aspect you could bring back from this image to use in everyday life. Just one thing will help you to begin the change from having to be on your own because of fear.

Perhaps you can see already how useful the art of visualization can be for traps.

Using images

The 'either/or' dilemma gives us two quite specific images to work with. Take the dilemmas you have identified in your life and ponder on them using your imaginal level. See if you can find images, shapes or colours for how you feel at each end of your dilemma. Joanna identified 'bottling up feeling or making a mess' with 'having to give in to others', and with 'having to do what others want', and found that her main dilemma in terms of relating to other people was that she felt she was either a *battering ram* or *modelling clay*. She felt that she had been modelling clay all her life, giving in to others, doing what they wanted. But if she expressed some of her feelings or was assertive in any way, she felt as if she were a battering ram. One week she spontaneously reached a middle position which married the positive value of each pole of her dilemma. Her image and her new position and aim was to be 'like springy steel'.

Once we have realized the images, we need to explore them. There are several ways to do this.

Imaging

Stay with the image in your mind's eye, either sitting or lying down with your eyes closed. Just let the image be there before you and ponder on its shape, colour, size, what it is made of, what, if anything, is around it, the age, sex, function, feeling, description, and every possible detail of the image. Even if you just get a red blob you can still explore: what kind of red; what shape is the blob; is it moving or still; is there anything else around it; does it have a name; does it remind you of anything? Each answer might lead to something else. In each case LET THE IMAGE TELL YOU. Give it time. Do not force it to do anything.

If you are co-counselling someone, just let them stay as long as they can with the image by softly encouraging them: repeating the name or sense of the image in the same voice they used to describe it to you; asking simple questions that will help amplify the image and expand its meaning.

With imaging techniques we may stay just with one image at a time, or we may see where the image wants to take us. We may put two or more images together, either imagining them side by side, or feeling first into the language of one and then moving on to the other, seeing how they may change or what they may need from each other.

Painting and drawing

Images may be anchored by painting or drawing. Keep these as spontaneous and natural as possible. Do not judge your spontaneous drawings as if you were in a class and looking for an exact replica. Many people are upset that their drawings do not represent the richness or vividness of the images they carry inside them, but what we are looking for by anchoring the drawings is a reminder of the nature of our images and their details. Making the paintings or drawings as soon as possible after the encounter with an image (it may be from working with the imagination or from a dream) means that we keep all the detail and intricacies of our experience and later on may wish to interpret or find meaning for them. Sometimes we may not understand the exact nature of an image until later, when something happens and the impact of the image becomes clear. Once we become accustomed to using our images creatively, as part of our lives, we are rewarded by other images and other insights into the potential use and meaning of our images, and we realize that we have inside us a rich resource for future assistance with struggles and difficulties.

As well as painting or drawing we may like to model something in clay or Plasticine, Playdoh, papier mâché or whatever is handy. Drawing and painting are best done on the floor, as if we were playing, using colours freely without constraints. We may also like to use magazine or newspaper pictures to conjure up the images or feelings of what we experience inside. This is not the same thing as using our own images, but sometimes seeing a photograph or picture can trigger or inform us of memories and feelings, and we may prefer to use this method. If you cut out pictures, you might like to stick them onto a paper as a collage or a wheel with different segments to portray the nature of your dilemma or trap.

When you have arrived at the image that suits you, keep it somewhere where you can look at it every day – in your wallet, diary, over the cooker, by the bathroom mirror, etc. Be proud of what you produce. Do not judge it or take notice of anyone else's judgement, save that of the loved ones you respect or who have your interests at heart. Don't cast your pearls before swine!

Exploring traps or dilemmas through the body

Images or feelings may also be enacted by finding a body posture to capture those feelings or images. Stand, sit, lie or get your body into a position that describes your image or your feeling. Stay with the posture and let your body tell you something of the nature of this posture as you hold it.

One woman I know wanted to use this technique to get in touch with the tremendous tension she felt. In letting her body tell her about it by forming itself into the position that would encapsulate the feeling best, she found herself literally trying to climb the wall. She was shocked to find how extreme this was and how evocatively her body behaved when asked to express itself.

Another person who described their dilemma as 'either I'm a doormat or one of the Furies' manoeuvred her body into the position of a doormat and experienced the sensation of everyone walking over her. When asked to describe the nature of the doormat, its colour and shape, she said, 'It's soft and brown and it's got WELCOME written on it'! In contrast, her body position for the Furies involved spinning, spitting, scratching, kicking, hissing and twirling. Her 'Furies' had never really been explored but remained hidden and repressed, and this had frightened her, thus aiding and abetting her doormat side. In this exercise she moved between the two position, spending a few minutes in each. Gradually a third position appeared, as her body spontaneously placed itself straight upright, looking ahead, arms swinging to and fro freely, shoulders back, knees supple. 'I'm ready for action,' she said, 'I can move fast or be still as I wish.' In this third position she felt in control, and in charge of her choices. In the other two positions she had felt trapped, caught, unable to respond in any other way than the limited and extreme nature of the dilemma demanded.

Sometimes we are able to explore how we feel by actually being aware of what our body is doing in different situations. Becoming aware of how we sit or stand when talking to difficult people can be helpful in our appreciation of the extent of our feelings; being aware of how we use our body, either when we are on our own or with others, can help us to examine the feelings that are being expressed unconsciously through the body. A person who is unaware of body language can declare with a sunny smile, 'I had a very happy childhood', while their body is tight, twisted, with arms wrapped around their chest and legs crossed tightly, telling another story altogether.

From this section we have established there are two main ways of using our observation of body language: (1) by a general awareness of what we do with our bodies and what others do; and (2) the direct use of body postures to act out the drama of an image or feeling, to allow us to take on board the full extent of our feelings, and to bring about change. Sometimes the smallest body change, from arms tightly folded when talking about the narrowness of our life, for example, to those same arms opening out widely to embrace something new, can begin an actual change, as what is depicted by the body change is taken into life experience. The woman who got into the position of the doormat never did it again in quite the same welcoming way, nor was she hurled about inside by the Furies. Something memorable always happens when we work directly with the body.

Exploring traps, dilemmas and other problems through objects

Make for yourself a box of small objects of a mixed kind, containing some you like, some you don't like, some to which you feel indifferent –

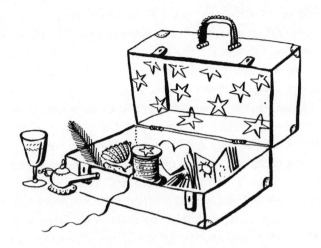

shells, stones, toys, sticks, glass, ornaments, eggs, bits and pieces you have in your room or around your house. Get down on the floor, either on your own or with your co-counsellor (this is great fun either to do alone or to help someone with). Clear a space for the objects you have chosen. Decide which trap, dilemma, decision, family scene or relationship struggle you wish to depict. Choose first an object for yourself, to represent you. Don't think too hard, just go for something you really respond to that will stand for you as you are now (or perhaps as you were in the past, if you are depicting a past situation). Hold your own object for a while and get the feel of it; get to know it well. When you are ready place it in the centre of your space on the floor. Next take an object to represent one of the people in your current drama. That could be father, mother, uncle, aunt, sister, brother, friend, colleague, neighbour, animal – anyone you wish. After you have chosen the object, say a little about why you have chosen it for this person. If you don't know as yet, this might become clear as you go on with the drama.

Go on choosing objects until you have one for everyone you intend to include. Place each one on the floor as you imagine them to be currently in your life, or as they were in the scene you are recapturing. Notice the spaces between each one and ponder on what they might mean. If some are close, how close are they? Notice if some block others in their closeness. If others seem far apart, ponder on this and the nature of the apartness. If you are depicting a scene from your past, for when you and your siblings were together, you might like to get the feel of what happened when the scene changed, as when someone left home or went into hospital, or when someone new entered. When you do this allow the objects to show you their picture, let the objects themselves take on the drama and give you the impact of what happens rather than concentrating upon which object is which person.

It is quite fantastic what strong feelings this exercise can evoke when the objects are allowed to unfold their story. For example, if you have chosen objects of similar size and then a huge one is suddenly introduced; if the objects in one group are of a certain material and when one leaves that material is changed or becomes vulnerable; if there are distinct groups of very different substances; if, in order to communicate with certain members, you have to make huge leaps across the floor. Everything that happens in terms of the objects is useful in portraying family structures: pairs and triangles; sizes and shapes; who is easy to approach and who isn't; what is needed in terms of change or movement; what needs to happen for one object to reach another; how it feels for the rock that is your father to approach the tiny shell that is your sister or the piece of string that is wrapped around your uncle.

Spend no more than half an hour with the objects. This is a powerful exercise. Let it inform you, and give you an idea of how you would like the patterns of things to be in your own life.

Writing letters you never send

This is useful when there are many things left unsaid to people who are perhaps dead or unapproachable. Start the letter, 'Dead Mum . . .' or whoever you wish to write to. Then begin with something of what you feel. For example, 'I am writing to you because I could never find the words to say what you meant to me', or 'All my life I feel you have put me down'. Go on into the letter and let out all the feelings you have never dared embrace. Writes as if your heart would burst, that your aches, longing, griefs are so full they would spill over. Write as if this were your last chance fully to express what that person has meant to you or brought out in your life. Do not flinch from any word or image that you use. Do not let guilt get in the way, or any moralizing about blame or fairness or pride. You will never send this letter, but you need to make it as if you were having a vibrant conversation with a living person. In Chapter 6, 'Writing our life story' we read Stephanie's story. Here is the letter she wrote to her father:

Dear Dad,

I tried to feel what life would have been without you; it was unimaginable except for the feeling of an immense weight lifting from me. Life without that burden. When I tried to imagine life without my mum, I could imagine some other good woman looking after me well enough.

I tried to think of an image to describe how it felt to be your daughter. What came to mind was that when I was small, over a period of time you slit me open, placed a box of maggots between my heart and my stomach and slowly and deliberately sewed the scar away. Your living legacy was that I could never again feel peace, goodness, satisfactions – just rottenness at the core. That shocks me. It is like hating and blaming my own limb to hate and criticize you. You seem old and often very pathetic, and nothing at all to do with the person who came and planted the maggots. I feel very sorry for you, but it becomes confused with feeling sorry for myself.

I do feel like I have been tortured enough, and I would like you to let me go now please. You and Mum tut tut about the relationships with men that I form, but each is modelled on the way things were with you. I had to learn to trust and love somebody who hated parts of me, loathed others, merely criticized most and demanded that I thrive and flourish and serve their every need.

I was at Uncle Jack's house lately. He thinks you have been a pretty dreadful father to me. I was there for an evening and he wanted to do something nice for me. He offered me a drink and brought me a cup of coffee – no strings. It made him feel good because he had done a nice thing. It made me cry, because in twenty-seven years my own father has never done such a simple act of kindness for me.

Guilt and mixed feelings apart, I think that I have to tell you that you have been a complete bastard. It fills me with an anger which I transfer to many people, and in particular all of the men I meet. Every skill you gave me you used against me; you tutored my brain, then devoted yourself to undermining my intelligence. I have many an amusing story to tell on these subjects; if someone is treating me badly I can't call you in to protect me because you would agree with them, etc. But the humour is a thin veneer on top of hate and anger.

Such a small and pathetic man, not content with losing his own chance of happiness and satisfaction, you had to have mine too. I would like to destroy you. I would like to spit all that hatred back at you. Strange that I should think you smaller and more pathetic than your own child. Strange that I should believe that even a fraction of the hatred you gave to me could destroy you. And you had my mum completely devoted to salving your every need from the moment you met aged fifteen. She has become quite a contortionist to be able to constantly feed your every need and still remember to keep herself alive.

Life with you has been like living in a minefield. Allan picked his way through first, but you set a different pattern for me and threw in a few booby traps for good measure. Jane made notes and tiptoed round the edge. They have got to the other side now, but I find I am still searching for mines years after the fight is supposed to be over.

I wish I had had a different father. I hope I can trust enough to allow the manly half of the human race to make some positive contribution to me and my life.

Monitoring your progress with problems and aims

Make yourself a chart like the one in Figure 16. Use this rating chart containing your problems and aims every day. Keep it in your diary or pocketbook so that each day you can at least glance at it to remind yourself particularly of the aims. Once a week have a concentrated look at the chart, and mark on it how much the aims have altered, if at all. There are lines for 'no change'; 'better' and 'worse', and you will need to mark where you feel you are in terms of your aim according to these markings. As the weeks progress your marks will form a graph. Some weeks will be better and others worse. When you mark the rating down one week be sure to understand why that is, what happened to put you off your aim and perhaps led to your being caught up in an old pattern. Don't be discouraged, but use the information to help you understand your need for change, and let yourself have some compassion for the struggle this part of you may well be having. Sometimes our progress with one aim drops as others are achieved, because we are testing out traps and snags. We may well feel 'snagged' by getting more assertive or stronger in some aspect. Marking this on your chart will help to highlight these problem areas and to focus upon them. Do not judge how you are doing or be tempted to mark all the ratings as high as possible. Just stay with a realistic view of how things are. Make sure that the aims you have given yourself *are* realistic. If you begin with the more straightforward aims, such as getting out of the traps and becoming more assertive, you will be encouraged to challenge some of the more

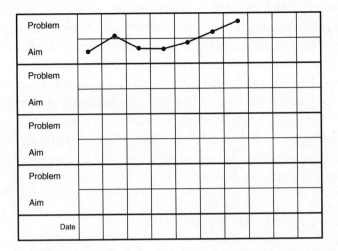

Figure 16 Monitoring your progress

difficult problems, like fear of dependency, sudden mood swings and more embedded difficulties with anxiety or physical symptoms.

Change is best consolidated if achieved slowly and thoroughly. Take your time, quietly focusing upon your task. A major change may already be happening, that of self-reflection and self-observation. This change will already be bearing fruit. Once you have begun to accomplish small changes you might like to make a new chart, including other problems or a more detailed version of your existing problems and difficulties.

Dreams

> He dreamed of an open window
> A vagina, said his psychiatrist.
> Your divorce, said his mistress.
> Suicide, said an ominous voice inside him.
> It means you should close the window
> or you'll catch cold, said his mother.
> His wife said nothing.
> He dared not tell her
> such a
> dangerous dream.
>
> 'The dream' by Felix Pollak

213

Dreams are the language of the unconscious, a rich symphony of yet undiscovered material which reach the daylight of consciousness through their imagery, motif, story, feeling and transcendence. We all dream every night, but not all dreams are remembered. When an important dream occurs we wake up and we know that something has happened. The feeling evoked by a dream can stay with us throughout the day and beyond, and is informing us about itself so that we can follow it through. Dreams contain messages and insights that help our daily journeying and development. They offer a balancing influence upon consciousness by making us aware of our unconscious longings, symbols and unfinished business.

How to work with our dreams

Keep a dream notebook to record your dreams. Write them down as soon as you wake, even if it is in the middle of the night. If a dream wakes you it is important. If you go back to sleep thinking you will record it in the morning, it will slip back into the unconscious and will be lost for that time. If the message conveyed by a dream is important it will come again, but we need to listen for the dream messages for they keep us alive psychologically and help to restore balance and make us whole.

When you have written your dream down, ponder on it, on its images, motifs, its general shape. Note the feeling of the dream. Notice the time and place in the dream – current time or past time, your age if you are represented in the dream. Note the time of day and consider its meaning. Morning or afternoon, evening or night.

The most important question when pondering on your dream is: what does this mean to me? If you appear as age seventeen in your dream and you are in fact thirty-five, what aspect of your seventeen-year-old self is being represented in the dream? What was this time about for you? What does it remind you of? Does the figure seventeen hold any other significance? What does the memory or meaning of being seventeen mean for your life as it is now? Why are you now having to think back to when you were seventeen? It is helpful in the amplification of your dream if this approach is followed for all other aspects, symbols or images of your dream. If there is a house in your dream, what kind of house is it – colour, shape, size? Is it familiar? What country or place does it remind you of? Where are you, the dreamer, in relation to the house?

Another important aspect of amplifying your dream is to consider the order of events in the dream. There is no linear time as we know it in dreaming, and dreams know nothing of death as we understand it as mortals. Death in a dream is a symbolic death and may be interpreted on many different levels – as an ending, a transformation, a dying off, a falling away, as the death of a particular aspect of your life. Look closely at the order of the events in your dream and see if you can understand some of the links between sequences, events or images. For example: 'In the dream an old lady rides a bicycle down a steep hill. At the bottom of the hill she is stopped abruptly by a small girl bearing a bunch of flowers. She wants to keep going, to use her downward speed to help her gain impetus to ride up the hill, but has to accept the flowers from the child first. She then begins her difficult ascent up the hill, but as she is going more slowly she sees the view of the fields more closely.' The order of the dream indicates that the old woman (an aspect of the dreamer) has to curb her irritation to stay with the child, and in doing so the dream shows how she gets another view of the fields as she travels on her way. The event of the child and the flowers precedes the climb and has to be encountered before the nature of the climb can be revealed.

Sometimes dreams come in series, and the series may occur all in one night. In these cases the series forms one whole dream which is trying to communicate a theme, a development and an idea over a number of dreams. This is one way in which the psyche alerts us to an unconscious process that is ready to be made conscious.

Dreams may produce images which are frightening, startling or powerful and which bear no resemblance to anything we know rationally. When this occurs, what is hidden in the image that is of importance to us wants very much to be noticed and understood before incorporation into our everyday living. Draw, paint or act out the nature of your dream figure, and share it with another person if you feel the dream content to be too disturbing or worrying. Although the figure in the dream may represent something you don't like, once explored and made conscious the figure and what it represents is never so frightening or overwhelming.

If you become interested in your dreams and in knowing more about them and how to work with them in your life, you may be helped by reading any of the books listed on pages 254–8. Taking our dreams seriously and learning how to weave their wise and eerie notes into the fabric of our life can be an ever-enriching, enlightening as well as restoring and confirmative experience.

Assertion and aggression

Whenever we change and revise old patterns of thinking and behaviour, inevitably we need to be more assertive about our ideas, thoughts, needs, wants and desires. We can easily get trapped into confusing assertion with aggression and thus hold back from expressing ourselves, and this can impede the process of change. You may be well aware already, having got this far, that it is difficult for you to be assertive, and this may indicate a deeper difficulty tied up with some of the traps and dilemmas you have identified with. Sometimes we feel that if we express ourselves assertively, if we state our needs or thoughts clearly, then we are being aggressive, and this will lead to our hurting others or being seen as too 'pushy'. If we avoid being assertive out of this unrevised belief, it may be that others will tend to ignore or take us for granted, because *they* actually do not know what we think or feel. Then, when we feel put upon or ignored, we can become childishly angry, hurt and sore, or be tempted to sulk, withdraw or have a tantrum, bursting out with a built-up anger that is out of proportion to the situation.

For all of us, being assertive is perfectly acceptable. People who do not respect our rights as human beings must either be stood up to or left out of our life. Learning the art of assertion may be an important part of your change. Once you realize this is a skill you lack and which you need to learn, there are many places where this can be achieved and practised. Joining a group or class to practise the art of assertion can really help to consolidate the changes you may wish to make. Having a living person or group to whom one practises saying 'no', or saying what one thinks, or with whom one tests out the new-found ideas or strengths is a potent and lasting way of keeping hold of change.

Part 5
Changing Within a Relationship

One of the secrets of equable marriage is to accept one's partner for the person he or she is. Each can have only what the other has to offer. Expecting more leads to frustration and disappointment.

Susan Needham
London Marriage Guidance Council

Relationships *always* bring our individual procedures to a head. Whether they are relationships with people at work, in groups, within our families or with friends. And intimate relationships are most likely to press us on the core pain we carry: on our fears associated with getting close, feeling dependent or needy, our fear or rejection or abandonment, of feeling jealous and envious. It's possible, through revision of our individual procedures and the way these interact with those of our partners, to elicit changes that free us to enjoy relating.

It seems too, that collectively we need to make relationships with others in a clearer way. Duty, religious belief, social tradition or just love are not enough to sustain relationships through the current times in which we live, and the basis upon which people live together must meet a new challenge. The increasing divorce rate and the number of children born outside marriage, together with a sense that the family has failed, points to a human struggle about relating. While this book will not debate political or sociological issues, Cognitive Analytic Psychology can contribute ideas about how we might establish more flexible relationships with ourselves and with others. By understanding our core pain, our control patterns and our reciprocal roles, we change how we become entangled or enmeshed with others' core pain and roles.

Idealization and reality in relationships

In his book *Love is Never Enough*, Aaron Beck writes about how marriage or intimate relationships differ from other relationships. He describes how the intensity of living with someone fuels dormant longings for unconditional love, loyalty and support, and sets up expectations and desires. These are often based on an idealized image of love and acceptance. Idealization is present in every hope and is useful for initiation, but it can set up impossible and unrealistic standards that cannot be met by another person. People with a history of early losses or poor bonding sometimes develop an over-idealized image of how relationships should be in order to compensate. While dreaming about this imaginative, 'happy ever after' world helps us to cope with a miserable home life, it cannot serve as a basis for relationships with others. When there is an over-idealized idea of how relationships 'should' be, whatever a partner does or does not do tends to be judged against a variety of these expectations or desires. Relationships can then become stuck, as each individual blames the other for their disappointment and sense of failure. And relationships can become blocked when each person carries one end of the reciprocal role and there is no room for flexibility. The relationship then remains at this superficial level and the deeper layers of potential within the couple cannot be reached. Relationships can only be truly satisfying when we learn to live with the other flesh and blood person we are not trying to reform.

Falling in love and sexual attraction are only the initial (but important!) triggers that draw two people together. *How* two people live together and sustain differences and difficulties is a test of maturity, generosity, endurance and humour. If we remain individually limited in our thinking and movement, we lack the flexibility required to dance in time with another, perhaps very different, person. Revising individual beliefs when they are redundant or damaging can be the beginning of allowing a relationship to flourish.

We have seen in Chapter 3 how the internal core pain from our childhood is carried by the internalized child self and maintained by both the learned procedures based on old beliefs and by the internalized adult or other. Thus it's easy to understand how, until revised, we may choose partners from our internalized child self who confirm the old beliefs of that child self and maintain the core pain. Someone with a crushed child self who expects a conditional other will tend to be drawn to someone whose attitude will confirm this; or, they will tend to see only the conditional response in the other, and react to this in the old way. Even when there is goodness between two people it can be undermined by these old, now outdated procedures. Someone with an over-idealized view of relationships who was neglected as a child will long for fusion and closeness, and yet at the same time fear being abandoned. They may set up impossible demands which force their partner to flee, so confirming their belief that it is not worth getting close because everyone always neglects or leaves you in the end. What needs revision is the procedure for dealing with deprivation. Instead of longing for fusion or perfect care, the internalized child self needs to be recognized and cared for first, so that we do not expect this hunger to be met totally by another. The core procedures that dominate relationships and maintain pain need to be revised together.

We have seen many other patterns of relating throughout this book. Someone who, when close to another person, becomes 'mother' or 'father' taking care and control of the other and denying their own needs, only to feel used and lonely. We have seen how the fear of loss of control can lead someone to seek to take charge of every interaction, creating a suffocating atmosphere where sooner or later one person will either explode or hit out, so establishing the very chaos the control pattern was designed to avoid.

Suggestions for couples

This section is for couples who are concerned about their interaction with each other and wish to make changes.

Read through Chapter 3, 'Problems and Dilemmas Within Relationships'. Make your own individual chart for reciprocal roles. It might help to notice how you feel with your partner at certain times when things seem to go wrong. Are you feeling like a crushed child or a furious parent? A critical carer who can only be martyred or a rebellious infant who wants to stamp its feet and run away?

Keep a journal individually (without reference to the other), for one week, of the times in which you have been pressed on a core pain place, or pushed into that bottom-line 'as if' core pain statement. Try not to make assumptions or judgements, but simply keep a record.

Having read through the chapters on traps, dilemmas and snags, write down which of these apply to you, and which procedures for coping with core pain are most dominant in your life.

Complete your examination of traps, dilemmas and snags by predicting which your partner would identify. Then look together at how each of you see the other, and how this differs from your individual identification of traps, dilemmas and snags.

As part of gathering information, you might also like to go back in time and make a note of the qualities that attracted you to your partner in the first place. Qualities such as spontaneity, warmth, fun, humour, caring, depth, perception, strength, intelligence. What were you hoping for from these qualities? Having made this note, make another column to record how you feel about these qualities now. If they seem to have changed, ponder on this. Sometimes when we are drawn to certain qualities in a person it is both because we like and respond to those qualities, and also because he want to develop them in ourselves.

Drawn to opposites: Frances and Mike

Frances, an only child, grew up in a very serious household. When she met Mike, who came from a large, noisy, fun-loving family, she was immediately attracted to what she had not experienced. For Frances, living with Mike was both a rebellion against her serious parents, who thought Mike a renegade and drop out, and a challenge to her own learned seriousness. She hoped that Mike would help to heal her loneliness and allow her to expand her spontaneity. While this was ultimately a healthy option for her, in their first years she found herself being snagged by feelings of guilt for choosing such a different life from her aloof parents, as if her fun was at their expense. She had visions of their lonely existence in front of the one-ringed gas fire while she was dancing the night away. This made her anxious, but she dared not confide in Mike because she did not want to spoil their enjoyment. She began to have panic attacks and to fear going out, returning instead to lying alone in bed and to the idea that she was not, after all, meant to go out and enjoy herself. A revision of her 'magical guilt', and speaking to Mike and her parents about the reality of their lives, helped her to begin to claim the life that she had chosen.

Drawn to similarities: Bill and Emily

Bill chose Emily because she was just like his mother. Bill hated change, which he saw as rocking the boat. He wanted someone to be there for him when he came home from work, who would look after him and serve his needs. For Emily, who came from a rather cold background where she had had to placate in order to feel a sense of worth, it was heaven to be so wanted. But over time, because the glue that bound them together was based on earlier needs, they began to come unstuck. Bill found Emily boring and demanding – just like his mother in the *bad* sense. And Emily found his need of her oppressive and began to have angry outbursts and tantrums. She felt that he never listened to her but was always demanding, and she started to dream of being alone, of leaving, or of having an affair with someone she was attracted to at work.

If each set of individual procedures is locked together unhelpfully, without revision, the relationship can reach crisis point where the only solution seems to be to get out. This does not have to be so.

Hidden complementarities: Frank and Maggie

Frank and Maggie find it difficult to live together without continual angry rows, when things get said which are regretted only to be used as fuel for the next argument. They have separated several times, but found it equally difficult to live apart. Figure 17 is a diagram of how their relationship moved from initial closeness to anger, separation, and then loneliness and reconciliation.

Frank and Maggie had actually separated when they first came to see me, and saw our meeting as a last-ditch attempt to save the relationship, although both were pessimistic, and both were deeply entrenched in their survival modes. Maggie was frightened, shaking and withdrawn; Frank aloof, controlled, calm, but his face white and muscles tense. By the time we had worked on their individual stories they had got together again and were both moved when each read out their story to the other.

In the early days they worked by doing simple self-monitorings. Frank was to monitor each occasion when thought, 'I've had enough, this is terrible, I'm getting out'; similarly, Maggie was to monitor the

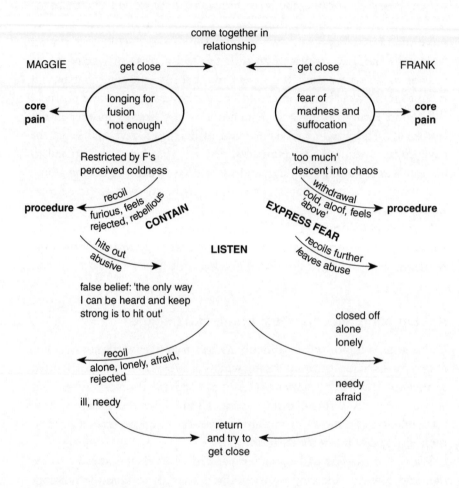

Figure 17 Frank and Maggie's relationship trap

times she thought, 'I want more, this isn't enough, this isn't how it *should* be'. It appeared as if these thoughts developed into a compulsion to act which, when followed through, served to keep the trap going. They found it very difficult to do this, and to contain the space this way of thinking created between them. But as they gradually came to understand more of the other's history and to allow for each other's fragility, they were able to hold on to the space long enough to listen, and later to have a discussion. To this end, they used their tape recorder to record conversations, later setting aside time together to listen to what had transpired between them. They were frequently shocked and moved by what they heard.

Frank and Maggie in therapy

This is what I wrote and then read aloud to Frank and Maggie:

The three of us agreed to look afresh at the situation within your marriage, which operated to make it difficult to live together or apart. You had been in different therapies, both individually and together, in a quest to find answers to the dilemmas you both face as a couple. A great deal of perseverance, time and effort has gone into this quest, perhaps indicating a desire to find a way to be together more harmoniously, and perhaps out of a yet not understood love for each other.

The individual reformulations (life stories) gained over three sessions, reveal similarities. You are both intelligent people with damaged siblings. There is considerable self-negation and disappointment in all four parents' lives. 'Magical guilt' is strong in both of your lives. You both learned not to appear too well or happy. Magical guilt presupposes that we have received something good at another's expense, and that if we have what we want later on in life someone else will be damaged.

In Maggie's case, her unconscious involvement with self-sabotage revealed itself immediately in terms of the appointments we made, and that it took us five arranged appointments to result in three actual sessions. It was 'as if' something operated in Maggie's life to prevent her from getting help, fulfil obligations or grow and become happier and more fulfilled. Maggie has recognized how she follows patterns of depriving and punishing herself in order to feel good about herself, and talked about the fact that she doesn't dress as well as she might because she feels she doesn't deserve it. All good things, because they make her feel 'bad' and guilty, have to be either denied or demolished in order to fulfil the unconscious pull of self-sabotage. Maggie's self-sabotage feels at its heaviest when it links in with the part of Frank she sees as 'Superman': superior, clever, successful, controlled and better than herself. Because her antennae are tuned to expect personal demolishment and criticism, it gets set up unconsciously, again confirming the myth of magical guilt. And when this happens, and she feels criticized or punished, she falls back on survival tactics, becoming either rebellious and aggressive or passive, ill and in need of care.

Self-sabotage in Frank's life seems to operate in the way he does not feel free to express himself emotionally or with any vulnerability, and in the fact that he feels compelled to 'walk on eggshells' for fear of triggering Maggie's wrath or abuse. Early in his life, control, success and intellect were very important, and emotion and feeling were associated with chaos and madness. His professional life is successful and free of chaos. But in personal relationships there is another challenge. He was possibly drawn to Maggie because it would enable him to become more in touch and comfortable with a whole range of feelings. At difficult times he experiences emotional inertia and feels stuck, putting up with unpleasantness and appearing cold and unresponsive, or, more recently, allowing anger to surface.

Magical guilt carries with it the fury and rage at the restrictions it imposes. Each of you offers the other a vehicle for this magical guilt. Freeing yourselves individually from this would mean that it would not have to be played out in the drama of marriage.

The other area that links you together negatively at present is the struggle around closeness and intimacy. It seems as if you have opposite ideas, and idealized ideas of what being close means. For Frank, closeness is self-contained and intellectual, and anything else feels suffocating and frightening, out of control. For Maggie, closeness is fusion, being constantly together, contained and safe, perhaps reflecting an inner longing to be held in a complete, symbiotic way. If you keep holding on to these polarized ideas your relationship will be a constant battle. Perhaps if you question the validity of these ideals and work towards making them less absolute, you could find a reasonable place from which to be close to each other. Freeing yourselves from magical guilt would mean that you could allow for, and maintain, good feelings and closeness, without having to sabotage it by all the 'as ifs' we have mentioned.

This is what Frank and Maggie wrote in return:

What we've taken home

We are learning that each of us carries substantial burdens from the past, which result in 'snags'. For example, for different reasons, each of us has difficulty with intimacy. Rage and frustration always get in the way of our being close. We are each well advised to make the effort to accept the reality and validity of these snags in the other, even though we may not always like the resulting behaviour. To deny and reject these personal characteristics in the other is futile. It also devalues the other person and therefore causes unhappiness.

So, we need ways to cope. We must learn to use them effectively. First, we can understand them and empathize. We can also gracefully fall back and use and cede space. Apartness need not be rejection, and sometimes can be constructive.

On top of this, we realize that each of us has difficulty delivering on some of the other's primary needs. These were detailed by Liz in one of her reformulation documents. Just sensitizing ourselves to this reality is a step forward. We must also think constructively and take more initiatives.

Finally, it should be said that our continuing resolve and application shows that we love and need one another. But it's a rocky, non-placid road that we are gradually learning to travel. The good times are worth it.

Frank and Maggie are still struggling to listen to and contain the feelings produced by their very different responses to getting close. Although their relationship is not easy, they are still together, and there are some good times which make the effort feel worthwhile.

Sean and Mary

Sean and Mary sought help as a couple because of the painful rows which threatened their relationship. Their dreadful quarrels seemed to develop a life of their own and escalate out of control. The each began to look at their individual traps, dilemmas and snags, and kept a record of exactly what happened, what they were thinking, what was said, and when they had a row.

Sean's early experience was of a critical father, before whom he felt inadequate. Mary felt that Sean constantly criticized the way she did things. Her own pattern was to take the blame for any disagreements. After one of their rows, each drew up their own diagram (see Figures 18a and b).

One row occurred when they were laughing and joking, and about to make love. Mary said something which she thought was very funny but which had a dramatic effect: Sean turned away, seemed to lose all interest and became very angry. Mary became upset, and very soon they were deep into a conflict from which they could not extricate themselves. When Mary had made her jokey remark Sean had experienced her as the critical and contemptuous castrating father. For Mary, Sean's withdrawal was devastating. She needed desperately to please in order

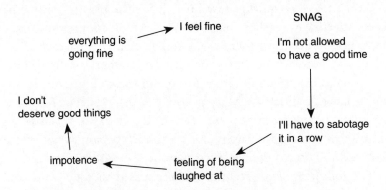

Figure 18a Sean's dilemma diagram

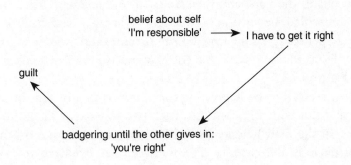

Figure 18b Sean's trap diagram

not to be rejected. She took the blame for the row and badgered Sean to tell her what she had done. This only increased Sean's feeling that he was being harried and put down, and that he must give in to Mary even though he did not agree with her. Following the row, and Mary's appropriation of the high moral ground, Sean withdrew, which left Mary feeling frightened and abandoned, just as she had experienced as a child.

Sean and Mary quickly saw how their responses to each other had been affected by earlier maladaptive ways of communicating, which were now preventing them from seeing each other clearly. For Sean, Mary had become the castrating, rejecting father; and for Mary, Sean represented the rejecting father for whom she could never do anything right. It was a shock for Mary to discover that Sean's perceptions were entirely different from her own. One of the values of working together in this way is the opportunity it gives to each person to hear the other's side and to witness their learned patterns of response.

The following is an account of the focused therapy Sean and Mary had with two cognitive analytic therapists.

The previous hypotheses of Sean and Mary's traps and dilemmas were given added confirmation during the following session. Once again they had had a row which had lingered on in a desultory fashion. It was as though Mary had to keep picking at Sean in an attempt to put things right, trying at the same time to do and be what she thought he wanted of her, and in the process ignoring what she wanted. Sean, unaware of Mary's needs and feeling only a sense of being smothered and of her underlying withholding of approval, retreated behind his paper resigned to the fact that the situation could not be resolved. Later they decided to go out to the park and then on to an AA meeting. This, however, only intensified the tension between them, because Sean had to wait for Mary to get ready, all the time becoming more and more irritated at the delay. From this we were able to tease out the trap that Mary was in (see Figure 19a).

What seemed to be happening for Sean was that he felt, once again, he could not win. This brought back two important memories of his father. In the first, he and his father were staying with a much loved, jovial uncle in the country. The two men had arranged to go somewhere. Sean's father, up and ready early, stood in the middle of the room, jingling his keys and almost bursting with irritation at his brother who was taking his time putting on his boots, completely unconcerned by the other's impatience. Clearly, in the incident with Mary it was Sean who had become the irritated, impatient father, while Mary had assumed the role of the laid-back, disorganized uncle.

The second memory involved Sean's desire to become a car mechanic. His father, however, had wanted him to have a more respectable, higher

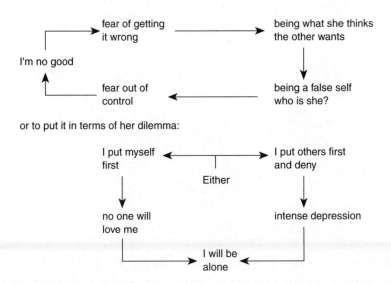

Figure 19a Mary's trap diagram

status career in management. Unable to go against his father and choose what he wanted to do, but equally reluctant to go along with his father, Sean fell between two stools and ended up in a series of jobs where he did just enough to get by. It was as though if he were to succeed, particularly at something his father disapproved of, he would incur not only his father's envy but also his anger. On the other hand, if he failed he risked his father's contempt. It seemed as though the only course was simply to get by. This was seen not only in his work but in his behaviour at home. He would start something – putting up shelves, decorating etc. – have piles of wood all over the flat, and then leave the jobs half-done, a source of irritation to Mary and incomprehension to them both. We were able to see here how the memory of his father once again seemed to be intruding (see Figure 19b).

In the fourth session we linked their responses to the relationship between them to possible past modes of behaviour. For example, in response to the first trap, avoidance, Mary felt responsible for Sean and for the possibility that they might split up, so she had to prevent this by trying to do what he wanted. This had parallels with her earlier life, when she had needed to be both in control of her siblings and respon-

231

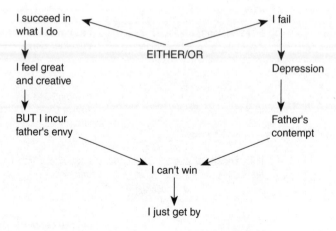

Figure 19b Sean's trap diagram

sible for their welfare, particularly after her mother died.

With Sean, his fear of standing up to his father leads to a self-fulfilling prophecy that he is no good, followed by inevitable depression. What became very clear was that his fear of succeeding in his relationship with Mary stemmed from his conviction that he must pay for success, and so he has to sabotage it.

Both Sean and Mary were very afraid of something within them that seemed out of their control. Sean's other procedures were his avoidance of his feelings about partings and loss, and his destruction of his creativity, which he longed to enjoy. For Mary we highlighted her need always to take responsibility for others' feelings, and her pattern of being unable to value, and thereby destroying, her creativity.

The nub of the work over sessions 6–15 focused on analysing together any rows they had had during the week, and seeing where their individual false beliefs got tangled up with the other's in these quarrels. Sean and Mary became very good at this, which gave them a sense of control that they had never experienced before. The weekly sessions became both a safe place to defuse explosive feelings held about the other, and a place to learn techniques to take with them for the future. Both Mary and Sean liked the idea of seeing their often repeated procedures caught on paper for them to refer to, and would regularly point out where they saw themselves as being on their diagrams. Sean put it this way, 'It's like opening a book and seeing all the stuff in my head laid out plain on the page. I can see how all my life I have got into the same patterns.'

In the early and middle weeks of our work the reported rows were fierce and felt catastrophic, but it was exciting to see how quickly Sean and Mary began to recognize patterns from childhood in their behaviour. Both came to see how their fathers' voices chimed in on them so often and stopped them from being themselves and expressing their spontaneity. In session eight, Mary talked about her struggle to confront her daughter's unjust and hurtful behaviour in saying things about her to a third party that were untrue. We saw her caught in the now familiar dilemma (see Figure 19c).

She was able to see that the exit here was to hold on to the right to her own feelings, and to express them. Sean witnessed her struggle with this problem and was able to be protective and supportive in a helpful way. At the end of session eight we suggested each of them compose a description of themselves, as if written by a loving friend. Mary, we found, was able to really enter into this and present herself as the warm, ebullient person she is, but Sean found it hard to see himself in a favourable light and could only come up with a description of how he would like to be. This brought home to Sean how hard it was for him to be appreciative of himself. His father's critical voice was pervasive.

In the middle of our work, in session nine, there was a big row that

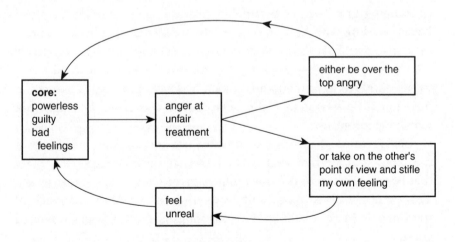

Figure 19c Mary's diagram of Sean's false beliefs

seemed to be connected with their feelings about the therapy coming to an end. Apparently they felt they were not getting enough from us, and were taking out their anger about this on each other. Mary said she had left the last session without feeling the closeness to Sean that she usually experienced at the end of a session. She felt let down, and this was transferred onto Sean. She said Sean seemed depressed, and in swung her need to jolly him out of it: if he were down, it must be her fault (as with her parents when she was a child). She then felt guilty and that Sean was critical of her (when in actual fact he did not feel that at all at the time). It was clear to see how plugged in to each other's moods Mary and Sean had become. They could see this and were able to identify the points at which they had each pinned their own feelings on the other.

A key issue for Sean came up at this time. Mary was bringing to the sessions her painful feelings at the death of a close friend, which in turn resonated a whole untouched area of feelings about the death of her father. She was able to express her rage and hurt forcefully, and explore some key issues about the rejection by her sister and mother. This was so hard for Sean to witness, as his pattern has always been to swallow feelings about loss and endings. He was surly and irritated at Mary's outpouring of feelings of grief at the death, and by the fear, anger and hurt she displayed at the thought of losing us. Sean was able to say it frightened him. We noticed at this point that his false belief charts showed that no progress had been made on changing his usual pattern of avoiding grief, so this became an area of focus. We realized we had been colluding with him on this. As the weeks went on he was able to make two significant steps in dealing with this problem: (1) to actually tell his son, when he was leaving to return to Ireland, how hard it was to say goodbye to him and how much he loved him, and (2) to tell us how much he would miss the sessions and was afraid he might not manage without us.

Another area that Sean confronted in the middle sessions was the child part of him that needed constant reassurance from Mary that he was allowed to do something (e.g. watch football on television). This pattern worked quite well between Sean and Mary for much of the time, as Mary would be the reassuring mother to Sean's reassured child.

At this point the therapists sketched the following diagrams.

Problems

We think that you quite often feel uncertain of yourself, expecting to be found unworthy, not good enough, or to be humiliated (father's voice) so when you do find happiness (as with Mary) you are anxious and almost expecting things to go wrong and your good potent feelings not to last. For example you are often expecting rows will blow your relationship apart.

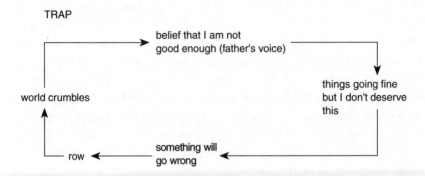

TRAP

Figure 20a Therapists' diagram of Sean's false beliefs

EXIT. Argue with the voice that tells you you are not good enough. Be aware that you expect to be humiliated and choosing the right moment, talk to your partner about your feelings

Perhaps Sean you feel caught in a kind of inertia wanting to succeed in your own individual way, but not ever getting to do what it is you want to do. We feel the stalemate your father put you in may still be operating.

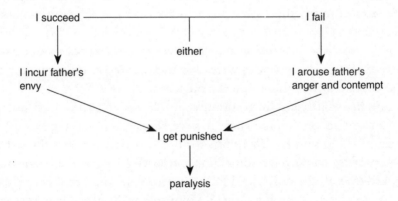

DILEMMA

Figure 20b Therapists' diagram of Sean's dilemma

EXIT Perhaps to experiment with planning and carrying out your own individual goals.

235

At times, however, his need would exceed Mary's ability to keep giving, and we traced the rows that ensued. Yet another pattern for Sean was his jealous and rivalrous feelings when Mary paid attention to others. (She was a sponsor for other AA members.) They would often phone, and she would spend considerable time talking to them, sometimes adopting what Sean called a flirtatious manner. He would then become sullen and withdrawn, which would in turn evoke Mary's need to take responsibility for his feelings and her sense of guilt – his moodiness was her fault. Both were able to recognize this pattern, as well as the way in which Mary's attention to others evoked the insecure jealous child who was afraid of rejection in Sean. These feelings also came out in a dream Sean brought to the session at this time. He dreamed he was on a coach sitting beside Mary who was making love with the man next to her. In the dream Sean went off and sat by himself away from Mary.

A breakthrough came in another session over the escalation issue. There had been a small row over a football match. Sean and Mary had both been watching the game on television. Mary left the room to do something during a break for advertisements, but Sean failed to call her when the match started again. The reason for jubilation was that Mary, rather than nursing her anger and allowing it to swell inside with a kind of masochistic pleasure, was able to let go and the row did not escalate. We all four felt triumphant at this (see figures 20c and d).

Another issue that surfaced at this time was that of differences. We all noticed and discussed how different were Sean's and Mary's patterns of response to situations. Mary tended to feel anxious and insecure if Sean saw things differently from her – for example, if he took an opposing view to her at an AA meeting – and could see how this was linked to the hurt she had felt as a child whenever differences arose between her parents. She and Sean were able to say, 'We are different, and it is acceptable to be different, to be ourselves'.

In the twelfth and thirteenth sessions the focus turned particularly to Sean's sense of despondency at never finishing anything creative he planned. He said he felt things would be better between himself and Mary if he could have something purposeful to do. We laughed and joked over all the unfinished DIY jobs, the half-completed bed. He was able to clearly hear his father's voice telling him nothing was good enough. The exit from this snag was 'to have a go', he said.

The last four sessions were full of feelings about the ending and

We suggest that these feelings lead you into the following traps and dilemmas:

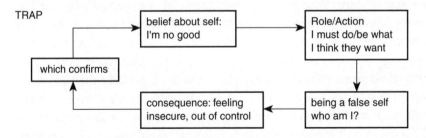

Figure 20c Therapists' diagram of Mary's trap

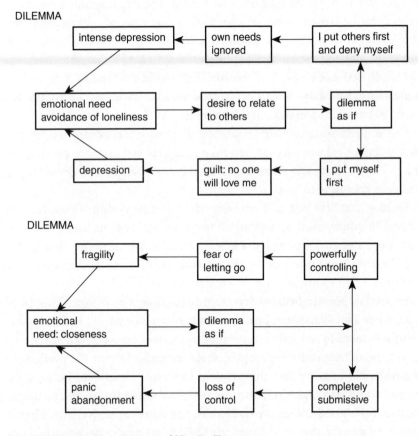

Figure 20d Therapists' diagrams of Mary's dilemmas
Either you are powerfully controlling and expect Sean to do what you want *or* you give into him completely and go along with whatever he wants.

reported activities. Sean and Mary expressed their great disappointment that their respective son and daughter had let them down at the last moment by cancelling plans to visit them. This deprived Mary of her fantasy of creating a warm, happy, safe family, and she saw how her hurt over this could have been directed at Sean. This session revealed the pathological part of each of them, how the terrible, enraged, hurt, afraid child could burst in and destroy good things, especially their relationship. It was a sobering session. Mary had told Sean to leave and not come back when, or so it seemed to her, he had put his daughter ahead of her. Sean had replied, 'If I do it might be fatal', and Mary was then able to tell Sean that she hadn't meant it and they managed de-escalate the row. We reminded them that it is alright to get angry and have rows.

The next session focused on how hard it was to bring our sessions to an end and on their sense of not having had enough. Even Sean was able to name this. There was some anxiety that there hadn't been a row. On one occasion Sean had felt resentful of Mary's laughter over the phone to someone else and he had been able to express this and be understood by Mary. Sean said in this session, 'Nothing in my life has made a bigger impression than this work'.

In the next session Mary reported that on three occasions she had succeeded in taking care of her own interests rather than putting the other person first. She was triumphant at her refusal to be domineered, and was encouraged in this by Sean.

During our last but one meeting the issue of ending came up very forcefully. Mary strongly vented all her fears and rage at losing us. Sean was more hopeful, saying he wished he had more time but that he felt they had the tools to go on by themselves. We confirmed that we would meet for a follow-up session in December.

In our last session Sean arrived with a package which turned out to be a painting that had given him great pleasure to paint. This was a great delight to all of us. We exchanged goodbye letters, ours being a joint letter to the two of them with separate sections for each of them. We spelled out again the patterns we saw that tripped them up, the enormous progress we had seen them make in finding exits from these snags, traps and dilemmas, and the good things we had got out of working with them. They in turn each gave us their goodbye letters. Each in their very individual way let us know what a landmark experience therapy had been for them. Sean's letter was much longer than Mary's, and once again we saw how they each felt the other must have performed better, as Mary convinced herself that Sean's letter must have been far more thorough that her own. Again we emphasized that it is alright to be different from one another. Both Sean and Mary felt they had gained a great deal of good experience and understanding to enable them to defuse their quarrels themselves, and both could see that using their creativity brought good feelings and was helpful in the relationship. They each expressed their thanks and sadness. We talked of all the changes we had witnessed, their courage, hard work and tenacity, and gave them more forms to enable them to continue the work of monitoring themselves.

Sean and Mary were able to use Cognitive Analytic Therapy to change their relationship. They were able to defuse their quarrels, to laugh at the tangles they got into and to confront things in the 'here and now' rather than carrying them around like a time bomb. Overall they had less devastating rows, which is what they originally set out to achieve in therapy. This change came about because they were each able to see how a lot of the anger and disruption really belonged to childhood experiences. For each, the procedure of trying to placate a powerful father loomed large and got in their way.

Sean recognized how the presence of his father's critical voice inside him created a trap, preventing him from enjoying his creative abilities and reducing his efforts, as well as ensuring that he withdrew from Mary whenever he heard his father's voice in her. He decided to 'have a go' and to enjoy himself, as well as reassuring his inner child and encouraging him to express himself.

Mary came to understand her fear of putting her own needs first for fear of others' rejection. Her difficulty with expressing her own needs remained hidden under her urge to punish when feeling rejected by being critical or withdrawing. When she began to express what she was feeling, particularly her fear at losing someone, this had a powerful effect on Sean, who was able to share and respect her feelings.

Sean and Mary write that now, five years on, they are still using the diagrams made in their therapy, and are communicating well.

Exercise

Write your individual life stories, separately, using the third person. It helps if we can step back and reflect – for example, let 'I' become 'he' or 'she'. Pick a time when you can be alone together and each read your own life story aloud to the other. Put your observer hat on and just listen to and respect the note of the storyteller and the drama behind the story. Be as objective as possible and *really listen*.

Try not to *judge, criticize, ridicule, object to, take personally, overrule or rationalize* the other's story. To do so would be to fall into a negative, internalized parent trap. If you do find yourself doing any of the above, just make a note of it so that you can refer to it later. Do not act upon it. Listen for the tone of the person who is trying to emerge, and communicate through the drama of the story. Note the way in which your partner has observed their own procedures and how they have survived their early life.

Give some time to the effect of reading the stories together and for each other's response.

Write something together about how your individual core pain and your procedures for coping affect the other.

Make a diagram for yourselves about the ways in which you repeat the ritual of your procedures during a row or difficulty. Note:
(a) the assumption or 'false belief' that leads to the behaviour ('I believe that . .');
(b) how this is received by the other which triggers their assumption ('so I do this . . .');
(c) how this assumption results in behaviour ('he/she sees that I believe that . . . so this makes me do . . .').
Each keep a copy, so you can check where you are if you get into difficulties.

Spend the first week just observing and noting with each other what is happening. *Don't* yet try and change anything, but use your recognition *not* to get into the trap or dilemma to which your relationship usually falls prey. See what happens to the space, see what emerges or wants to emerge.

If you find yourselves having strong feelings, write them down, and see where or to whom they belong. How are the feelings connected to your core pain, and how can you best begin to relieve it?

When the energy in a relationship is not taken up with fighting old procedures there is time for other things. Experiment with *how* you like being together, and give feedback to each other on what works and what doesn't.

Storytime

Begin together to look at some of the powerful myths which you can see operating in your own histories, families, environment and culture. One reason for doing this is to evaluate where some ideas about relationships, and particularly marriage, originate. Another is to check how much influence these myths still have over you and your relationships, and whether they too need revision.

As you read, see which of the myths could be still influencing you in your life now.

Role myths
In my family:
Men always came first.
Women served men.
Men never worked.
Mum and Dad stuck together through everything.
Women never worked.
Dad was always there for me.
Mum was always there for me.
What happened within the family was confidential/secret.

Development myths
In my family:
We had to better ourselves.
No one read books.
We always knew our place.
There were no divorces.
Marriage was for ever.
All the men/women were labourers, white collar workers, professionals, etc.
To be ambitious was to be selfish.
Any change was bad.

Sexual myths
In my family:
We never talked about sex.
Men were always unfaithful.
Women were always unfaithful.
Sex was OK for men but not for women.

Change for the Better

Sex was dirty.

Mum and Dad never had sex.

Men have got to have it, but women can wait.

Sex always led to trouble.

Sex was very difficult.

Sexual attraction myths

Men only like 'good girls'.

You have to play a game to get a man.

Only if you are a size — will you get a man.

Never trust a man until he's put a ring on your finger.

You have to look — to be sexy.

Sex appeal – you've either got it or you haven't.

Independent women are not sexy/are very sexy.

Men can do and look as they wish and still be sexy.

A man doesn't have to be sexy to get a woman.

Girls will be as sexy as they can until they've got you hooked, and then they turn into their mothers.

Myths about feelings

In my family:

No one was close.

We believed, 'Never wash your dirty linen in public'.

Anger was a dirty word.

Feelings were bottled up.

Mum/Dad/Gran/sister/brother, etc. had the monopoly on feelings.

Women could have feelings, men couldn't.

Myths about caring and love

Caring means looking after/being looked after.

Love means being strict/harsh/hurting.

Love is only for special people.

Love and caring means never being cross.

Love and caring means giving into others.

Love and caring means sacrifice: others are more important.

If you love a person of your own sex you are homosexual.

Moral and religious myths

Only God knows.

Marriages are made in heaven.

God can see everywhere and he knows you are bad.

To break a commandment means being punished for ever.

God gave you to us so we can mould you for Him.

To be good and loving is to serve God in forgiveness, even those who have hurt you.

Mother and Father always know best.

Family relationship myths

Should be happy ever after.

You make your bed and lie on it.

Should always be hard work or they're not worth anything.

Should come naturally or they're not true.

Should be as good as Mum and Dad's, Gran and Grandpa's.

Being in a relationship is better than being on your own.

Relationships make you whole (joining a 'better half').

Myths about behaviour

You can never do anything right.

You always make me unhappy.

If you really cared or loved me you would . . .

You will only be happy when you've . . .

You must win to survive, life is a contest of winners and losers.

Be seen but not heard.

If you get what you want you will be unhappy.

Only if you get what you think you want will you be happy.

Waiting for the 'perfect man/woman'.

Exercise

Predict which myths rule your partner's actual thoughts and beliefs, as well as their *hoped* for myths.

Name the myths which *together* you feel dominate your relationship.

Write the myths as you would like them to be!

Part 6
How to Hold on
to Change

How to hold on to change

In this book we have been challenging old beliefs and seeing how they can influence the thinking we have about ourselves and about other people. Self-monitoring and writing down help to move what were hidden ideas from the obscurity of our minds into the daylight and allow us to look at them afresh. Some of us might be amazed at the influence of an apparently simple but mistaken belief. Often this awakening alone is sufficient to bring about change. Many problems, however, result from strongly built up defences against early woundings, and the difficulty in changing these defences appropriately comes about because the fear involved is very great. We said at the beginning that change takes courage. It takes courage to risk feeling into our fears rather than avoiding them. It takes courage to go with anxiety rather then letting it ground us. And when we have become used to staying with fear and anxiety, staying with difficult feelings, we are giving those parts of ourselves a life, often for the very first time.

Staying with, and feeling into, are not the same as giving in to or being passive. We tend to give up on new ways or revised ideas because we lose heart at keeping them going. Anything freshly learned needs time and practice to become established. If we think that the old patterns of thinking have been around for most of our lifetime, it is not too much to ask that we give a proportion of time to practising the revised patterns.

There is usually relief, but there can also be loss, when we change how we think and what we presume. If we have built relationships largely upon our 'survival' self then these patterns of relationships will be challenged. Someone who has been used to us pleasing them, giving in to them, caring for them, may be disgruntled at first when they see us operating differently, and they may even be actively discouraging or threatening. Change does challenge all levels of our life and in particular those we are closest to. Living with what may feel like the opposition of our partner or closest friend or colleague is hard, but it is important that this opposition does not put us off. If it does we are colluding with the original fear that kept our old beliefs unrevised, and things will go back to being just as they were, with our 'seed' self still hidden and struggling.

What I have found is that when friends and colleagues realize the importance of change to the person trying to change, and how much relief there is when old redundant patterns are eradicated, they too are pleased. Only when relationships have become fixed and one-sided do things tend to get more heated. Then each of us has to make a choice. And the choice is frequently 'him (or her) or me?' If we risk losing others because they want us to stay the same we must ask whether we really want or need those others in our lives. If we lose the friendship of one or more people during our path of change, we need to question what kind of friends they were to begin with, and how much they may have been holding us back in terms of development. We must go forward and believe that we will make new friends and acquaintances.

The first priority for holding on to change is therefore courage and the determination to stick with it. What follows is a checklist of ideas for holding on to change. Not all will need to be considered. Pick out four or five which are helpful and write them out for yourself. Look at this checklist everyday to encourage yourself to stay with the changes you have chosen.

- Keep up your courage and strength to carry out the changes you have decided upon, even when others seem to discourage you or disapprove. Internal changes which need to be made to release more of the 'seed' self will not harm other people; rather they will tend to enhance your exchanges with others.
- Believe in what you are doing and allow others to see your quiet conviction.
- Recognize yourself for what you are. Stop trying to be like other people or as other people demand you to be.

- Know that there will be times when you will need to go through a 'pain barrier'. Changing is not easy, and many fears are being challenged. Know that sometimes it will be hard and that you must just keep going and stick with your newly made story and aims.
- Develop tolerance for yourself instead of feeling you have to give in to the demand for instant gratification, which could lead to slipping into the old habits you are trying to change.
- Celebrate your feelings and your needs. Don't let them isolate you.
- Know your fears and take them with you.
- Know you are anxious and take your anxiety with you by the hand. Don't muddle it up with, 'I shouldn't be like this, I'm silly'.
- Learn the art of listening to yourself and to others. Listen to yourself speak and note the tone you use. Listen to what your body is telling you, notice your body language.
- Be aware of the destructive power of negative thinking and don't let it get you. Be firm when you have a negative thought and tell it to go away.
- Be aware of the power of positive thinking and the healing that can be achieved from letting good vibes in.
- C.S. Lewis wrote that, 'Only a real risk tests the reality of a belief'. Take risks and check out your own beliefs.

- Make sure that you laugh every day. Be with people who make you laugh or with whom you have fun. Read or watch things that are amusing.
- Use your images in your everyday life. 'It is like . . .', 'I feel like . . .'. Let the symbols or images that have emerged during your reading be useful to you, so that you can say, 'Ah yes, this is how I'm being . . . this is where I am right now . . .'.
- If you get stuck at times or feel faint-hearted, say to yourself, 'It doesn't have to be like this', or 'This isn't all there is'.
- Every day give yourself permission to change and to hold on to change.
- Give space for your 'seed' self to begin to emerge. It might be raw and new at first. Let it have a proper life: give it the soil, light, air, water and careful nurturing that you would give to a precious seedling entrusted in your care.

Finding a therapist

Having read this book you may feel that you would like to consult a therapist, and the material raised by this book may be pressing you to do so. The subject of 'what is a good therapist' is still hotly debated in both professional and lay circles. You may find someone with excellent qualifications with whom you have no rapport; you may be seduced by someone's kindness and friendliness, only to find they have no stamina when the going gets tough. Finding a therapist with recognized qualifications is important, because it means that they have had to meet both personal (all good therapists have to have their own therapy or analysis for a required period of time) and professional standards and commitments. A useful guide is published by the British Association for Counselling. Their accredited members have to meet a wide range of standards and requirements and be in regular supervision.

If you are attracted by the ideas in this book, which come from Cognitive Analytic Therapy (CAT), write to: Mark Dunn, Munro Clinic, Guy's Hospital, St Thomas's Street, London SE1 for details of any therapists or other professionals working with CAT in your area. There are now a growing number of CAT-trained therapists working in different fields – doctors, psychiatrists, psychiatric social workers, community nurses and psychiatric nurses, occupational therapists, social workers, GPs, counsellors and psychotherapists – who are being trained to work in short-term therapy using the methods outlined in this book.

What is a 'good enough' therapist

A good therapist should have completed a recognized training, be in regular supervision and should receive you as a client or patient with equality, acceptance and an open mind. Every therapist will have his or her own individual style, just as you will do. The chemistry in the working therapeutic partnership is crucial. Do not feel duty-bound to put up with a therapist who:

doesn't speak to you properly, or at all, for the first month;
abuses their position by trying to be overpowerful, over-interpretive, or who does not adhere appropriately to boundaries (for example, the therapeutic hour is yours: a therapist who is continually late, takes phone calls, leaves early or who is frequently distracted is not adhering to the boundaries of the therapy, for which you may well be paying fees);
who is judgemental or disparaging about your feelings and your life;
seems overly interested in some aspect of you for his or her own personal purposes.

It is not helpful if a therapist talks too much about themselves or their own life. Whereas there may be times when personal disclosure is timely, appropriate and a real gift to you as client or patient, too much too soon destroys the freedom and sanctity of the professional hour. The same can be said for physical contact. Some body-orientated therapies such as bioenergetics include touching within the therapy as long as it is within the context of the physical work. Therapies which are unclear about touching and physical contact can create confusion, and as a client or patient we can feel invaded. A therapist who hugs you when you arrive and when you leave, or who touches you in some way during the session when this does not seem appropriate, may feel cosy and accepting at first, but this situation can create difficulties, confusion and misinterpretation of motives, as well as lack of freedom later on. Again, there may be times when one hug or hold is exactly right for the moment, and is mutually anticipated, but these genuine moments are rare, and a lot of woolly mistakes in the name of 'warmth' occur when physical boundaries are not adhered to with integrity and honesty.

Transference

There may be times during a therapy when you have very negative feelings for your therapist: anger, fury, fear, hate, despising, contempt. These feelings are usually part of what is generally known as 'transference' (i.e. they are 'transferred' from some other person who has affected you, and who may have originally produced such feelings, or from part of yourself). They form a useful part of the therapy, which can be discussed, interpreted and understood, and although painful can be liberating. If you have any negative feelings, or difficult feelings, like being attracted to your therapist, talk about it and allow it to be part of the work. If your therapist does not allow such feelings to be part of the work, but takes them personally or judges you for them too harshly, you may need to be challenging and confrontative, and to leave the therapy if the issue does not reach a satisfactory conclusion. There is no therapy which is 'perfect', and the 'perfect' therapist should not be sought. A 'good enough' therapy will allow you to explore most things, at the same time as keeping an appropriate containment for the more frightening, diffuse feelings which we carry unconsciously.

Practicalities

Most therapeutic 'hours' are fifty, fifty-five or sixty minutes. Reliable time-keeping is important. Many areas within the NHS now offer psychotherapy or counselling. In the private sector there are many more therapists and a wide range of training. Fees vary from between £15 to £40 per hour. The higher range of fees tend to be charged by therapists who also have a medical background. Most good therapists work on a sliding scale of fees if they possibly can. The value of a short-term therapy is that the cost is known in advance and limited. If you feel that your therapy is not going well, or if you have any reservations about your therapy after reading the above, talk about it to your therapist. If you are not satisfied with the response you are perfectly free to go elsewhere. Everyone who enters therapy needs to feel that they are receiving something useful before too long, no matter how obscure the nature of the usefulness, which will be personal and individual to all people who become clients or patients. As a 'consumer' looking for a therapist you are allowed, indeed entitled, to feel valued, respected and to be given help by the therapist.

Having decided upon your choice of therapist, take along your note-book of findings, drawings or personal recollections and realizations that you have gleaned from this book, and share them, at whatever pace you choose, as part of your process in therapy.

Resource addresses

Association of Cognitive Analytic Therapists
Munro Clinic,
Guy's Hospital
London SE1 9RT

Write for information about the availability of this therapy in your area.
Cognitive Analytic Therapy is also available in Greece, Finland and Spain.

British Association for Counselling
1 Regent Place, Rugby,. Warwickshire CV21 2PJ.
Information line: 01788 578328.
Offers information about counselling and training in Great Britain.

Eating Disorders Association
Sackville Place, 44–48 Magdalen Street, Norwich, Norfolk NR3 1JU.
Offers information about groups in different parts of Britain, and a topical
magazine SIGHNPOST.
Information line: 01603 621414.

In your local telephone directory you will find addresses and phone numbers
for your nearest branch of:

MIND
The national association for mental health in Britain. Offers help and guide-
lines for people searching for appropriate resources in their own locality.

Samaritans
Samaritans offer confidential telephone or one-to-one conversation and
befriending particularly for those feeling desperate or suicidal.

Further reading

If you have found the self-help approach useful, you may like to consider
some of these titles for your own further reading. I have compiled the list
with help from colleagues, friends and patients.

General

Bruno Bettleheim *The Uses of Enchantment*
This book is an analysis of fairy tales. We frequently identify with a figure

from folk lore or fairy tale, and this can help us in our understanding of ourselves and our patterns.

John Bradshaw *Healing the Shame That Binds You*
Helps us to look at how shame can be the core problem to many of our difficulties and behind many presenting problems. Includes exercises for releasing shame.

David Burns *Feeling God, Feeling Fine,* and *The Feeling Good Handbook*
Two extremely popular and positive books based on cognitive therapy and self-help.

Erika J. Chopich and Margaret Paul *Healing Your Aloneness: Finding Love and Wholeness Through Your Inner Child*
A practical and powerful guide to inner healing.

Carl Jung *Memories, Dreams, Reflections*
Classic autobiography of the famous Swiss psychologist.

Barry Kaufman *Happiness Is a Choice*
This book shows how people *can* change by changing their attitude. This positive philosophy is the outcome of Kaufman's pioneering work bringing children out of autism.

Dorothy Rowe *Depression and the Way Out of Your Prison*
A practical and sensible approach to self-help and depression.

Cognitive Analytic Therapy

Anthony Ryle *Cognitive Analytic Therapy*
The classic textbook of this effective short-term focused therapy now used widely within health service settings.

Relationships

Aaron Beck *Love Is Never Enough*
A practical, sensible approach for couples to understand the way their distorted thinking undermines communication problems.

John Sandford *Invisible Partners*
This is a Jungian approach to looking at the inner male and female components of men and women. Useful for readers wishing to explore their inner lives more thoroughly.

Maggie Scarf *Intimate Partners*
A well-researched book offering insight, into how inherited emotional and family history affects our pattern of relating.

R. Skinner and John Cleese *Families and How to Survive Them*
A classic book. Psychology is made accessible, helping us to understand how our current patterns grow from our background.

Bereavement and separation

Elisabeth Kubler Ross *To Live Until We Say Goodbye*
A very moving book about the dying process of close friends and family.

Judy Tatelbaum *The Courage to Grieve*
A sensitive and creative book for those suffering from loss, taking readers through the processes of grief and mourning, with stories and suggestions for how to complete the mourning process.

Allegra Taylor *Acquainted With the Night*
A beautifully written and thoughtful account of the author's work with The London Lighthouse. Allegra Taylor is also a healer.

Denise Vaughan *Uncoupling*
Separating or divorcing a partner and all the emotional and practical difficulties.

J. William Warden *Grief Counselling and Grief Therapy*
A helpful guide to the different stages of grief and mourning.

Alison Wertheimer *A Special Scar*
An extremely sensitive and well-researched book about the painful experiences of people bereaved by suicide.

Eating disorders

Julia Buckroyd *Eating Your Heart Out*
This book links the misuse of food with emotional hunger and gives practical advice for change.

Peter J. Cooper *Bulimia Nervosa and Binge Eating: A Guide to Recovery*.
A self-help manual offering techniques for recognising and preventing triggers to problems. Based on Cognitive Behaviour Therapy.

Sarah Gilbert *The Psychology of Dieting: Tomorrow I'll Be Slim*
A practical and useful understanding of how dieting can be a trap.

Susie Orbach *Fat Is A Feminist Issue*
Still a classic look at how current social thinking affects women's image and capacity for control and power.

Geneen Roth *Feeding the Hungry Heart*
Helpful uses of visualization to discover the real source of hunger within.

Mira Dana and Marilyn Lawrence *Women's Secret Disorder: A New Understanding of Bulimia*
A compassionate and useful guide to giving up bulimia.

Sexual abuse

I am grateful for this list to Marjorie Orr, founder of Accuracy About Abuse. Her address is P.O. Box 3125, London NW3 5QB.

Ellen Bass and Laura Davis *The Courage to Heal*
Popular book offering comprehensive and sensible help and encouragement.

Sylvia Fraser *My Father's House*
A compelling and moving account of the author's own experience and her creative use of her wounding.

Linda Sanford *Strong at the Broken Places*
A practising psychotherapist interviews survivors.

Jacqueline Spring *Cry Hard and Swim*
The true story of a damaged childhood and healing therapy.

Moira Walker *Secret Survivors*
Stories of survivors and the journeys they have made.

Phobia – Fear – Addiction

Susan Jeffers *Feel the Fear and Do It Anyway*
An excellent self-help book about befriending phobia and fear.

Linda Leonard *Witness to the Fire: Creativity and the Veil of Addiction*
A marvellous and hopeful book about addiction with examples from artists and writers and the author's own experience with alcoholism.

Further Reading

Isaac Marks *Living With Fear*
Written by a well-known expert, this book looks at anxiety and obsessive compulsive difficulties.

Dreams

Ann Faraday *Dream Power*
Popular book about recognizing and using the power of dreams.

John Sandford *God's Forgotten Language*
A lovely contribution from a Jungian to ways of looking at dreams.

Carl Jung *Man and His Symbols*
A look at the use of images and symbols in our everyday life. Many illustrations.

Imaging and visualization

Gregg Furth *The Secret World of Drawings*
Shows us how drawings and doodles can be helpful in our understanding of unconscious processes. The author worked with Elisabeth Kubler Ross.

Ronald Shone *Creative Visualisation*

Women's Dictionary of Symbols and *Women's Dictionary of Myths and Symbols*
Edited by Barbara G. Walker
Two stunning books amplifying images and symbols from different cultures from a modern cultural perspective.

M. Scott Peck *The Road Less Travelled*
A lovely book that offers a philosophy of hope that ignites our imaginations. On the bestseller list for over ten years.